BEYOND THE MINARETS

A BIOGRAPHY OF HENRY MARTYN

BEYOND THE MINARETS

A BIOGRAPHY OF
HENRY MARTYN

KELLSYE M. FINNIE

Foreword by Bishop Dehqani-Tafti

Illustrations by John Finnie

STL BOOKS

PO Box 48, Bromley, Kent, England
PO Box 28, Waynesboro, Georgia 30830, USA

British Library Cataloguing in Publication Data
Finnie, Kellsye M.
  Beyond the minarets.
  1. Martyn, Henry 2. Missionaries—
  Great Britain—Biography
  I. Title
  266'.3'0924 BV3705.M3

ISBN 1 85078 026 9

STL Books are published by Send The Light
(Operation Mobilisation), PO Box 48, Bromley, Kent,
England, BR1 3JH.

Cover and text illustrations by John Finnie. All rights reserved.

Typesetting, production and printing in England by
Nuprint Ltd, Harpenden, Herts, AL5 4SE.

Contents

Foreword

Reading biographies is one of the best ways of strengthening our faith and receiving purpose and vision in life. Situations change from one generation to another, but principles remain the same. Things were very different when Henry Martyn sailed for India as a minister of the gospel during the last century, but the obligation for Christians to witness to Christ remains the same today, through total commitment and being prepared to pay the price for one's faith at any time.

The life of Henry Martyn and his untimely death have influenced many people throughout the world. He lived in the city of Shiraz, a centre of learning and religion, for one year. Here he tried to share his faith with Muslim priests and to understand their points of view. Others who have attempted any serious religious dialogue with Iranian Shi'ite leaders will realise how difficult this task is. Suspicion, hate and contempt can form antagonising barriers between faiths, often expressed by aggression.

The story goes that while making a point during a religious discussion, Henry Martyn was met with verbal abuse about Christ. This brought tears to his eyes and filled everyone with amazement to see his non-aggressive reaction and the depth of his love for his Master. This affected them far more deeply than any intellectual arguments.

There have been several attempts by various scholars to write about the life of this genius of the faith and humble servant of his Lord, without whose tireless efforts the church in Iran would probably not have taken root, and people like myself might not have become Christians.

I have the pleasure of recommending this sensitive biography of Henry Martyn by Mrs Kellsye Finnie to everyone, especially young people in search of a meaning in life.

H. B. DEHQANI-TAFTI

Former President-Bishop of the Church in Jerusalem and the Middle East (1976–1986), and Bishop in Iran

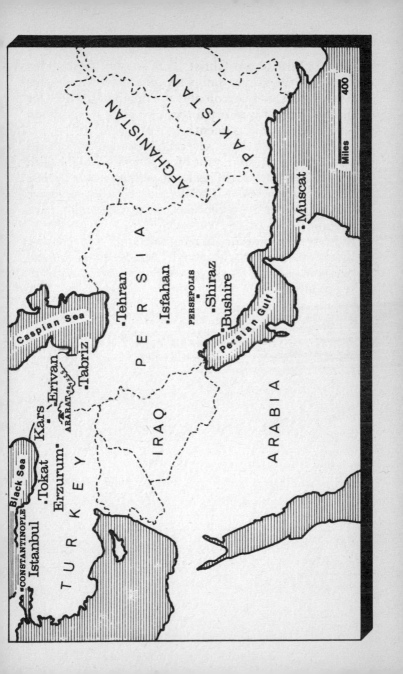

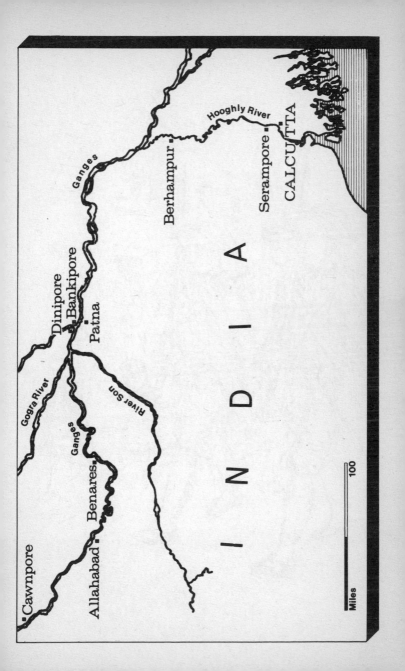

I

A Cornish Boy

His face alight with excitement, the small boy raced along trying to keep up with the soldiers marching over the cobbled streets of Truro, his Cornish home town. He knew that as usual his young sister would be trailing somewhere behind him but this time he did not dare wait for her or he would lose sight of the marchers.

The usually quiet city of Truro was alive on this August morning in 1789 for it was filled with soldiers waiting for the noisy protest march of the desperate tin miners. The miners were on their way over the rolling hills to demand the higher wages they needed to survive.

'Henry! Wait for me, Henry!' Above the clatter of the marching soldiers the boy could hear his sister calling. Suddenly there was a loud wail indicating all too clearly that she had fallen, and he stopped. A hot anger surged up within him for he knew he would have to go back to her. Now all thought of keeping up with the soldiers was gone, and soon he would lose sight of them completely.

Scowling darkly he walked back to the crying child. But when he saw her distress the storm within him vanished as quickly as it came, and his thin plain face lit up with brotherly tenderness. The anger had given way to loving concern.

'Never mind, Sally.' He picked her up from the ground. 'Don't cry. I've come back for you.' Carefully he took from his pocket a small periwinkle shell. 'I'll wait for you and here, look at my new shell that I found this morning by the water. If you stop crying I'll give it you. You can have it for keeps, Sally.'

This caring concern for his small sister had become natural to Henry Martyn, as for the last six of his eight years there had been no mother to offer comfort when needed. The two youngest children of the family had drawn close in a bond that was to last their whole lifetime.

The noise and the shouting of the protest march did not last long and when the excitement was over the city soon returned to its normal remoteness beside the Fal estuary, to its peaceful fishing and the sound of the curlew over the water.

In France, just across the sea, the stormy Revolution was just breaking out. But few of Truro's citizens had travelled far outside its boundaries, and news of the outside world was brought to them mostly by the arrival of the stage-coach.

This was a time when in Britain that outside world was one of harsh justice, particularly for the petty criminal, and the death sentence could be passed on a young person for stealing five shillings from a shop, cutting down a tree in any avenue, or even for impersonating a Chelsea Pensioner!

Not surprisingly the prisons had become more and

more crowded and began to burst at the seams. Something had to be done and Britain, more eager to build up her Empire abroad than to deal with trouble at home, decided to rid herself of 'undesirable characters'. This was done by shipping boat-loads of convicts over to the other side of the world.

Australia, discovered some years earlier by Cooke, was thought to be a suitable destination for these miserable sinners, and transportation had come into being, with the First Fleet sailing from Portsmouth in 1787.

But the influence of men such as Wesley and Whitefield, the preachers, Wilberforce with his anti-slavery ideals, and many other good men, was penetrating the conscience of the country. Guy's and other hospitals were founded in London, and charity schools were opened, and Robert Raikes had opened his Sunday schools in 1780. Here children were being taught to read by easy methods based on light theology, chiefly by recitation. 'A is for angel who praises the Lord; B is for Bible, His most holy Word.'

This was the background against which the young Henry had been brought up by his twice-widowed father, John Martyn, a gentle but enthusiastic Nonconformist, anxious that his children should learn to appreciate spiritual values as they grew.

John Martyn was an intelligent man of business, a self-taught mathematician. He held the position of chief clerk to Thomas Daniell, local merchant and mine-owner, and the Martyns lived comfortably in a house looking out over the estuary. On the opposite side of the road was the Coinage Hall where Wesley sometimes came to preach and the glad sound of the rousing services echoed round the area. The hymns

Wesley introduced in his meetings became the tunes whistled by the family in the house across the way.

In 1789 the family consisted of a son John, by the first marriage, and from the second the three children who had survived infancy. Laura was two years older than Henry, and Sally a year younger than he was. There is no record of any female relative or housekeeper in the home to take the place of the mother who had died soon after Sally was born. The father, devoted to his young children, managed the upbringing on his own. But this lack of feminine influence in the home was a serious loss to the sensitive, inward-looking younger boy, who had so much affection to give.

John Martyn was quick to realise that his son showed unusual scholastic promise and when Henry was seven entered him at Truro Grammar School.

In those days the standard curriculum at grammar schools was of a severely classical nature, and Henry would be given a good grounding in Latin and Greek. Mathematics, in which he was to specialise later, was not added to the school curriculum until about 1805.

The Headmaster, Dr Cardew, noticed that the small nervous boy with the ready answers was being teased and tormented by bigger pupils who enjoyed watching him get into a bitter rage. He decided to put an end to this trouble by placing Henry in the special charge of a senior named Kempthorne, a kind and popular member of the school. Under his protection the new boy overcame many of his fears and gradually his friendly, cheerful spirit returned.

Although more than usually bright, Henry was not at that time particularly studious in school but often trusted to his quick wits to see him through.

By the time he was fifteen he had done so well that

his father and Dr Cardew suggested he entered for a scholarship to Corpus Christi College, Oxford. He agreed to do this and, young as he was for such an ordeal, travelled completely alone by coach to Oxford.

He was not successful in winning the scholarship and continued his education at Truro for one more year, his father still keeping before him the ultimate goal of a university career. While he was still at school the war with France became a certainty, drawing all Europe into a bitter struggle, and this continued during the whole of his life.

2

Cambridge Student

By the time Henry was finishing at school, Kempthorne, Henry's friend and something of a hero-figure,
had entered St John's College, Cambridge, where
records show he was excelling himself in mathematics.
Whether this influenced Henry is not known but, with
encouragement from his father, he became convinced
that mathematics was an important subject to study.
In October 1797 Henry followed Kempthorne and
became a student at St John's .

Coming from the remoteness of Cornwall, Henry
felt himself to be in a new world. He was quick to
appreciate the beauty of Cambridge, with its many
small streets inviting the inquisitive to explore. He
walked by the calm waters of the river, his mind filled
with thoughts of the new life facing him. He admired
the stately austerity of the College building with its
richly-decorated gateway topped by the figure of St
John.

Henry listened with delight to the music of King's
College chapel and, perhaps with less pleasure, to the
constant buzz of conversation from fellow students.

But more than anything this was the place of learning, of adventure into new fields of thought and ideas, and his eager mind was ready for this.

But at first his studies proved a disappointment. His tutor found the undersized youth something of an enigma, for although he had a good knowledge of the classics he was completely unable to 'make anything of even the First Proposition of Euclid'. And, after all, mathematics was the subject he had come to study.

After a time of struggling the tutor asked a second-year man named Shepherd to see if he could help Henry to get started. Shepherd invited him to his room and persevered, but all efforts appeared to be in vain. Henry became so disappointed over his lack of ability to get a grasp of the subject that in despair he was ready to give up and return home to Cornwall.

He had already packed when Shepherd called at his room to try to persuade him to stay on and to give the lessons one more chance. This gave a boost to Henry's confidence and he agreed to have another go. From then on it seemed that gradually the problems began to straighten out, and at last comprehension of basic mathematical principles began to dawn. Once over the first hurdle Henry went from strength to strength, at last passing everyone on his way to the top.

This early encouragement to persevere was to become a formative characteristic of his later years, pursued—even against the advice of others—to the unfolding tragedy of his early death.

But life at Cambridge was not to be all plain sailing. Henry was of course still an immature teenager, living away from home for the first time. He was torn by emotional problems, ambitions, fears and frustrations, liable to fly off the handle in a sudden rage.

In the dining-hall one day an argument developed between two or three students. It was a trivial matter and could have been settled in a matter of minutes, but Henry's temper was roused. The others tended to laugh at his angry outbursts and this was something his intense nature could not stand. Suddenly he picked up a knife from the table and hurled it.

Fortunately his aim was as erratic as his temper and the knife missed its intended target, wedging itself in the wall opposite. With shocked surprise the laughter ceased and the meal continued in subdued silence.

For most of the time Henry's more usual attitude, gentle, courteous and kind, gave little indication of the storms within. For his many friends and those he loved he maintained a deep warm affection.

Gradually he settled down to his studies with serious, dedicated application. At home there was his father, eager as Henry to hear examination results as they came through. His sister Sally was more concerned for her brother's spiritual progress. Near at hand to guide and encourage was the dependable and trusted Kempthorne, who was not afraid to criticise if necessary.

At one stage he thought Henry was too concerned with the praise of others and seemed to be studying chiefly with that in mind. 'Shouldn't you also be doing it for the glory of God?' asked Kempthorne.

Henry listened politely to what he thought was strange and unnecessary advice, but paid little attention to it. Only later would he realise the importance and wisdom of his friend's good counsel.

3

Learning New Values

During Henry's visit home in the summer of 1799 Sally often brought up the subject of religion but he was not particularly interested in the subject, becoming irritated if she persisted.

'I spoke in the strongest language to my sister and often to my father if he happened to differ from my mind and will. What an example of patience and mildness he was, and I love now to think of his excellent qualities.'

When October came Henry returned to Cambridge, leaving his father in good spirits, highly pleased at the academic success of his son. At the end of the year he was able to add to this by writing to tell his father that he had come first in the examination.

Unfortunately, as it turned out, Henry decided to stay on at Cambridge for the Christmas vacation, knowing all was well at home. This would avoid the long coach journey to Cornwall, tedious enough in the summer but hazardous in the bleak days of winter snow and ice.

He missed being with his own folks for the festive

season and filled in the time with extra study. He was
sitting alone in his rooms in the early days of the new
century when a letter was brought to him. It was from
his step-brother John and the contents completely
stunned him, telling as it did that his father, who had
appeared to be in good health, had died suddenly.

For a long time he sat with the opened letter in his
hand, unable to take in the full meaning. It was hard
to believe it was true, and in desperate isolation he had
to face the first great sorrow of his life.

Where could he find comfort? He remembered his
neglected Bible. How many times he had promised
Sally to read it, only to fail to do so once he had settled
back into college life? Now he reached for his copy
lying under a pile of books, and began to read. No
peace came with the words and he was turning to look
for other reading when there was a knock on the door.

Kempthorne, that faithful friend, that link with
home, had come to bring consolation and, at his
suggestion, they read together helpful verses from the
Scriptures. By the time his friend left Henry had
decided to study the Bible for himself, not only for
comfort but as a guide for daily living.

'I began with the Acts, as being the most amusing,
and when I was entertained with the narrative I found
myself insensibly led to enquire more attentively into
the doctrine of the Apostles.'

As he read more he realised that his childhood
memories of the teaching of the revivalists in Cornwall
corresponded with what he was finding out for himself.
He was not used to praying and his first attempt was
simply to thank God for sending Christ into the world.

Like William Carey, the great missionary pioneer,
Henry had no sudden vision but he had started on a

gradual searching for God. As he read of the offer of mercy and forgiveness through Jesus Christ he asked that this might be his experience and he found, not a doctrine, but a personal Saviour and Friend. Later evidence showed that Christ now held the central place as Lord of his life. Before the nineteenth century was through its first month Henry was ready to commit that life to the claims of God.

His natural characteristics were still there of course, and he remained for all time a man of intense emotions, moving quickly from the mountain top to the slough of despair. He could be enraptured by music or the beauties of nature, devastated by personal failure or weakness, but he was no longer dominated by his previous passions.

Henry now shared with Sally his spiritual awareness and they wrote long letters to one another, encouraging or, if necessary, criticising. He had other Christian friends at Cambridge, but the chief leader along his Christian path was the famous preacher, the Rev Charles Simeon of Holy Trinity Church in Cambridge, which Henry attended regularly.

Simeon was a fearless man of God and in his preaching was a vehement earnestness unusual at that time. The three-fold purpose of his preaching, he said, was 'to humble the sinner; to exalt the Saviour; to promote holiness.'

The teaching of this gifted minister was one of the greatest blessings that came to Henry and it was to strengthen and fortify him to the end of his days. There developed a wealth of warmth and mutual admiration between them, each fully recognising the other's qualities.

Simeon held what he called 'Conversation Parties'

for students, and here the tea-drinking was inter-spersed with discussion and fatherly advice, mostly on the subject of Christian living. It was here that Henry met John Sargeant, the man who became one of his closest friends and who probably understood the somewhat unpredictable Henry best of all.

By the end of the third year the student who had made a slow start at Cambridge had worked himself to the first place in all his college examinations. When his finals came in January 1801, just before he was twenty, he maintained his high position as the mathematician of the year, and gained the honoured position of Senior Wrangler.

'I obtained my highest wishes but was surprised to find I had grasped a shadow.' Perhaps he was thinking of those words of Kempthorne during his first year. 'Shouldn't you be studying for the glory of God as well as for the praise of others?' From now on that was to be his chief aim.

To his fellow-students Henry was something of an unknown quantity. He was a man who walked alone with his thoughts, sometimes serious to the point of aloofness, yet ever ready for courteous consideration of others. One of his colleagues wrote of him, 'Not-withstanding his unassuming manners and almost childlike simplicity, Martyn was perhaps superior in mental capacity to any one of his day in the University.'

In March 1802 Henry was chosen to be a Fellow of St John's, and gained first prize for his Latin essay.

For the long vacation in 1802 Henry went home to Cornwall to be given a hero's welcome. He spent an enjoyable holiday with relatives and friends, and he and Sally had long, interesting discussions on the things closest to the heart of both. He had much time for private Bible study and quiet meditation, a blessed relief after a strenuous term at Cambridge. It was for him a memorable visit which left, he said afterwards, a fragrance on his mind.

4

Wider Vision

When Henry returned to Cambridge after the long vacation in 1802 his first visit was to Simeon, and over their many cups of tea the talk turned to the subject of missionaries. Simeon had been impressed by reading reports of William Carey, the Baptist minister and shoe cobbler who had sailed with his family for India in 1793. He spoke so glowingly of what Carey had already accomplished with his translation work that the younger man was captivated. He walked back to his rooms that evening with his mind full of the need for more and more people to take the gospel of Jesus Christ to those who had not yet heard of it; for more translators to follow the example of Carey and make it possible for the Bible to be available in every language.

He started to read books on David Brainerd, that dedicated man who had preached to the North American Indians, wearing himself out in the service of God, finishing his earthly course at the early age of thirty-two. Henry longed for Brainerd's devotion to God and his holy living. 'Read David Brainerd today and yesterday and find as usual my spirit greatly

benefited by it. I long to be like him. Let me forget the
world and be swallowed up in a desire to glorify God.'

The influence of Simeon's teaching and the thought
of Brainerd's life as a missionary filled his mind.
Earnestly he prayed for more missionaries to carry on
the work, until he began asking himself the arresting
question. Why not me? Was it for this that God had
given him a gift for languages? Was this what he was
preparing him for?

At first the thought appalled him. He had hoped to
make a career among the learned intellectuals of his
day, to live and work in his beloved native country. He
could not accept the challenge, for his fastidious spirit
loved refinement and culture too much. He could not
live in conditions that were repellent to him, travelling
along rough and dangerous roads away from all
comfort. It was too much to ask of him.

So he struggled for many hours and weeks. But
before the end of the year he knew there was nothing
he could do but accept the missionary call. 'Lord, here
am I, send me.'

Henry's decision came like a thunderbolt to those
who knew him. Some saw it as a waste of scholarship
and a brilliant career. Sally, in true sisterly style, told
him plainly he was too inexperienced and not suitable
for such a project. Simeon saw it as a triumph of faith.

Henry himself was not sure what his plans for the
future would be, for sometimes he felt drawn to China
where there were not yet any Protestant missionaries.
At other times it was the country of India that tugged
at his heart.

Through it all he began to see that Sally was right
when she said he was not yet ready for missionary
work. The Christian fellowship he shared with Simeon

served to reveal to him his own lack of spiritual growth and depth. His self-examination as usual was without mercy, and to help him clarify his thoughts he began to keep a journal.

'My object in making this Journal is to accustom myself to self-examination and to give my experience a visible form, so as to leave a stronger impression on the memory and thus to improve my soul in holiness. For the review of such a lasting testimony will serve the double purpose of conviction and consolation.'

Henry kept up the journal faithfully to the end of his life, writing down an honest account of his thoughts and actions as he analysed them daily, never feeling satisfaction with his spiritual progress. Everything was recorded, his struggles and failures, unconscious as he was of the advances he was making in the Christian life. The journal showed the literary style of a good writer as it portrayed his self-analysis.

The journal was a private thing, not written for publication, but when after Henry's death it was eventually opened by his friends, they found an authentic record of the way in which this young Christian sought to discipline himself as he determined to follow Christ more closely. It remains for succeeding generations a treasure of great price.

5

Preaching Problems

The Rev Charles Simeon was a dominant character, ever eager to emphasise to young Christian men the joy and privilege of entering the ordained ministry. Rightly or wrongly, he influenced Henry to consider this possibility. Maybe this was a mistake, for Henry, brilliant as he was in other ways, was never particularly suited to the duties of a parish priest. Although he developed an absorbing devotion to the 'cure of souls' of every nation, his gift lay in personal contact rather than in preaching from a pulpit.

Without any strong conviction that God was leading him along the path, and keeping India and missionary work on the horizon, he was eventually persuaded to seek ordination. Apprehensive of the responsibilities this would bring, he found little joy in the ceremony when he was made a Deacon in Ely Cathedral. As he walked the sixteen miles back to Cambridge he could only feel ashamed of the unworthy self he was offering to God for what Simeon called 'the transcendent excellence of the Christian ministry.'

He was now curate to Simeon, and the following

Sunday he was booked to preach in the village church attached to Holy Trinity. He had been given no theological college training, for in those days a candidate was left to his own devices to prepare himself as best he could. The only training in preaching he had was by listening to the sermons of Simeon and others. He spent a worrying week preparing for Lolworth's pulpit but it was not a success. One member from the pew stayed after the service to suggest that Henry's missionary call was due to immature enthusiasm only, for he appeared not to be strong enough in mind or body for that sort of life.

The second week he felt more optimistic until he read over his written sermon. 'I was chilled and frozen by the stupidity of it.' But in the evening of that day he was more composed as he read the Prayer Book Service at Holy Trinity before Simeon preached. His depression returned when the congregation told him they had not been able to hear him and that his reading should be altogether more solemn!

For a young man who had recently achieved the highest success in his university, these setbacks were a blow to his pride. He had not anticipated this kind of failure and it was hard to take. With a certain amount of legitimate arrogance mixed with a desire for humility, Henry wrote honestly in his journal 'I began to see for the first time that I must be content to take my place among men of second-rate ability'.

As a member of Simeon's staff there were other duties for Henry to carry out, one of them being the work of visitation in the parish. Although he was of a compassionate and caring nature, he did not find himself equipped or suitable for this, although he carried it out faithfully. Often he was appalled by his lack of interest in those he was ministering to and he would leave with the feeling that he had been no help to them at all. Yet he could write in his journal, 'With my Bible in my hand, and Christ at my right hand, I can do all things. What though the whole world believe not, God abideth true and my hope in Him shall be steadfast.'

Apart from his clerical duties there was still time for other outlets. For three years he was examiner in the classics at St John's College but however busy he might be he was determined not to neglect the study of the Bible in ancient languages. For his own delight he read the Old Testament in Hebrew and the New Testament in Greek. His excellent memory helped him to learn much of Scripture by heart and this was to stand him in good stead later when he journeyed in the solitary places of the earth. He set himself to learn the Epistle to the Romans in Greek, and also studied Bengali and Arabic languages.

One friend thought he spent too long alone in his rooms, and complained that it was not necessary for a Christian to become so much of a recluse, neglecting social duties and deadening the fine feelings we should cultivate. 'His amazing volubility left me unable to say anything, but I kept my temper pretty well.'

Henry did not tell his critic that, in fact, since he had become a Christian his taste for painting, poetry and music had been intensified, refining his mind and making it more susceptible to the sublime and the beautiful.

6

A Problem Solved

Henry's mind was still set on missionary work, confident that God was calling him to India. He finally decided to offer himself to the recently formed Society for Missions to Africa and the East, which later became The Church Missionary Society.

This decision had not been easy and with it came the anguished realisation of what it would mean, putting an end to his cherished dream of a scholastic career among the intellectuals of his day. He would be leaving all he held dear; his family, his friends and his country. But having made up his mind he remained unshaken in his resolve to obey the command 'Go and preach to all nations'.

Then out of the blue came a plan-destroying problem. He learnt of the sudden loss of the small fortune left to him by his father, which was his only means of support. Sally was dependent on him and he had to provide for her, but the allowance the Society could be expected to allocate would only be sufficient for his own needs.

Now the doubts crept in. Was God not calling him

to missionary work after all? He could see no clear way ahead and in despair he confided to his friend, John Sargeant, 'The door to India seems to be closing.' Henry's friends, concerned at his obvious disappointment, gathered round to offer advice and eventually a new plan was suggested.

Although the war with America had ended the year after Henry was born, when the States had gained their independence, England's war with France was a continuing reality. But her Empire in India was being strengthened and enlarged and the power of Great Britain on land and sea was a force to be reckoned with.

The East India Company, founded by Elizabeth the First's Charter of 1600, held the monopoly of trade with the East Indies. The Company had regiments of soldiers in various parts of the Empire to guard their interests. They must be kept ready for attack by Dutch and Portuguese rivals as well as by world-wide pirates.

Their ships, built and manned for both war and commerce, were used to transport to Britain stocks of tea, coffee, spices and rich silks from China and India.

The Company was known to be opposed to the idea of missionaries going to other lands to seek to convert the heathen—'leave them happy in their ignorance' —but there could be a way in which Henry could take advantage of their assistance.

The directors of the East India Company, maybe through the powerful preaching of Wesley, had for some time been concerned for the welfare of their soldiers across the sea. They realised the need for spiritual help and guidance for men serving in units far from their native land.

Charles Grant, Chairman of the Board of Directors,

was at this time looking for dedicated men of evangelical faith to fill the positions of chaplains to their units in Bengal. They were offering a substantial salary for the job.

'Why not,' said Henry's friends, 'approach them and get to India that way?'

Henry listened to their suggestion but at first he was sceptical, doubting the wisdom or success of such a move. Was he suitable for such a position? He wanted to be a missionary, the work to which he felt God had first called him. His desire was to get among the people of India to talk to them of God's love. How could he do this if he were to be chaplain to one of England's regiments?

It was only after serious consideration of the matter that he finally decided that if this were the only way he would be willing to accept it.

Interviews were arranged in London for prospective candidates and there were visits to India House. At Leadenhall Street Henry met Charles Grant who put his name forward to the Board for consideration, and indicated that he would hear from them in due time.

For the man born and bred a Cornish countryman, a visit to the London of the early nineteenth century was an exciting experience. Henry found it a new world and he availed himself of every opportunity to see as much as possible. Among other places he visited the British Museum, revelling in its proud exhibitions. He attended musical lectures, called on John Newton the hymnwriter, and in company with William Wilberforce went to the House of Commons to listen to the persuasive voice of William Pitt.

Henry was delighted to be invited to go with Charles Grant to stay at the home of Wilberforce, and as they journeyed there in the coach Grant talked of the India so prominent in both their minds.

The aspiring missionary heard that Bengali was the language most widely used, but that Hindustani, which included Arabic, Persian and Sanskrit words, was used in many areas. Immediately Henry, ever eager for more knowledge, decided there and then to study them all!

Dinner that evening in the home of Wilberforce was a lively meal. The conversation ranged over a wide area and the youngest guest at the table listened spellbound. His university training had fitted him to take his place among these important men of high standing and intellect. He appreciated the value of their guidance as he waited for direction from the East India Company.

When at last he went to bed his mind was so overflowing with plans that sleep was impossible. India filled his whole horizon.

7

Comfort and Conflict

It was good to be going home once more, Henry thought, as in July 1804 he travelled to Cornwall, expecting this to be his last visit before sailing for India. Both his sisters were now married, Sally's husband being Mr Pearson, vicar of Lamorran and St Michael Penkevil, about five miles outside Truro. Her new home was open to the brother she was always so pleased to see.

The journey on the coach took several days and there was time for meditation, something Henry was always ready to indulge in, writing up his thoughts later in his journal. 'Most dreadfully assailed by evil thoughts, but at the very height prayer prevailed and I was delivered. During the rest of the journey enjoyed great peace and a strong desire to live for Christ alone, forsaking marriage...'

This was a definite step of renunciation for, as only Henry himself knew, he was already in love.

When they reached Plymouth he stayed for a few days with his cousin Tom Hitchin and his wife, Emma Grenfell, greatly enjoying their Christian hospitality.

Then he set off for Sally's home at Lamorran.

When the family greetings were over, news exchanged and commented on, Henry settled down to enjoy the peaceful setting, looking out with tired eyes through the window at the Cornish hills that had surrounded him in his childhood.

Gradually the hectic university life of learning and study faded into the background. He was a boy again, throwing pebbles over the Fal; listening to the exciting tales of the fisherfolk; finding a robin's nest; and on one well remembered day seeing the soldiers marching through the streets of Truro.

He loved it all, and in a letter to a friend he wrote, 'The scene is such as is to be frequently met with in this part of Cornwall. Below the house is an arm of the sea, flowing between the hills which are covered with wood. By the side of this water I walk in general in the evening, out of the reach of all sound but the rippling of the waves and the whistling of the curlew.'

This was his first visit home since his ordination and he was hoping to use his time in preaching in his native surroundings. His brother-in-law invited him to the pulpit of his two small churches, where Henry felt more at home than he had been at Lolworth.

His old church in Truro thought what they considered his Calvinist views to be too severe, and they declined to extend an invitation to him.

It was a novelty for Henry's family and friends to see him in the pulpit and Sally, in particular, enjoyed her brother's sermons. He was encouraged by the fact that Laura, the sister who had previously shown little interest in spiritual matters, was 'deeply affected' by his preaching, and he enjoyed a long talk with her on the things that matter.

'In the evening I walked by the waterside till late, having my heart full of praise to God for giving me such hopes of my sister.'

But Henry's mind was on other things beside sisters. Talking with Emma Grenfell on his way home had revived a train of thought that persisted. The Grenfell family had long been friends of the Martyn family and, still living at home in Marazion, near Penzance, with her somewhat possessive mother was Emma's sister, Lydia, five years older than Henry. And Henry loved Lydia. He must see her once more before he left England for good.

One morning he went over to Marazion and called at the Grenfell house. After greeting the family he persuaded Lydia to walk with him through the country lanes, mentioning nothing of his feelings for her. But before he returned to Lamorran he realised Lydia had crept further into his heart.

The knowledge of this caused tumult within. He wanted to be faithful to his conviction that God had called him to a life of missionary work in India. He had accepted the call at a time when he felt marriage was not for him; before he had realised he was falling in love with Lydia. He could not ask her to share what must inevitably be a life of isolation and hardship in a foreign land, even supposing she returned his affection. One moment he was tormented with the idea of settling down with Lydia to the alluring prospect of a parish appointment here at home. The next moment he knew this was impossible. Whatever the sacrifice, his call to India was clear.

During the night he wrestled with his conflicting thoughts and eventually, unable to sleep, he went out to walk in the garden, seeking the peace that eluded him. 'I could think of nothing but her excellencies and spent two hours reasoning with my perverse heart.'

With his usual concern for others Henry kept his sadness to himself and devoted the rest of his holiday to his sisters until it was time to return to Cambridge. Not expecting to see them again, he said goodbye to his friends.

He called again at the home of Tom and his wife at Plymouth and Emma confided to him the secret that she knew his affection for her sister was not altogether one-sided. While this news could not help but thrill his heart, it made him at the same time even more sad.

Henry spent another day in London with Charles Grant before going back to Simeon in Cambridge 'to preach the gospel to my fellow-creatures that they might obtain the salvation which is in Christ Jesus.'

He wrote to Sally, 'Pray that I may know something of humility ... How it smooths the furrows of care and gilds the dark path of life. It will make us kind, tender-hearted, affable, and enable us to do more for God and the Gospel than the most fervent zeal without it'.

Had he perhaps been reading 'We are afflicted in every way, but not crushed; perplexed but not driven to despair'? (2 Cor. 4:8 RSV).

Determination to persevere and proceed along a difficult path, whatever the cost, proved to be a characteristic feature of Henry Martyn which, under God, resulted in his fine achievements.

In the meantime students, hearing that he was back in the district, were eager to contact him and make use of his well-known talents. Difficulty in mathematics perhaps? Help needed for one studying classics? Even children for extra tutoring? They all came knocking on his door, and none of them was disappointed.

8

Ordained Priest

When in January 1805 Henry heard from Grant that the chaplaincy with the East India Company had been granted and would soon be finalised he wrote in his journal, 'I could have been better pleased to have gone out as a missionary, poor as the Lord and his apostles.' He was asked to be ready to sail during the month but this was not possible as he was not yet ordained as a priest. This could not take place until a candidate was twenty-four years old, so Henry had to wait until his next birthday, on 18 February.

He stayed on with Simeon as his curate, still caring for the small parish at Lolworth, encouraged continually by his long talks with Simeon at the end of the day. This great man was aware of the limitations and mistakes of his young friend but he loved him as a son. He slipped seeds of valuable advice into the fertile mind of the one who would soon be setting off into unknown paths. There were warnings about the danger of being drawn into situations where secular interests could hinder the spiritual work of evangelism. Simeon stressed the necessity of reaching out to Asians in their own language and culture. Henry listened, and remembered.

On one of his visits to London Henry met Dr Gilchrist, a colleague of Carey in Calcutta, and he was able to give valuable help with the subject of Hindustani. Little by little the new chaplain was gaining information and experience while he waited in the wings.

He was asked by the Rev Richard Cecil to preach at St George's Chapel in Bedford Row. 'After I had preached Mr Cecil said a great deal to me on the necessity of gaining the attention of the people and speaking with more warmth and earnestness. I felt a little wounded at finding myself to have failed in so many things, yet I succeeded in coming down to the dust and received gladly the kind advice of wise friends.'

On 10 March 1805 Henry was ordained as a priest in the Chapel Royal of St James's in London. He also received a degree of Bachelor of Divinity conferred upon him by mandate from the university. Now nothing remained to keep him in Cambridge. 'I felt more persuaded of my call than ever.'

The continuing war with France made it difficult to fix sailing dates. Napoleon, with his lust for power and dominions, constituted a real threat of invasion, and the ships might all be needed in home waters.

For this reason Henry was advised to live in London while waiting, so that he would be available as soon as a date could be decided on.

Eager now, as any young man would be, to get on with what he had concluded was to be his life's work, he could not help but find this further delay a tiresome necessity.

Henry hurried to Cambridge for a short farewell visit to Simeon. 'I supped with Simeon alone. He prayed before I went away and my heart was deeply moved.' He went to Lolworth for the last time on Palm Sunday and in the evening preached to a large congregation in Trinity Church.

Like a swarm of bees the students gathered at Henry's lodgings early next morning, ready to accompany him right to the coach. As he looked back over the past seven years in this noble palace of learning where he had been taught so much, formed so many friendships and grown—unknowingly—in the ways of God, the morning mist came down over the river and the stately spires of Cambridge disappeared for all time from his sight.

The war situation, with reports of activity of the hostile fleets of France and Spain, kept Henry in London for a further three months. His official appointment as chaplain for the East India Company was confirmed on 24 April 1805, when he took the oath at India House.

He was given an interview at Lambeth Palace, where the Archbishop stressed the importance of the appointment and cordially wished the new chaplain every success.

Henry paid another visit to John Newton and they discussed the work Henry would be engaged in, the visitor adding that he might not live to see much fruit. 'You will have a bird's eye view of it which will be better,' was the wise reply.

'When I referred to the opposition I was likely to meet with he said he supposed Satan wouldn't love me for what I was about to do!' The old man prayed before Henry left, adding his own benediction.

At last came the final preparation for departure, luggage packed and roped, and farewell parties with new and old friends in London. At one of these he met a fellow-student from Cambridge, Daniel Corrie, and was delighted to hear that he too expected to be going to India to serve Christ in that land.

On 8 July Henry left London and on his way to Portsmouth to board his ship he called at the home of John Sargeant, his Cambridge friend who had recently married and was living in Sussex. But the strain of the past weeks—waiting in uncertainty, the hectic round of farewells and the preparation necessary for a completely new life as chaplain—had finally caught up with him. He had never been very robust and as he was getting ready for bed that evening he collapsed. When he came to he was in much pain.

Henry confided details of this incident to his journal but, stoic that he was, he appears to have told no one else about it, for nobody seems to have been sufficiently perturbed by it to query his physical fitness for the life ahead. And by the next day he was so far recovered that he could continue his journey to Portsmouth.

What a sight met him when he reached the quay! A whole fleet of ships, too numerous to count, lay at anchor, with only the hovering seagulls to indicate there was life aboard. A forest of tall masts swaying in the ocean breeze hid for the moment the distant skyline. And among this array of ships was *The Union* which was to carry Henry and the 59th Regiment to their base some 15,000 miles away.

Sailing date was still uncertain as the convoy hoped first to hear of Nelson's return from the West Indies before they left. Simeon and Sargeant with other friends had gathered in Portsmouth with a view to seeing Henry off, and together they settled down to wait.

For a further week the ships dragged impatiently at their anchors and still Nelson did not return. So early on 17 July there came signs of movement throughout the convoy and orders came for all ships to be cleared of their visitors. Simeon said goodbye to the pale young man he loved as a son, clasping his friend's hand in both of his, and the many farewells were over.

Across the noisy docks came the sound of clipped commands, the shouting of the crew working as a team, the crack of the sails as they snapped open into the wind, the clanking of chains, lifting of the anchors and the firing of the gun signal by the Commodore.

One by one the wooden ships began to glide farther out toward the open sea to manoeuvre their position in the convoy, and the watching people on the quayside began to disperse.

It was a triumphant moment for Henry, at last to be actually on his way to the country he had been thinking of day and night for many weeks and months. It was true he was not going as a free missionary but as one under orders, but his whole being radiated praise for the way God was surely leading him to the land where he hoped to live and work to the end of his days.

At that moment the mountain top on which he stood was lofty, but the ship was not many miles out before the new chaplain was in need of prayer as much as any of his flock. He lay in his cabin in the depths of despair, homesick, Lydia-sick—and violently seasick!

9

Delay at Falmouth

The fleet kept fairly near the coastline as it moved slowly westward and two days later Henry found himself looking out on a familiar scene. They were anchoring in Falmouth Harbour. Tantalising thoughts began to creep in, reminding him that his sisters, Truro, his friends, and above all Lydia were almost within reach, and yet so far away.

The following day they learnt that Napoleon's invasion fleet had embarked from Boulogne, bringing the possibility of trouble from the French. The British convoy was likely to be held at Falmouth for some time and shore leave was granted. What could stop Henry from satisfying his intense longing to see Lydia once more?

'But I dare not; let the Lord open the way if it is His Will,' wrote Henry in his journal. But as the days dragged on Henry's own will weakened until in desperation one morning he caught the early coach to Marazion, this time determined to declare his love.

The family were at breakfast when he arrived, startled at the sudden appearance of one they thought to be away on the high seas. Mrs Grenfell may not have been too pleased to have this earnest missionary-minded young man back on her doorstep, for although her daughter had reached the age of thirty Mamma liked to think the apron strings were still tied!

Henry and Lydia spent most of the day together and, with a shy reticence, Henry told of his deep abiding love for her. He asked if she would be willing to come out to him in India, should it be God's will for them to be married. She was hesitant and would give him no firm answer, suggesting there were obstacles such as the shortness of time to decide. That was understandable, but there was a deeper reason for her indecision and this she did not reveal.

In the past Lydia had suffered a broken engagement and—foolishly perhaps—she was unwilling to enter into another marriage contract while her ex-fiancé remained unmarried. Had she been able to discuss this with Henry at the time, it is possible much heart-break for both of them might have been spared.

Poor Henry! Perplexed and despondent he went back to his ship. Yet in his cabin that evening he could write 'May the Lord give me grace to turn cheerfully to my proper work and business.' And away in Marazion Lydia was confiding to her diary 'May the Lord moderate the sorrows I feel at parting with so valuable and excellent a friend.'

On Sunday the new chaplain preached on board *The Union* and tried out his stumbling Hindustani on the Indian crew but found little response. 'How I long to know their language so that I can preach the Gospel to them.'

Rumours abounded on the ship, and one was that they were to go to Ireland first and then on to the Cape of Good Hope; but for the time being they just stayed on where they were, anchored in Falmouth harbour. It was too tempting for Henry, who could not resist making several more visits to see Lydia although she was not always at home when he called.

She wrote her secrets in her diary. 'I learn from our servant that he called and left a message that he would be here tomorrow. My future happiness and his, the glory of God, the peace of my dear mother, all are concerned in what may happen tomorrow.'

But when the next day dawned the wind was blowing from the north and the fleet at last decided to sail. The signal gun was fired but the chaplain was nowhere to be found. When news of the preparation for sailing reached Marazion there was no time to be lost and it had to be a curt and hasty farewell. In the flurry of the moment Lydia raised no objection to Henry's repeated suggestion that she would come to India, although she would not enter into any agreement.

A horse was made ready and Henry galloped away, his one thought now to reach Falmouth in time. His heart sank as he came in sight of the harbour and realised it was almost empty. But the anchor chains of *The Union* had fouled other lines and, mercifully for the harassed chaplain, this had delayed its departure with the rest of the fleet. With a thankful heart he scrambled aboard, careful not to let anyone know why he had been missing or where he had been.

The next morning the spire of St Hilary's Church near Marazion was still visible and his thoughts flew to Lydia and their frantic parting. She had said, he remembered, 'We had better go free.' What had she meant? What *had* she meant? The one who filled Henry's mind as his ship carried him past the Cornish coast was writing up her diary. 'My affections are engaged beyond recall. It is now fairly understood between us that he is free to marry where he is going and I shall often pray the Lord to find him a suitable partner.' Not quite what Henry had in mind!

He had finally left England, his missionary vision dominant, his chaplaincy a means of realising it. As his native land slipped farther and farther into the background his one aim was to live for Christ in the place of his calling.

But his highly-strung nature was tormented by the remembrance of all he had loved and lost, while his merciless self-examination rebuked him for his lack of dedicated holiness.

10

The New Chaplain

The fleet went first to Ireland where the invasion threat kept them for another two weeks. On 28 August 1805, accompanied by warships, they left the safety of Cork Harbour for the wild waters of the Atlantic, made more dangerous by the manoeuvres of the English and French navies leading up to Nelson's victory at Trafalgar.

Henry was thankful to have a cabin to himself and this was stacked high with his books. They were his only companions, for among the crowded decks he felt not only friendless but a complete foreigner. He was a 'raw academic', taking his meals with officers and cadets in the cuddy; pleasant and orderly enough, but the talk was all of regiments, war and firearms.

He spent much of his time on deck, seasick and cold in the howling wind that whipped through the rigging. Troubled thoughts plagued him, chasing through his mind with the pointed finger of condemnation. 'The world has a hold upon my soul and the spiritual conflict is consequently dreadful.'

They reached Funchal, capital of Madeira Island,

on 29 September and left the rolling ship for four blissful days on 'terra firma'. To everyone he met on the island Henry talked about the Lord Jesus Christ, fearlessly disputing with those who put forward mistaken ideas. He also found time to write a letter to Emma in Plymouth. 'God knows how dearly I love you and Lydia and Sally and all His saints in England, yet I bid you an everlasting farewell almost without a sigh.' Not altogether complimentary perhaps but, while his courteous spirit shied from causing unnecessary offence, Henry's nature was too deeply serious for trivial pleasantries.

Another forty days passed before they reached Brazil and throughout the journey the chaplain continued his personal programme of Bible study, prayer, meditation and memorising parts of Scripture. His duties included a weekly service when some two hundred soldiers came, but they were not very attentive to his preaching, finding his sermons difficult to take. They were too demanding, they said, and set too high a standard.

One young soldier confided to Henry that he had been a choirboy, and this was the chaplain's opportunity to enlist his cooperation by asking him to start singing sessions. Henry himself had a rich deep voice and the singing proved a great success.

'Where's the chaplain?' became the common question, for this one was everywhere. Like a true shepherd he looked for his flock in every corner, below deck or on the gun deck, chatting with sailors among the hammocks or having an earnest conversation with a man working in the boatswain's berth. In the afternoons he would read to a small group of soldiers and their wives, introducing them to the delights of *Pilgrim's Progress* by Bunyan.

Often he would go quietly down the ladders to visit those who were ill in the cockpit, groping his way to where they lay in the dark, taking them water and nourishment for their bodies and an uplift for their souls.

The chaplain's uncompromising presence in the ship made its own impact, and although some were offended by his ruthless warning of judgement there were others who decided to follow Christ whatever the cost. A cadet's officer named MacKenzie became a true friend, eager to discuss spiritual matters and to progress along the Christian path. A faithful few met often in Henry's cabin, learning from him something of the hardships as well as joys of discipleship.

In his leisure time Henry continued the study of languages that were to fit him for missionary evangelism, and tested out his vocabulary on the Lascar sailors. Constantly his prayer was for the setting up of Christ's kingdom in the world, never losing sight of the solemn responsibilities of his vocation, always longing for greater spirituality. He did not mind that one of his friends on the ship had said, 'He is a good scholar but a poor orator.'

11

Trespassing in Brazil

The voyage was not without incident, and soon after passing the Equator the whole fleet came on to a dangerous reef of rocks. Horror-struck, they saw that two of the ships were lost but miraculously the look-out man on *The Union* saw what was happening in time and his quick action saved the ship from tragedy. Soon they came in sight of South America and, while one of the army captains was having a heated argument with the chaplain, blaming God for giving him the nature he had, the fleet ran into San Salvador.

Brazil, then a Portuguese colony, was made up of Brazilians, Portuguese, and coloured slaves, and it was a joy to the sea-weary Henry to mix with the friendly people with whom he was to spend the next sixteen days.

His curiosity for new scenery sent him exploring, and he wandered through an open gate before realising it was the private approach to someone's house. The trespass turned out to be the introduction to a fascinating and pleasant interlude, for as he decided to withdraw the owners came out, wondering who this

was in their garden. Henry apologised in French and
explained his mistake and the fact that he was a
stranger just off one of the anchored ships. The details
of his meeting with Senor and Senora Corre are given
in diary form in his journal:

'…I was very politely desired to sit down at a little table
which was standing under a large space before the house
like a verandah. They then brought me oranges and a
small red acid fruit, the name of which I asked but
cannot recollect. The young man sat opposite, conversing
about Cambridge; he had been educated in a Portuguese
University. Almost immediately, on finding I was of
Cambridge, he invited me to come when I liked to his
house. A slave, after bringing the fruit, was sent to gather
three roses for me; the master then walked with me
round the garden and showed me, among the rest, the
coffee-plant. When I left him he repeated his invitation.
Thus did the Lord give his servant favour in the eyes of
Antonio Joseph Corre.'

'Nov. 14. Senor Antonio received me with the same cor-
diality; he begged me to dine with him. I was curious and
attentive to observe the difference between the Portuguese manners and ours; there were but two plates laid
on the table and the dinner consisted of a great number
of small mixed dishes, following one another in quick
succession but none of them very palatable. In the end of
the evening we walked out to see his plantation; here
everything possessed the charm of novelty. The grounds
included two hills and a valley between them. The hills
were covered with coconut trees, bananas, mangoes,
orange and lemon trees, olives, coffee, chocolate and
cotton-plants etc. In the valley was a large plantation of
a shrub or tree bearing a cluster of small berries which he
desired me to taste; I did and found it was pepper, lately
introduced from Bavaria…Slaves were walking about

the grounds, watering the trees and turning up the earth…At night I returned to the ship in one of the country boats, which are canoes made of a tree hollowed out and paddled by three men.'

'*Nov. 18*. Went ashore at six o'clock and found that Senor Antonio had been waiting for me two hours. It being too late to go into the country I stayed at his house till dinner…At his father's house I was described to them as one who knew everything—Arabic, Persian, Greek etc. and all stared at me as if I had been dropped from the skies.'

'*Nov. 23*. In the afternoon took leave of my kind friends, Senor and Senora Corre. They and the rest came out to the garden gate and continued looking till the winding of the road hid me from their sight. The poor slave Raymond who had attended me and carried my things burst into a flood of tears and when I parted from him he was going to kiss my feet; but I shook hands with him, much affected by such extraordinary kindness in people to whom I had been a total stranger till within a few days.'

So could Henry win the friendship of both the uneducated and the scholarly, able to converse with each person at their own level, ever desirous of their spiritual welfare, pointing his hearer to the claims of the God he worshipped.

12

Back to Work

The last sixteen days had been beneficial to Henry in many ways, restoring as they did his old buoyant spirit. The trauma of leaving England with the events leading up to it, combined with the loneliness he felt in the new life on board ship, had obscured for some time the brighter side of his character. For although given to melancholy self-criticism when alone, with his friends he always had a gracious charm, ready to share a joke, often bubbling over with wit and gaiety. And at Salvador he had walked among friends.

But now he had to return to the serious business of being the spiritual adviser to soldiers who would shortly be exposed to the horrors and dangers of war. They had been told that their object was the capture of the Cape of Good Hope, at that time a Dutch colony. It was necessary for this to be retaken by the British in order to keep the sea route to the East open.

It took five weeks to reach the battle area and as the calendar turned to 1806 the fleet anchored near Cape Town.

The 59th Regiment landed and on 8 January the

fierce battle of Blaauberg was fought. There was a loss of almost a thousand men, most of them from the Dutch side.

As soon as the fighting ceased Henry was allowed to go on shore with a stretcher party and a doctor, to do what they could for the many wounded lying around on the sand or in the farmhouses that had been hastily turned into a hospital.

The battle had raged for two days before the Dutch surrendered and Henry found his time taken up with helping the wounded men and bringing what comfort he could. He was able to find lodgings in Cape Town and preached at the military hospital where he visited.

Appalled by his close contact with the result of warfare, he wrote, 'I felt considerable pain at the enemy being obliged to give up everything to the victors...I had rather be trampled upon than be the trampler.'

His journal records more of his thoughts. 'I prayed that the capture of the Cape might be ordered to the advancement of Christ's kingdom; and that England, whilst she sent the thunder of her arms to the distant regions of the globe, might not remain proud and ungodly at home, but might show herself great indeed by sending forth the ministers of her church to diffuse the gospel of peace.'

During his month at Cape Town Henry longed to find some Christian fellowship and friendship. When at Cambridge he had heard of a Dutch missionary living in Cape Town and decided to try and find him. He knew that eighty-year-old Dr Vanderkemp was an agent of the London Missionary Society, and at last he was able to locate his house. Henry received a warm welcome when he introduced himself and immediately

Dr Vanderkemp introduced his fellow missionary, Mr Read.

'I was beyond measure delighted. Meeting these beloved brethren so filled me with joy and gratitude to God that I hardly knew what to do.'

Henry spent most of his leisure time with the missionaries, joining them in their family worship. Sometimes they would sit at night in the open, with Table Mountain in the distance, and Henry listened avidly to their account of the missionary work they were engaged in. Nothing could have done more to encourage him in the path he had chosen.

'Talking with Read on the beach, we spoke of the excellency of missionary work. The last time I stood on the shore with a friend, speaking on the same subject, was with Lydia at Marazion, and I mentioned her to Read. However I felt not the slightest desire for marriage and often thank God for keeping me single.'

When Henry wrote that, it may have been he was trying to convince himself that this was the case, for the truth was that his love of Lydia was still as strong as ever.

In one of his talks with Vanderkemp before he left Cape Town, he asked the elderly missionary if he ever regretted spending his life as a missionary. Like a shot came the reply. 'No. I wouldn't exchange my work for a kingdom.' These were encouraging words for the one whose great longing was to get started on the mission-ary pathway.

On 4 February the fleet set off for Madras. Illness among the passengers, rough and stormy seas, increasing heat and a shortage of food combined to make this part of the voyage the most difficult. But Henry was encouraged by the continuing fellowship of

MacKenzie and a few others who came to his cabin for prayer and Bible study.

They caught sight of land on 21 April and the following day reached Madras. Henry was intrigued by all he saw, eager to learn quickly all he could about the country he had thought of for so long.

As soon as Henry and his possessions were on shore he was surrounded by a great crowd of coolies, all eager to transport his luggage. They picked up one box after another, going off in all directions and he was forced to run after them to stop the dispersion! Only when he had managed to get all his things together again was he able to get to the Custom-house. Even then he was closely followed by four coolies, an umbrella-carrier, and a boy called a 'waiting-man', who attached themselves to him without invitation. At dinner that night they were waited on by turbanned Asiatics.

'Now that I am actually treading on Indian ground, let me bless and adore my God for doing so much for me; and if I live let me come hither for some purpose.'

As a change from Henry's constant study of Hindustani and Persian languages he left his lodgings one night to go to see an Indian village accompanied by his servant Samees. In the main street there were about two hundred terrace houses, and in the little winding paths were a number of detached ones. 'Here all was Indian—no vestige of anything European.'

On the Sunday Henry preached at Fort St George before the Governor who was so impressed he asked for a copy of the sermon.

13

New Friends

It was very hot as the ships left Madras and edged their way up the Hooghly River until they reached Calcutta.

The next day, 16 May 1806, Henry stepped ashore as soon as it was light and went to enquire for the East India Company's senior chaplain, David Brown. He was disappointed to find that he was not at his Calcutta address but was staying at his suburban home, Aldeen.

It was a poor welcome into a strange land for someone who had travelled 15,000 miles to get there. But arrival time for ships was so unpredictable that it was not possible to make arrangements beforehand.

After further enquiries Henry found someone who could direct him to the missionary base of William Carey, the Baptist translator who had been in India since 1793. The meeting of these two men must have been an emotional experience for them both, for it was through hearing of Carey's translation work that Henry had come. When he was a young ordinand drinking tea with Simeon in his rooms at Cambridge, listening to his host's story of William Carey, he had

been first alerted to the needs of India and her people.

For Carey there was the thrill of not only receiving a visitor from England, but one who had the same aspirations as his own.

As they sat at breakfast the two men, from different backgrounds but alike in literary gifts and evangelical fire, talked chiefly of missions and missionary outreach. Then after family worship with the servants Carey went back to his study to continue translating with his pundit from the Sanskrit manuscript, leaving his guest to explore his new surroundings.

As soon as David Brown heard that Henry had arrived in Calcutta he came to fetch the new chaplain to stay with him and his family at Aldeen. Mrs Brown, always ready to make room for another guest at her large family table, soon made him feel at home.

The house was set in a mound of foliage; mango, bamboo and teak growing in abundance in the hot climate. There was a large green lawn under the trees where the Brown family played and where their parents could relax.

Henry soon made friends with the children for in their company he could be as a child, romping with them, playing 'lions and tigers' on all fours or carrying the smaller ones on his shoulder. 'Here comes Uncle Henry,' they would shout as soon as they saw him coming over the lawn, and there would be a race to reach him first. His merry laugh would mingle with their shouts of welcome that rang out over the treetops.

Mr Brown realised that Henry would need a quiet place for study and he prepared an ancient pagoda that stood near the river at the end of the garden as his special sanctum. This one-time temple was a strange place, with its vaulted cells and walls showing carvings of Hindu gods, now echoing the prayers of this dedicated Christian who walked so near to the living God. Henry wrote, 'I like my dwelling much, it is so retired and free from noise. It has so many recesses and cells that I can hardly find my way in and out.'

Here he wrote out his sermons to preach for David Brown to his English congregation at the Old Mission and the New Church in Calcutta, and his friends now began to hope he would stay on with them. They were deeply concerned about his health when a serious attack of illness and high temperature put him out of action for many days. It was obvious he was not robust, and rather than the strenuous life as a chaplain in an inland army centre, they felt that Calcutta was more suited to his particular ministry and linguistic gifts.

He was also in close touch by this time with what was known as 'the Serampore trio'; Carey, Marshman and Ward, and ever the talk between them was of oriental languages and grammar. 'Three such men so suited to one another and to their work are not to be found in the whole world.' They too would have liked their new friend to stay and join them at Serampore and give himself to the study of Urdu (Hindustani) and translation. The many kind suggestions for his future interested and intrigued him. 'I was perplexed and so excited I could get little sleep.'

But as chaplain he was not a completely free agent and his first duty was to the East India Company and the men of the regiment. He knew he must wait to hear where his posting would be.

Apart from that he longed to get among the native people, to mix with them and learn something of their hopes and fears, their traditions and frustrations. He remembered the wise words of Simeon when he had stressed the necessity of reaching out to Asians in their own language and culture.

While he waited at Aldeen he set himself to continue more ardently than ever with his study of Urdu, Sanskrit, Arabic and Persian. His zest for learning seemed endless and the Brahmin who was now helping him was usually the first to tire of the day's lesson!

On some days Henry went for tutoring in oriental writings to Fort William College, where Carey was now one of the Professors.

But all study went by the board the day Henry heard that his old friend from Cambridge days, Daniel Corrie, had arrived at Calcutta. He too had come out to take up work as a chaplain and there were lively scenes of joy when the two friends met. Corrie was later to become Bishop of Madras.

14

A Letter from Lydia

Ever since that abrupt parting at Marazion, Henry's thoughts had never been far from his beloved Lydia. Although he seemed to be resigned to the fact that she would never be his wife he knew that his love for her would remain.

Before they had reached the end of the voyage he had, as he imagined, come to terms with it and he wrote a final farewell to her. 'Never will you cease to be dear to me; still, the glory of God and the salvation of immortal souls is an object for which I can part with you.'

It is difficult to understand Lydia and her vacillations. It would appear that, although she was a committed Christian, there was something of the nature of a coquette in her make-up. She certainly seemed to trifle with the affections of this man who was sufficiently naïve not to realise it.

She had been willing to send him away to India without her, but as soon as he had gone she sent him a letter to keep fresh in his mind the memory of the woman he had left behind. At this juncture one would like to have whispered to him, 'Think no more of her, Henry. She will probably break your heart.' But he would not have listened.

Henry's whole nature was filled with love, firstly to God and, fulfilling the second commandment, loving his neighbour as himself. Every incident of his life, joy or sadness, was brought in prayer to God with a childlike, trusting faith and a willingness to accept his will for every step on what often proved to be a prickly path.

Only towards himself was he merciless, and sometimes his self-condemnation seemed to be outside the bounds of common sense.

Lydia's letter arrived with the first mail from England on 12 July. It told him she thought of him in prayer every day and the whole letter sounded full of promises to his lovesick heart, rousing the old longings. His peace of mind was disturbed and he began to wonder if after all it could be God's will for them to marry.

The thought persisted and eventually Henry discussed the whole matter with David Brown, asking him to read the letter. The older man was convinced that the lady was waiting to be won over and he advised Henry to send a suitable reply.

Later that evening a lonely figure sat in his pagoda, his mind in a whirl, writing out a courteously restrained love-letter, with a definite proposal that she should come out to him as soon as possible. So sure was he now that Lydia would one day be with him in India that he asked if she could be ready to sail in the February fleet. In the event it was actually well into March before she even received his letter.

The sun was rising in the dawn sky before Henry

put down his pen and in his heart rang the sound of wedding bells.

From then on he began to prepare for Lydia's arrival, brightening up his spartan home as much as possible. Among other things he sent an order to Josiah Wedgwood, Queen Charlotte's potter as he was called, for a set of his latest 'Queensware' cups and saucers being produced in the English county of Staffordshire.

Henry talked over plans with David Brown and his wife and it was arranged that Lydia should come initially as their guest. Mrs Brown would go down to Calcutta to meet her and take her to Aldeen to stay until the marriage could be arranged.

Everything seemed to be slipping into place and the optimistic Henry was as excited as a schoolboy!

15

New Appointments

On 13 September 1806 Henry received his appointment to Dinapore, the European suburb of Patna, which was then the fifth largest city in India, stretching for some fourteen miles along the Ganges. Patna was predominantly Muslim. In the army settlement there were four hundred troops under the command of General Clarke.

Having become accustomed to the pleasant way of life at Aldeen, Henry had now to adjust again to the more arduous and lonely life of a chaplain. But it would also mean he would be fulfilling his great desire to get among the people of India and tell them of Jesus and his love. 'I think that when my mouth is opened I shall preach to them day and night. I feel that they are my brethren in the flesh.'

The Serampore missionaries with other friends joined the Brown family for a farewell meeting in his garden pagoda, and on 15 October he had to say goodbye to them all. He was comforted by the verse David Brown had quoted from the first chapter of the book of Joshua 'Have not I sent you?' But it was with mixed feelings he boarded the barge-like budgerow

waiting to take him along the river to Dinapore.

Now for the first time he was alone with native people, and on a trip that would last many weeks, calling at local places on the way. Progress was slow as they glided over the water, giving opportunity to enjoy the passing scenery along the river bank and to watch the rare birds that flew overhead. Here and there they saw white-washed temples with broad steps leading down to the water's edge.

Although the sun was merciless during the day, the mornings and evenings were chilly, so when at sunset the budgerow was moored the boatmen lit their supper fire and settled round it. Many were the tales they told as they sat smoking their hookahs before bedding down for the night.

Traffic on the river came to a standstill and boats were moored along the bank. In the eerie stillness the cry of a distant jackal would break into the soporific sound of water lapping against the sides of the vessel. Then the lonely traveller's thoughts would go to his well-loved sisters in Cornwall and his friends at Cambridge, and with a clutch at his heart he longed for that expected reply from Lydia.

During the day he studied with his native language secretary (moonshee) and on 20 October he records the fact that he had started translating the book of Acts into Hindustani (Urdu), writing it out in Persian characters. He realised that the best method of acquiring a knowledge of the various oriental tongues was to study Sanskrit, although he found difficulty in trying to conquer the grammar and wrote, 'I cannot say whereabouts I am in it, being enveloped at present in a thick cloud with the exceptions, limitations, anomalies etc.'

He also records that later that day he shot a bird which he handed over to the cook and looked forward to a meal that would be a change from curry!

He went often on shore to meet the local people and found little difficulty in getting into conversation with them. His sensitive ear was quick to notice the change of dialect as he passed from village to village. He also went into the markets on the river bank to distribute copies of the New Testament to those who said they could read. In this way, watching and listening, Henry learnt more and more of the beliefs and traditions of the country he had adopted as his own.

On 27 October they moored at Berhampore and he went ashore to visit an army hospital to minister to the European soldiers who were patients. When he met the surgeon he was surprised to find him to be an old school-fellow from Truro, and invited him back to the boat to spend the evening, giving them both the chance to talk of days gone by.

Another day he visited a village school at Mirdy-pore. 'The little boys, seated cross-legged on the ground all round the room, read some of the New Testament to us. While they displayed their powers of reading their fathers and mothers crowded in great numbers round the doors.' Proud parents—the same the world over!

And so at last, after six interesting weeks, the chaplain came to his new parish, and moved into barrack quarters on 26 November 1806. There was no welcome for him and there had been little preparation for his coming. His duties were to include taking services, but he found no church, so they had to be conducted either in a barrack room with no seating or in one of the squares which provided no shade from the hot sun. It was little wonder the soldiers were apathetic in their response.

Henry also tried to introduce Church services at Bankipore, the civilian settlement, but here again he was discouraged by the attitude of his own country-men. In fact they seemed to resent his presence among them and particularly his friendly approach to the native people.

He continued with translation, working on the Parables and the Book of Common Prayer. By June 1807 he could write, 'In Hindustani translation I begin to feel my ground and can go on much faster than one Moonshee can follow.' Increasingly he was aware that his gift as a linguist exceeded his suitability as a chap-lain. His evangelistic sermons were not popular and seemed to make very little impression on most of his congregation. They wanted their religion to be a little less severe!

Henry was, however, kept busy with army matters and fulfilled his duties with sincerity and compassion. There were funerals to conduct and there were also sick men in hospital to visit and to these he brought cheer and comfort.

On one occasion he needed to travel seventy danger-ridden miles in an uncomfortable covered litter (palanquin) to preside at the wedding of two of his parishioners. Before setting off he left work for his *moonshee* to get on with in his absence and prudently made out his will!

His friends, Brown and Corrie, wrote to him regu-larly and their letters came to him as refreshing as snow in summer heat; their support was invaluable to this solitary worker. The only friends near at hand were Major and Mrs Young, who invited him often to a meal in their home.

Henry had a flair for mingling with the 'man in the street'; learning as he talked with them, finding out more of the prejudices, aspirations and attitudes of Asian people. His scholarly mind delighted in discussion specially when the subject was that of the varying forms of worship and religion. After listening courteously to the opinion of others he would lead his hearers back to the truths found in the Scriptures. 'My thirst for knowledge is very strong but I pray continually that the Spirit of God may hold the reins.'

When the hot dry winds that scorch the upland plains made barrack quarters unbearable Henry was allocated a spacious bungalow in one of the 'cantonment' squares. He immediately put aside the large central room and verandahs for a church and kept only the smaller rooms for his personal use. He put in benches to seat the congregation and a table behind which he stood to take the services, while the army band led the singing.

It was encouraging that there was now a small group of soldiers who came to his room during the week for Bible study and prayer, and sometimes he spread out a 'fair white linen cloth' and held a Communion service for them.

There were many Indian and Portuguese women who had become an institution in camp life, and for these there was no shepherd. Though nominally Catholic or Muslim they understood little of any faith and Henry was concerned for their spiritual welfare. So he arranged to have a special service in the native tongue and asked the Sergeant-Major to give public notice of the fact, with the result that about two hundred women turned up for the first service. But he could never be sure how much they understood of his faltering Urdu.

His next concern was for the native urchins that haunted the bazaars, learning nothing but the ways of the world. He set up primary schools, and for the pupils who learnt to read he prepared in Urdu some of the Bible stories as their text book.

During the year he was distressed to hear from Cornwall that his older sister, Laura, had died from tuberculosis, and that Sally too was far from well. The news emphasised and multiplied the many thousand miles that separated him from his family. His own health was also causing him concern.

But there was sunshine among the clouds, for although the transfer of Major and Mrs Young to another district had left Henry feeling destitute of close friends, there were to be others to take their place. Paymaster Sherwood of the 53rd Regiment was on his way to Cawnpore with his wife, and when they reached Dinapore they decided to leave their budgerow and call on Henry, and he invited them to stay at his bungalow for the night.

Mrs Sherwood was a writer, and with skill she recorded her impressions of people and places. Her book *The Life of Mrs Sherwood* includes her description of the first meeting with Henry Martyn and it gives a much more realistic picture of the man than can be deduced from his journal. 'He was dressed in white and looked very pale, which however was nothing singular in India. His hair, a light brown, was raised from his forehead which was a remarkably fine one. His features were not regular but the expression was so luminous, so intellectual, so affectionate, so beaming with Divine charity, that no one could have looked at his features and thought of their shape or form—the out-beaming of his soul would absorb the attention of every observer. There was a very decided air, too, of the gentleman about Mr Martyn and a perfection of manners which, from his extreme attention to all minute civilities, might seem almost inconsistent with the general bent of his thoughts to the most serious subjects. He was as remarkable for ease as for cheerfulness, and in these particulars his Journal does not give a graphic account...

'After breakfast Mr Martyn had family prayers which he commenced by singing a hymn. He had a rich deep voice and a fine taste for vocal music. After singing he read a chapter, explained parts of it and prayed extempore. Afterwards he withdrew to his studies.'

She described him as 'walking in this turbulent world with peace in his mind and charity in his heart.'

That peace of mind was once again to be shattered and Henry desperately needed what Mrs Sherwood called 'charity in his heart'.

On 24 October 1807 the longed-for reply came from Cornwall. To his dismay Henry read that Lydia was not coming out to him in India. It was a long, obscure letter, giving as her only reason the fact that her mother would not give her consent.

As a mature adult Lydia did not need this before taking any action, and here again her behaviour is difficult to understand. Was it a strict adherence to parental authority or an excuse to cover up doubts in her mind? Did she love Henry enough to follow him to the ends of the earth? No one can say.

Henry was thrown back on his faith as he attempted to conquer his grief and disappointment. In his answer to the letter he wrote, 'I shall have to groan long perhaps, with a heavy heart; but if I am not hindered materially by it in the work of God, it will be for the benefit of my soul...'

But when he wrote to David Brown with the news, his words showed more of the heartache that he hid from others. 'It is as I feared. She refuses to come because her mother will not give her consent. Sir, you must not wonder at my pale looks when I receive so many hard blows on my heart...The Queensware on its way out to me can be sold at an outcry or given to Corrie. I do not want Queensware or anything else.' This was not a petulant outburst but more a sigh of resignation.

But even as Henry was suffering the loss of so much of the world's joys and compensations, his devotion to Christ remained as strong as ever; the guiding principle in every part of his life.

16

Translation and Sabat

There had been a request from the Baptist missionaries in Calcutta for Henry to translate the New Testament into Urdu, and also into Arabic and Persian. David Brown wrote that they were sending an assistant to help with translation work. This was Sabat; an Arab who had become a Christian and wanted to serve the God he now worshipped.

In due time Sabat arrived and brought with him not only his wife but his wild prickly nature that had not yet been wholly refined by grace! Again it is the writing of Mrs Sherwood in her autobiography that gives a vivid picture of this 'son of the desert'.

'Every feature in the large disc of Sabat's face was what we should call exaggerated. His eyebrows were arched, black and strongly pencilled; his eyes dark and round and from time to time flashing with unsubdued emotion, and ready to kindle to flame on the most trifling occasion. His nose was high, his mouth wide, his teeth large, and looked white in contrast with his bronzed complexion and fierce black mustachios. He was a large and powerful man, and generally wore a skull-cap of rich shawling or embroidered silk...This son of the desert never sat in a chair without contriving to tuck up his legs under him on the seat...The only languages which he was able to speak were Persian, Arabic, and a very little bad Hindustani; but what was wanting in the words of this man was more than made up by the loudness with which he uttered them for he had a voice like roaring thunder.

'He would often contend for a whole morning about the meaning of an unimportant word; and Mr Martyn has not unseldom ordered his palanquin and come over to us, to get out of the sound of the voice of the fierce Ishmaelite.'

As was to be expected, Sabat proved both a joy and a trial to Henry, and many were the storms encountered, as recorded in Henry's journal. When one of the servants offended the giant he vowed revenge, trembling with uncontrolled rage until, finally soothed by the patient, understanding chaplain, 'the wild beast fell asleep!'

Sabat was provided with a bungalow but worked and ate with Henry. At first neither approved of the plans and ideas of the other but his master persevered with this new firebrand and in their own way each influenced and helped the other.

Sometimes the proud Arab was tearfully remorseful and confessed his failure in the Christian life. 'Why am I like this after believing for three years? Every day I determine to keep Christ crucified in my sight, but I forget to think of him. I rejoice when I remember God's love in Christ, but I am like a sheep, feeding happily while he looks at the grass—but when he looks behind and sees the lion he can't eat.'

His faithful friend assured him that all Christians

experience a disappointment in themselves but, like Paul the apostle, they learn gradually that with Christ at the helm they will be able to say, 'I can do all things through Christ who strengthens me' (Philippians 4:13).

Sabat was also jealous of Mirza, the Muslim who arrived shortly after Sabat to help with the Urdu translation of the New Testament, and spoke of him only with contempt. He was angry that Henry did not hate him too, quoting the Arabic proverb that a friend is the enemy of a friend's enemy.

But Henry liked Mirza and found him invaluable in the work they were doing together, although the continual conflict between his two helpers caused him distress. At last, in spite of Henry's appeals to stay until the translation was finished, Mirza found it impossible to put up with Sabat any longer and he resigned before the four Gospels were completed.

In the meantime Henry's health was steadily deteriorating and in January 1808 he wrote, 'I found pains in my chest for the first time, a consequence of over-speaking.' At the end of the day he would be breathless and completely exhausted. 'I had better take warning in time before I am put on the shelf.' He suffered an attack of fever in September and had to cancel engagements 'because of the weak and sore state of my lungs.' As he sought to regain strength he had a great longing to feel again the bracing air of his native land instead of the humid atmosphere of the Indian rainy season.

Then in April 1809 Henry heard from the military authorities that he was being transferred to Cawnpore, three hundred miles farther up the river. Even for someone in good health it would have been a daunting journey to contemplate in the hottest part of the year but, leaving Sabat to do the packing with instructions to follow later, Henry set off in a palanquin to tackle the many wearisome miles on land.

It was indeed a foolish mistake for Henry to attempt such a journey at the hottest and worst period of the year. He could have asked for permission to postpone it to a more suitable month, or he could have arranged to go to Cawnpore in a budgerow along the river. Instead he suffered the discomfort of the palanquin, deciding to travel only at night when the hot winds, which blew like a furnace fire, would be less severe.

But on reaching Allahabad he found there was no stopping-place between there and Cawnpore, so this meant continuing the journey for two days and nights without a pause. The uncomfortable palanquin could do nothing to keep out the fierceness of the hot winds, as the four bearers jerked it along the dusty path.

It was a mercy that Henry's friends, the Sherwoods who had stayed with him at Dinapore on their way to Cawnpore, were now installed there with the 53rd Regiment. On 3 May the Sherwood family were about their various tasks; the paymaster at a table with his account books while behind grass screens under the cloth fan (punkah) the pregnant Mrs Sherwood lay on her couch resting.

On a diminutive chair at her side sat Annie, the little orphan girl rescued and adopted by the Sherwoods. The long black plait hanging down her back looked strangely heavy against the small contented face of the child as she played. Near her was a small green box complete with precious lock and key, and in this were stored her few treasures.

Quiet as a little happy mouse she dressed her doll or looked up verses in her Bible, marking the place carefully with minute pieces of paper.

It was too hot for much conversation and only the click of the punkah or the wail of the hot wind outside broke the silence. Then suddenly there came the sound of footsteps and Mr Sherwood went to the side of the house to investigate. His wife heard him exclaim 'Mr Martyn!' and a moment later he led in the exhausted chaplain, who collapsed on the floor.

The lethargy of the household disappeared in a frantic preparation to find the coolest place to put up the obviously ill traveller and a couch was brought into the central hall. There Henry lay for many days, too ill to lift his head from the pillow. The heat of the journey remained in his blood and the motion of the palanquin stayed in his brain to torment him. Much later he wrote to David Brown, 'I transported myself with such rapidity to this place that I nearly transported myself out of the world.'

When the hot winds subsided they left a stifling stillness which was even more unbearable for the invalid, but Mrs Sherwood cared lovingly for him, treating him as one of her household. As he recovered strength his old cheeriness returned, and with his precious books around him his convalescence in this home proved to be a happy contentment.

The child Annie, her large eyes gazing sympathetically at the man who had lain day after day on the couch, gradually overcame her shyness. Then she would bring her chair and her green box to sit quietly beside him. He asked to see her treasures and she showed him also the Bible verses she had marked, and it was not long before they were the best of friends.

This highly qualified man, who in his Cambridge days had won the honour of being Senior Wrangler,

found it easy to interest himself in the thoughts and mind of an Asian child. He enjoyed her daily visits and they did their share in his healing.

Though Mrs Sherwood mothered him, she did not fully understand some of the religious views or the naïvety of her lovable invalid. She scolded him when she found out he had sent off one of the coolies to draw the salary which had accumulated during Henry's illness.

'What?' she said, 'With so large a sum there would be a temptation to any coolie to make off with it.' But the man returned safely with the money, and it was only the trusting Henry who expressed no surprise!

When he was well enough he went to look around his new station and prepare to take up again his chaplain's duties. His first impression of Cawnpore was a disappointment. There was no church for services, 'Not so much as the fly of a tent', and all he could do about it was to apply to Lord Minto, the Governor General, to requisition a building.

Eventually the authorities were willing for one of the existing bungalows to be adapted for church services. But the first one, on 14 May, had to be conducted out of doors on the parade ground. It was excessively hot and some of the soldiers dropped where they stood beneath the burning rays of the sun. It was amazing that Henry, who was still a convalescent, somehow received strength to carry on.

When the rains came all outdoor parades were cancelled and services were held in a riding school, where the lingering smell of horses could hardly produce an atmosphere of worship.

Henry bought two houses near one another; one for himself, and a smaller one for Sabat and his wife when they finally arrived with the furniture and goods from Dinapore.

Sabat settled down to work with a will, helping with the translation into Arabic and Persian. 'He is gentle and almost as diligent as I could wish. Everything seems to please him. His bungalow joins mine and is very neat. So from morning to night we work together and the work goes forward. The first two or three days he translated into Arabic and I was his scribe, but this being too fatiguing to me we have been since that at the Persian.'

But when the novelty of his new home wore off Sabat lapsed into apathy, eager to find any excuse to shut up books for the day, being satisfied to get through just one chapter.

Henry was also concerned about the quality of Sabat's Persian, but any criticism only made Sabat angry. 'I did not come from Persia to India to learn Persian.'

Henry heard from Mirza that he was willing to come back provided Sabat was not around, and although this meant constant vigilance on the part of the harassed peace-keeper, he felt it worthwhile to secure once again the help of this valuable language teacher. Revision of the Urdu New Testament was begun in earnest.

At this time Henry discovered an increasing fascination for Hebrew, which he found to be a help in understanding other languages. He wrote to ask David Brown to send him grammars and dictionaries of all the languages of the earth. 'Do not stare, Sir, I have no ambition to become a linguist, but they will help me in some enquiries I am making.'

Not a linguist? The man was already a dedicated and gifted student of languages and was applying his genius to the translation of the New Testament into the three great tongues of the Near East.

Yet for all his thirst for knowledge and learning he also wrote 'I would rather have the smallest portion of love and humility than the knowledge of an arch-angel!'

To counteract the strains and stresses of his busy life Henry would often go at sunset to call on his friends. Mrs Sherwood wrote 'Two or three times a week he used to come. He sat his horse as if he were not quite aware that he was on horseback, and he generally wore his coat as if it were falling from his shoulders!'

17

Death of Sally

When he was at home Henry's house was always full of
people, with scribes copying translations surrounded
by manuscripts and dictionaries; soldiers who were
keen enough to come for Bible study and prayer, and
beggars who knew where they would be given a handful
of rice. To the latter he let it be known that his alms
would be handed out only once a week. Each Sunday
his gates were thrown open to admit the motley crowd
and it was the unpredictable Sabat who suggested that
the chaplain ought to hold special services for them.

Accordingly the following Sunday, when some four
hundred had gathered in his garden, Henry addressed
them. He said he gave with pleasure what alms he
could afford but wished to give them something better
— the riches to be found in an understanding
knowledge of God. This was the first of the services he
was to hold for them right up to the time of leaving
Cawnpore, but it remained an exacting ordeal.

It was a congregation of mixtures, as Mrs Sherwood
recorded in her book. 'They were young and old, male
and female, tall and short, athletic and feeble, bloated

86

and wizened; some clothed in abominable rags, some nearly without clothes; a temperature often rising above 92° whilst the sun poured its burning rays upon us through a lurid haze of dust... I still imagine that I hear the calm, distinct and musical tones of Henry Martyn as he stood raised above the people.'

They were a noisy lot, often interrupting the preacher with shouts and sneers and curses, and he needed to wait for the storm to pass before continuing. Each week he needed to seek courage and when the service was over it would leave him in a state of collapse.

Henry often wondered whether he had been the means of doing the smallest good to any one of the strange people who, he believed, came chiefly for the coins he gave them when it was over. He never knew that on that first Sunday there had been a group of rich young men passing the end of his garden who were curious about the strange proceedings and stopped to listen.

One, a Muslim, a professor of Persian and Arabic, heard enough to want to learn more, though telling no one of his interest. He approached Sabat and became employed as copier of the Persian Gospel and one day was given charge of a complete copy of the Persian New Testament to take to the bookbinder.

He retained it long enough to read it all before passing it on, and he believed what he read, eventually accepting the truths for himself. Records show that this man was baptised by David Brown in 1811 under the name of Abdel Musseeh, going on to become a clergyman and a notable Christian leader.

Letters from England sometimes included one from Lydia, who seemed to have a flair for prolonging emotional situations. Each time Henry saw her hand-writing his heart beat a little faster, but her letters were only to emphasise her decision not to come to India and marry him.

Henry was deeply distressed to hear that his sister Sally was now suffering from the family complaint of tuberculosis, and within a few days he was given the news that she had died. Grief overwhelmed him. Sally was the dearest and the last of his family and now he was completely alone. In despair the words of Elijah came to him; 'I, even I only, am left' (1 Kings 19:14, RSV).

When writing to console him, Lydia suggested she might take the place of the sister he had lost and this began a new series of letters between them.

By April 1810 Henry's health was so bad he had to reduce his speaking engagements and found little strength for his other duties. He had to confess to his friends, Brown and Corrie, that his chest pains were becoming alarming, and Corrie was given leave to go to Cawnpore to help. He brought with him his sister Mary who had come out to India, and together they settled down to look after the invalid. Corrie took over the preaching, and Mary came each day from the Sherwood's house where she was staying, helping with domestic arrangements for Henry. This meant he was able to concentrate more fully on the translations without overtaxing his strength, and after four months his health improved.

With a 'dog-in-the-manger' attitude Lydia must have written to Henry about Mary Corrie, for in a letter to her he says, 'You thought it possible your letter might find me married, or about to be so. Let me begin with assuring you, with more truth than Gehazi did his master, "Thy servant went no whither". My heart has not strayed from Marazion or wherever you are.'

By June there had been great progress with the Arabic New Testament. Although Henry wrote, 'We shall never find in India so good a man as Sabat', he was concerned over the many inaccuracies that had to be corrected in the Arab's translation work.

For some time Henry's eyes had been turned toward Arabia and Persia and his conversation with Sabat increased his desire to visit these countries for himself.

He realised that in the Arabic translation Sabat's grammar needed more care, and that in the Persian his writing was interspersed with faulty Arabic phrases. But it was impossible to convince the bombastic Arab of anything wrong with his work.

At last Henry wrote to David Brown suggesting that the only way to succeed with the translations would be to take the Arabic New Testament to Arabia for improvement, 'having under the other arm the Persian to be examined at Shiraz. If my life is spared there is no reason why the Arabic should not be done in Arabia and the Persian in Persia, as well as the Indian in India.'

There had been great satisfaction among the missionaries in Calcutta over the Urdu New Testament, and hope for the Arabic, but the Persian was found to have too many Arabic idioms in it for it to be realistic for the average reader. So Henry's suggestion began to take root. This might be the answer.

Plans for him to travel to Arabia and Persia (modern Iran) were put into operation, and the army General at Cawnpore was approached with an application for leave of absence for the chaplain. There was no hesitation in granting him unlimited sick-leave.

On Henry's last Sunday at Cawnpore the building he had worked for was complete, and the new bell rang to call his flock to the opening service. Corrie read the prayers, the regimental band played for the singing, and Henry preached his first and last sermon in the new church.

Before he left Cawnpore he decided to burn all his memoranda but fortunately Corrie persuaded him not to do that, suggesting that all the papers should be packaged and sealed, and that he would keep them safe until Henry's return. Among other things the parcel contained Henry's precious journal, which was thus preserved safely.

18

En Route for Persia

On 1 October 1810 Henry said goodbye to his kind friends at Cawnpore and boarded the budgerow to take him down the river to the base at Calcutta. On the way they called at Allahabad, Benares and Patna to renew acquaintances but for most of the month the chaplain was alone with his books and his exciting dreams for the future.

It was four years since he had left Calcutta and it was very much like going home to be on his way to Aldeen once more. When he arrived the Brown family gave him a royal welcome; 'the children jumping, shouting, and convoying me in troops to the house. They are a lovely family and I don't know when I have felt so delighted as at family worship that night.'

For the next ten weeks he spent his time between Aldeen and the missionaries at Serampore, while he prepared for the journey to Arabia and Persia.

It was an added joy to meet an old friend from Cambridge, Thomas Thomasson, who had been Simeon's senior curate before following Henry to India to give the rest of his life to her service. Thomasson was now living in the heart of Calcutta with his wife and family, gathering a home together.

They were shocked at the change in their friend. 'He is much altered, is thin and sallow, but he has the same loving heart.' Knowing that Simeon was anxious to have the latest news of Henry's health Thomasson wrote to tell him, 'He is on his way to Arabia where he is going in pursuit of health and knowledge. You know his genius and what gigantic strides he takes in every-thing. He has some great plan in his mind of which I am no competent judge, but as far as I understand it, the object is far too grand for one short life, and much beyond his feeble and exhausted frame.... But let us hope that the sea air may revive him. In all other respects he is exactly the same as he was; he shines in all the dignity of love; and seems to carry about him such a heavenly majesty as impresses the mind beyond description....'

During this time of waiting at Calcutta Henry was able to fulfil a five-year-old promise to Simeon to have his portrait painted, and when completed this was sent home to India House to be collected. It was a 'striking likeness' but when Simeon saw it he was distressed to see the change in his former curate. 'I couldn't bear to look up on it but turned away... covering my face.'

In Calcutta there was nothing but praise for the Urdu New Testament, but again it was stressed that Sabat's Persian needed polishing, so Henry determined to go first to Persia, and after that maybe to Damascus or perhaps to Baghdad and into the heart of Arabia.

He had an interview with Lord Minto, the Governor-General of India, who listened sympathetically to the enthusiastic pale young man with the wide vision, and granted him leave to proceed with his fantastic plans.

Armenian friends in Calcutta wrote an introduction
for him to take to their relatives in Persia, commending
him to their fellowship and care. 'I now pass from
India to Arabia, not knowing the things that shall
befall me there, but assured that an ever-faithful God
and Saviour will be with me in all places whithersoever
I go. May He guide and protect me and after prosper-
ing me in the thing whereunto I go, bring me back
again to my delightful work in India.'

But it was not easy to find a ship willing to take this
disturbing clergyman, whose evangelical zeal was now
well known. One captain refused to have him on board
in case he tried to convert the Arab sailors, lest this
should cause a mutiny! But at last he managed to
secure a passage on a boat going to Bombay by way of
Ceylon and Goa, taking Mountstuart Elphinstone,
former ambassador in Kabul, to take up his post as the
new British Resident at Poona.

They were to sail on 7 January 1811. Henry could
not bring himself to say goodbye to his Calcutta friends
so he slipped quietly away. 'Leaving Calcutta was so
much like leaving England that I went on board my
boat without giving them notice.'

For the whole of the six weeks before they reached
Bombay Henry was to enjoy thoroughly the companionship of the kindly man who was to become the
Governor of Bombay. Elphinstone had a wide knowledge of India and the two men stimulated each other
as they discussed many intellectual subjects.

This important man seems to have been impressed
with his fellow-traveller and wrote to a friend: 'We
have in Mr Martyn an excellent scholar and one of the
mildest, cheerfulest and most pleasant men I ever
saw.'

The letter continues, 'He is extremely religious and disputes with the Abyssinian about the faith, but he talks on all subjects and makes others laugh as heartily as he could do if he were an infidel!' ... 'His zeal is not troublesome; he does not press disputes or investigate creeds. He is a man of good sense and taste, simple in his manners and character and cheerful in his conversation.'

When the boat called at Ceylon the two men went on shore and walked to a cinnamon garden along a pleasant road beneath groves of coconut trees. Amongst the trees were native tents and beyond them there were glimpses of the sea. Henry found time to procure a piece of the aromatic bark to send with his next letter to Lydia.

At the same time he described to her the Indian coastline they passed as they went on to Bombay: 'At a distance green waves seem to wash the foot of the mountain but on a nearer approach little churches were seen...Was it this maritime situation that recalled to my mind Perran Church...or made my thoughts wander on the beach to the east of Lamorran? You don't tell me whether you ever walk there and imagine the billows that break at your feet to have made their way from India.' Poor Henry! He kept searching the clouds for any break in them that would bring him comfort.

At Goa he visited the tomb of St Francis Xavier but he lost interest in the Italian paintings and bronze figures when the friar who was showing him round mentioned something about 'the grace of God in the heart'. Within minutes Henry was deep in earnest conversation with the man!

When they reached Bombay he became a guest at

Government House for five weeks and, thanks to his friendship with Elphinstone, was introduced to other important people there, including Sir James Mackintosh, Recorder of Bombay, who later wrote in his journal, 'Elphinstone introduced me to a young clergyman called Martyn. He seems to be a mild and benevolent enthusiast ... Martyn the saint dined here. We had the novelty of grace before and after dinner, all the company standing. We had two or three hours good discussion on grammar and metaphysics.'

Henry was also introduced to Sir John Malcolm, a soldier and diplomat who had twice been sent to Persia to establish British trade and prestige in that country. He was at present in Bombay writing a history of Persia and he was generous with his information. This was a valuable contact; someone with whom Henry could talk of Persia and her political and commercial aspects.

Sir John Malcolm gave Henry letters of introduction to important people he would be likely to meet in Bushire, Shiraz and Isfahan in Persia, and he also wrote to Sir Gore Ouseley, British Ambassador in Persia.

'I warned Martyn not to move from Bushire without your sanction. His intention is to go via Shiraz and Isfahan to Baghdad to try to discover ancient copies of the Gospels, which he and others are persuaded lie hidden in the mountains of Persia. His knowledge of Arabic is superior to that of any Englishman in India. He is altogether a very learned and cheerful man, but a great enthusiast in his holy calling ... I told him I thought you would require him to act with great caution and not allow his zeal to run away with him ... His good sense and great learning will delight you, while his constant cheerfulness will add to the hilarity of your party.'

It is of course possible that Henry had told Malcolm of a desire to include in his itinerary a search for old manuscripts, although this is not recorded in his journal. Perhaps Sir John had got it wrong. Certain it is that Henry's main interest in going to Persia was to live among the people, learn all he could of their customs and culture, and improve his knowledge of their language while translating the New Testament into perfect Persian.

While in Bombay he was, as usual, on the lookout for an opportunity to mingle with the local people. 'I am visited from morning till night by the learned natives who are drawn here by the Arabic tract I composed to help Sabat but which the scribe I employed has been showing round.'

He had many long discussions with his visitors, especially with a Parsee poet named Feeroz who spoke Persian and was familiar with Arabic. 'He is considered the most learned man here ... and possesses one of the most agreeable qualities a disputant can possess, which is patience. He never interrupted me and if I rudely interrupted him, he was silent in a moment.' Henry's gentlemanly nature appreciated courtesy in others.

Feeroz was not impressed with the New Testament translations Henry showed him. His criticism was helpful as it pointed out mistakes in Sabat's Persian, and he was amused by some of the Arabic words.

When Henry told him the translator was an Arab who had lived in Persia, Feeroz replied crisply, 'An Arab, if he live there twenty years, will never speak Persian well.'

One day the caller was a very young man, son of

Lord Wellesley's Envoy to Persia. At first Henry thought he seemed such a boy that there would not be much point in arguing with him, but when the visitor spoke it was obvious he had a powerful command of the Persian language, which was a delight to his listener. He was found to be familiar with all the arguments put forward by the Muslim scholars (mullahs), and the discussion proved helpful and interesting. 'I thought that perhaps his youthful mind might be more open to conviction than that of the hoary Mullahs.'

Henry's conversation and discussions with so many people added fuel to the fire burning within him, intensifying his desire to get to Persia itself and proceed with further translation. He planned to get to Shiraz, city of poets and learning, the centre of Persia's culture. Here he expected to find the facilities he needed for his study of all things Persian, taking with him the various letters of introduction he had been given.

With as much patience as he could muster, he explored the best way to bring this about as quickly as possible.

19

In Oriental Dress

In the month of March 1811 Henry was given a passage in an East India Company's ship *Benares* which was to cruise in the Persian Gulf, looking for Arab pirates. There were Europeans on board, to whom he could act as chaplain, but they were in no way demanding of his services and he had much time to himself for his continued language study.

'Every day I Hebraize. I resolve to read Arabic or Persian but before I am aware of it I am thinking about Hebrew. I have translated Psalm 16.' He thought of sending the translation to his friend Thomasson in Calcutta, but wanted first to make sure that each part of it was correct. Had his friend and counsellor been near at hand it is possible he would have advised the insatiable linguist to stay with the New Testament, where his translation gift was seen at its excellent best.

Apart from an initial bout of sea-sickness the voyage was a pleasant trip, the suspected pirates keeping well out of the way. 'You will be happy to know that the murderous pirates against whom we were sent, having received notice of our approach, are all got out of the way. So I am no longer liable to be shot in a battle, or to decapitation after!'

On 21 April the *Benares* anchored at Muscat where it lay for a week in a small cove surrounded by rocks which held the heat and kept out the air. Shore leave was not encouraged as the area around Muscat was unsafe, but Henry went with Captain Lockett to see some of the sights and to walk through the fascinating bazaars, accompanied by an Arab soldier and his African servant. The African boy was so keenly interested in talking about Muhammad and Christianity that the following day Henry gave him a copy of the Gospels in Arabic. It may have been the joy of possession that gave the boy so much delight but he took it away as a great prize to be treasured. And, as Henry fervently hoped, to be read.

After leaving Muscat the ship had a rough passage for some days in the great funnel of the Gulf, but before they reached Bushire Henry wrote in his journal '*May 7*. Finished a work on which I have been engaged for a fortnight—a new arrangement of all the Hebrew roots, classing them according to the last letter, the last but one, and so on.'

On 22 May they landed and Henry set foot for the first time on Persian soil; another step toward the fulfilment of his translation plans. He was determined, God willing, not to leave Persia until he had in his hand a New Testament translation that would satisfy the most fastidious Persian.

Henry always felt that the best way to get to know the people of a foreign land was to look as much like them as possible, so to travel into the interior Henry decided to wear Persian dress.

While this was being made for him he set about finding out Persian and Arabic reactions to his first translations. One day he called on the Governor, a Persian Khan; 'he was so particular in his attentions, seating me in his own seat and then sat by my side. After the usual salutations and inquiries the hookah [smoking-pipe] was introduced; then coffee in china cups placed within silver ones; then hookah; then some rose-water syrup; then hookah. As there were long intervals, often, in which naught was heard but the gurgling of the hookah, I looked round with some anxiety for something to discourse upon, and observing the windows to be of stained glass, I began to question him about the art of colouring glass...'

Another day a well-known Turk came to visit Henry. 'He is a great Arabic scholar and came to see how much we knew; or rather, if the truth were known, to show how much he himself knew!'

By 30 May the Persian costume was ready and it was time to start the journey to Shiraz. Friends back at Calcutta might have had difficulty in recognising the man who had slipped away from them without saying goodbye. He was still writing his journal and before starting for Shiraz he recorded, 'The Persian dress consists of first stockings and shoes in one; next a pair of large blue trousers or else a pair of huge red boots; then the shirt; then the tunic; and above it the coat, both of chintz, and a great-coat. I have here described my own dress, most of which I have on at this moment. On the head is worn an enormous cone, made of the skin of the black Tartar sheep with the wool on. If to this description of my dress I add that my beard and moustaches have been suffered to vegetate undisturbed ever since I left India—that I am sitting on a Persian carpet in a room without tables or chairs—and that I bury my hand in the dish without waiting for spoon or plate, you will give me credit for being already an accomplished Oriental!'

Henry's new servant Zechariah, an Armenian from Isfahan, livened the preparations with his cheerful chatter. He had the gift of being able to find something to say to anyone who would listen!

Most of the company travelled on mules but some rode horseback. The muleteer offered Henry his own horse, complete with the bell fastened round its neck. One of the travellers, a Bombay trumpeter, was on his way to join the Embassy at Shiraz and he was asked to announce the departure with a blow on his instrument. He might have been a learner or perhaps his trumpet was out of order, but the frightful sounds that emerged did nothing but startle the animals and cause amusement to the humans!

There followed a deal of jostling, arguing and restraining of recalcitrant mules before each one found his place, and in an orderly fashion the cavalcade moved out through the gates of the city.

It was nearing midnight, the fine moonlit night punctuated by the sound of tinkling bells and the tramp of hooves over the hard rocky ground of the Oriental scene. As night advanced the noisy party grew quiet and one of the muleteers began to sing softly a sad, plaintive song.

By sunrise they had completed about twenty miles and pitched tent under a tree. The heat became intense, rising to an unbearable 112°F. Henry wrapped himself in a blanket in an attempt to keep out the burning heat and keep in the moisture of his body.

When the fierce sun went down plans had to be

made to proceed and while the mules were being
loaded up Henry was able at last to get an hour's sleep,
waking refreshed in the cool night air. Henry's ebul-
lient Armenian servant was here, there and everywhere, talking incessantly and seeking to encourage
the party by word and gesture.

At the next calling-place the travellers quickly made a 'tatty', or matting of cuscus grass, with branches of a date tree, and employed a peasant to keep it well watered. By this means they were able to keep the temperature through the day below 114°F. Even so Henry needed to wrap a wet towel round his head and body. A neighbouring village was able to supply them with milk and food for their meal.

During the night they reached the foot of the mountains, but instead of the clearer air they expected they were greeted by a suffocating smell of naptha. 'We saw a river — what flowed in it it seemed difficult to say whether it were water or green oil. It scarcely moved and the stones which it laved it left of a greyish colour as if its foul touch had given them the leprosy'. An unpleasant experience, crowned by the fact that Zechariah fell from his mule and was rather bruised, putting a damper on the whole company. 'He looked very sorrowful and had lost much of his garrulity!'

Next morning the cavalcade found a grove of date trees and decided to camp, hoping for shade through the day, but the atmosphere at sunrise proved far hotter in the grove than the surrounding air. So that evening they welcomed the cooler, clear air as they began to ascend the mountains, although the going was more difficult. As they wound their way round the narrow paths on the high rocks overlooking deep and dangerous precipices, they had to be alert every moment. Here a false step could prove fatal and send them hurtling down the mountainside.

The animals they had to depend on were used to the terrain and fortunately their step was sure, for there was no room for mistakes. 'There was nothing to mark the road but the rocks being a little more worn in one place than another. Sometimes my horse stopped as though to consider about the way; for myself I couldn't guess where the road lay, but he always found it.'

The scenery was grand and impressive and Henry would have been the first to appreciate its grandeur, but the extra fatigue he felt through lack of sleep made him insensitive to all around him. Only his invincible spirit and determination to fulfil the task ahead carried him along.

They were able to ride briskly when they came to the mountain plain, still finding it necessary to travel in the night and try to get what sleep they could during the heat of the day.

Occasionally they descended into a fertile valley where they saw fields of wheat and barley growing, and an occasional tree, reminding Henry of an autumn morning in England, with the temperature a blissful 62°F. Another time it was a green valley near a stream where clover grew in abundance, and cattle browsed in the adjoining fields. With a thankful heart Henry wrote in his journal, 'He maketh me to lie down in green pastures and leadeth me beside still waters' (Psalm 23).

This was a journey full of contrasts. At one point, when the temperature registered 110°F, the cavalcade met a mountaineer travelling down to Bushire with a load of ice. At that moment his load was to the hot and thirsty travellers more precious than gold, and they persuaded him to sell it to them.

But the next night they climbed to a plain where the piercing wind cut like a knife and everyone was obliged to pile on all the clothes he could muster. And still they shivered!

20

Roses and Nightingales

On 9 June 1811 the travellers came in sight of the orchards and gardens of Shiraz. The sun had set and the gates were already closed, but all around was the scent of herbs and roses, and the sound of nightingales.

Thankful that the nine days' trying journey—which today would take but a few hours—was over, Henry and his party camped for the night in a garden outside the walls.

Next day he rode in through the gates as soon as they were open, along the cypress-lined avenues of the city, past the elaborate mosques and the superbly-tended gardens where Hafiz and other Persian poets lie buried. He caught sight of maidens, shyly peering out of the folds of their veils at the strange rider in his Persian dress, and gradually he reached the house of Jaffir Ali Khan. This was the leading citizen of high rank, to whom Henry carried his letter of introduction from Sir John Malcolm in Bombay.

It was refreshing beyond measure to arrive at this rich man's home and be graciously welcomed by Jaffir Ali who immediately called for food for his visitors.

'After the long and tedious ceremony of coffee and pipes, breakfast made its appearance on two large trays; curry, pilaws, various sweets cooled with snow and perfumed with rose-water, were served in great profusion in china plates and dishes. There were a few wooden spoons beautifully carved but being in Persian dress, and on the ground, I thought it high time to throw off the European, and so ate with my hands.'

In his gracious manner Henry seemed always able to sense the 'rightness' of things, and be able to adapt to the custom and culture of the company he was in. Surely a valuable asset to any missionary!

Jaffir Ali made arrangements for a room in his large house to be set apart for his guest, and here Henry was able to unpack the books he had brought with him, ready for a concentrated attack on the Persian translation. This was to be his home for almost a year.

He found his host to be an understanding man of courteous manners, ever on the lookout for ways of adding to the comfort and pleasure of his guest.

As they talked, mostly on religious topics, it was obvious there was a complete absence of bigotry and prejudice. Jaffir Ali listened with an intellectual interest to Henry's plans for a perfect Persian translation of the New Testament. He later introduced his visitor to his brother-in-law, Seid Ali Khan, 'who speaks the purest dialect of the Persian.'

This new contact was interested in all Henry told him of his translation plans, and offered to assist in making the new version. The offer proved to be a Godsend to the man who had come to Persia for the express purpose of 'getting it right'. Who better to help than one born in the country, who spoke 'the purest dialect'? So, in little more than a week after arrival in

Shiraz, Henry had started on the work he had come
from India to do.

He found both Jaffir Ali and Seid Ali to be open-
minded Sufis—the mystics of Islam—and their
friendliness was helpful to one who knew what it was
to be lonely in a crowd.

A stranger in a strange land, with only memories of
all he had left to keep him company, Henry longed for
Christian fellowship. He thought affectionately of
Simeon in Cambridge, Corrie and David Brown in
India, remembering their many words of comfort and
advice, thanking God afresh for them. Though separated by many miles, he was conscious that he still had
their support.

It would seem that Henry's health stabilised, if not
improved, while he was at Shiraz, although he still
had occasional bouts of fever and fatigue.

Henry had written several letters to Lydia since
leaving India, sending them by caravan to the coast or
by Tartar courier to Constantinople, but there had
been no reply. 'Since ten months I have heard nothing
of any one person whom I love. I read your letters
incessantly and try to find something new, as I
generally do ... I try to live on from day to day happy
in His love and care.'

So Lydia, truly loving but still rejecting him, flitted
in and out of his life and thoughts, but never from the
recesses of his heart.

2 I

Life in Shiraz

The British Ambassador, Sir Gore Ouseley, was in Shiraz for some weeks and Henry called on him, again with the letter of introduction from Sir John Malcolm. He was received kindly and was invited to preach to the household, after which he baptised their child.

As a stranger in the country Henry was anxious to pay due respect to the 'powers that be' and on 6 July he went to present himself to Prince Abbas Mirza, son of the Shah. 'Early this morning I went with the Ambassador and his suite to court, wearing agreeably to costume a pair of red cloth stockings with green high-heeled shoes. When we entered the great court of the palace a hundred fountains began to play. The Prince appeared at the opposite side, in his talar or hall of audience, seated on the ground. Here our first bow was made. When we came in sight of him we bowed a second time and entered the room. He did not rise, nor take notice of any but the Ambassador, with whom he conversed at the distance of the breadth of the room...'

There was much local curiosity about the European

who had taken up residence in the house of Jaffir Ali and mixed with the important people of the city. The lively Zechariah was for once silent but 'all ears' when he went shopping in the bazaar, carrying a list of his master's needs. He made time to mingle with the crowds, alert to any mention of the lodger in the home of Jaffir Ali, and what he heard he was eager to pass on to the one concerned.

'Zechariah told me this morning that I was the town talk; that it was asserted that I was come to Shiraz to be a Mussulman [Muslim], and should then bring five thousand men to Shiraz under pretence of making them Mussulmans, but in reality to take the city!'

But in spite of his eavesdropping Zechariah attended well to his shopping and made sure the requirements of his master were properly met. The journal records 'Victuals are cheap . . . such a country for fruit I had no conception of. I have a fine horse which I bought for less than a hundred rupees, on which I ride every morning round the walls. My vain servant Zechariah, anxious that his master should appear like an ameer [ruler], furnished the horse with a saddle, or rather a pillion which fairly covers his whole back. It has all the colours of the rainbow, but yellow is predominant, and from it hang down four large tassels also yellow.'

The journal from this point becomes mostly a record of the progress of translation work and of Henry's discussions and disputes with the learned scholars of the city, to whom he reached out in friendship. He laid before them all that he believed to be true. But through it all runs the thread of his solitary witnessing to the faith of Jesus Christ.

Quickly he realised he would need to scrap the Persian copy he and Sabat had worked on in India.

Without having his chaplain's duties to fulfil he would be able to give his whole time to translation, and with the help of Seid Ali he would start afresh and prepare a completely new version. Henry resolved to stay in Shiraz until this was finished, and wrote to tell Corrie in India of his decision, concluding the letter on a personal note.

'I go on as usual, riding round the walls in the morning and singing hymns at night over my milk and water—for tea I have none, though I want it! I am with you in spirit almost every evening and feel one with the saints of God all over the earth.'

The greater part of the day was spent in his room working with Seid Ali, but they had to cope with many interruptions. Some callers came with a genuine desire to learn more of the Christian faith, seeking proof for the religion of Christ. Others came only to argue, and some simply to scoff, but the grave and gentle stranger made himself available to all, ever ready to defend his faith.

One young scholar who on his first visit came to taunt, found his attitude changing as he listened to the calm reasoning of this man of God who knew that arguments are powerless until made effective by the Holy Spirit. Rahim returned many times until at last he was convinced of the truth. Before Henry left Shiraz he came again, this time to confess his belief. Later, when the Persian translation was finished, Henry gave Rahim one of the first copies which became his greatest treasure. One day he showed it to a Christian traveller he met, pointing to the words on the fly-leaf. 'There is joy in heaven over one sinner that repenteth.' This was followed by the signature of Henry Martyn.

There were many Jews in Shiraz and, eager as

always to learn, they were interested in the new teacher in the city. One of them who had become a Muslim came regularly to talk with Henry, asking him questions. 'He showed himself extremely well read in the Hebrew Bible and the Koran, quoting both with the utmost readiness. He said he must come every day and either make me a Mussulman or become himself a Christian.'

So great was the general interest stirred up by the presence of the zealous Christian translator that the authorities became concerned. After deliberation they arranged for a treatise, a *Defence of Islam* to be prepared by Mirza Ibrahim, who was known as the foremost of all the teachers. When this was presented to Henry with the idea of silencing him, he replied with a masterly series of tracts covering the whole controversy.

He was encouraged by the reaction of his helper, Seid Ali, to some of the passages of Scripture they were dealing with. 'The poor boy, while reading how one of the servants of the High Priest struck the Lord on the face, stopped and said "Sir, did not his hand dry up?"'

Another day, while dealing with the twelfth chapter of John, Seid Ali exclaimed 'How he loved those twelve persons!' 'Yes,' replied Henry, 'and all those who believe on Him through their word.'

The two men often chatted together after the day's work was done. One evening Seid Ali confided the fact that ever since childhood he had been trying to find the truth in religion and was still undecided. Never before had he been given the opportunity of talking with those of another faith. Gently Henry reminded him of the necessity of making up one's mind on such a subject, pointing him to the text they had recently been dealing with. 'If any man's will is to do his will, he shall know whether the teaching is from God' (John 7:17 RSV).

Henry explained that this had been his own experience and when he could at last say before God, 'What wilt Thou have me to do?' he had found peace.

During these talks Seid Ali was always reluctant to finish the conversation and one evening he said, with a smile, 'You must not regret the loss of so much time as you give me because it does me good.'

Henry began to realise that his helper no longer argued about the truths they were translating together, as he had been inclined to do at first. His remarks now became more serious. One day when they were discussing the need to be humble in dealing with disputes in religion, Seid Ali confessed that he had no humility. 'The truth is we are in a state of compound ignorance; ignorant, yet ignorant of our ignorance.'

But Seid Ali was justly proud of what Henry and he had achieved in translation work, and when his friends called he would immediately produce the latest results, even though they ridiculed his enthusiasm. Then he would point out that, supposing he had received no other benefit, he had learnt a lot. It was, he emphasised, much better to have gained so much knowledge about the Christian religion than to have frittered away the year idling in the gardens as they had done!

When July came Henry was given the opportunity to camp out. As a relief from the close confinement of life in a city house, his kind host had a tent pitched for him in one of the lovely gardens.

It was a tranquil spot beside a clear running stream beneath the shade of an orange tree and surrounded by clusters of ripening grapes.

Here the two translators were able to work during

the week with fewer interruptions, and here Henry
could enjoy a quiet Sunday on his own. The lone
worshipper wrote in his journal, 'The first Sabbath
morning I have had all to myself this long time, and I
spent it with comfort and profit. Read Isaiah chiefly,
and hymns, which as usual brought to my remembrance the children of God in all parts of the earth.'

22

A Break from Translating

Although Henry's dedicated mind seemed closed to trivial matters, he was acutely aware of the beauty of creation, the wonders of science and the history of past ages. During his stay at Shiraz he decided to set apart two days for a visit to the ancient city of Persepolis and see something of its fallen grandeur.

Persepolis, shrouded in mystery, unknown to the Greeks until the time of Alexander the Great, had once been the dynastic capital of Persia. It was here the many celebrations and festivals were held each year in the reign of Darius and Xerxes (about 400 BC). It was also the place chosen by Darius for his summer residence.

For the visit Henry arranged for two guards on horseback to accompany him and his servants, and when all was ready they started about two hours before the sun went down. 'We entered a vast plain and two or three hours before day crossed the Araxes (sic) by a bridge of three arches and coming in sight of the ruins we waited for day. I lay down upon the bare ground but it was too cold to sleep.'

Perhaps he was tired after riding through the night, or his mind was still on translation work, but the river was not the Araxes. This lies some thousand miles to the north of where he was, and the bridge they crossed on their way from Shiraz to Persepolis was over the river Kur Rud.

As soon as the sun rose Henry was eager to reach the ruins, filled with curiosity and anticipation, and it was with amazement he noticed the complete lack of interest displayed by the rest of his company. Perhaps, living as near as they did to Persepolis, it was a case of familiarity breeding contempt, but they had not the slightest inclination to look at this ancient place. From the moment they climbed the great terrace they all lay down and fell asleep.

They on their part could not understand why people should come from far away to look at nothing but ruins. One of the servants stayed awake long enough to say to Henry, 'A nice place, Sahib. Good air and a fine garden; you may carry brandy and drink here at leisure!' Poor man, expressing his idea of human happiness, he could only suppose that his master's whole purpose in making the journey to Persepolis was to have a drinking bout.

But for Henry, as he wandered alone among the remains of antiquity, his mind was filled with visions of the past; the banquets, the revelries and the songs that had echoed over the surrounding mountains.

He gazed up at the huge columns still standing sentinel, pointing ever upward like accusing fingers, their capitals almost as long as the shafts.

There was a certain awe in looking out over the plains beyond which, in ancient Babylon, Nebuchad-nezzar set up his great image of gold. Did Henry fancy he could hear that vast orchestra with its sound of the dulcimer, flute and harps commanding the people to bow down and worship the great king (Daniel 2)?

Here was the place where Daniel, the chief president of Darius, may have come with his king to the festivals, walking over these same flagstones (Daniel 6).

Many more of the names in the Old Testament history must have come vividly alive in the alert mind of this earnest student of the Scriptures as he walked around.

For generation after generation Persepolis had been the palace of kings, symbol of might and majesty; until that day when Alexander came marching with his Greek army to force their way through the band of defending tribesmen and burnt it to ashes.

Now all was silent and austere, hiding its secrets as if in shame.

The time had gone all too quickly and Henry realised that the sun was going down on yet another day. Soon it would be necessary to prepare for the return journey back to Shiraz.

He rode on into the next village to get a meal before rejoining his servants and the two guards. Then, rousing those who still wanted to sleep, they were ready to start for Shiraz.

On the return journey the company lost their way, not willing to be guided by Henry, who insisted that he remembered the way they had come and stressed that they were taking the wrong road.

Mile after mile they rode until they came across a group of villagers spending the night on their threshing-floor in the field, and asked for directions. To the astonishment of everyone but Henry, they were told to go back to the right way which proved to be the one he had suggested.

Now they were so impressed with his geographical skill that when it was time for them to stop for prayers they asked him to point the way. 'After setting their faces toward Mecca, as nearly as I could, I went and sat down on the margin near the bridge where the water falling over some fragments of the bridge under the arches, produced a roar which, contrasting with the stillness all around, had a grand effect. Here I thought again of the multitudes who had once pursued their labours and pleasures on its banks.'

In all the wide experiences of Henry's life in various parts of the world, he appreciated the quiet calm of sitting beside a stream in a pleasant place, or listening to the happy roar of a waterfall, prizing, as he did, the moments when he could draw aside from everything and be alone. 'Be still and know that I am God' must have been a favourite verse.

Once the Muslims had finished their prayers, Henry rejoined the group and mounted his horse. Not wishing to reach Shiraz before the gates were opened, they stayed at a caravanserai (inn) on the way. 'I put my head into a poor corner and slept soundly upon the hard stone.' Obviously not a four-star hotel!

The visit had not been without its value for it gave Henry the opportunity for discussion with the guards, who asked questions as they rode.

'What think you of Christ?' one asked.

'The same as you say—the Word of God.'

'Was He a Prophet?'

'Yes . . . but what it chiefly concerns us to know—He was an atonement for the sins of men.'

This time the man made no reply.

23

Completing the Task

During his months in Shiraz Henry was often involved in controversial discussions, boldly seeking every opportunity to show Christ to the people of Persia, while working incessantly to produce the New Testament in their language.

On Christmas Day he arranged a party for some Armenian friends and, at Jaffir Ali's request, he invited a Sufi master and his disciples. He hoped there would be some helpful conversation but in this he was disappointed. Although Seid Ali made an attempt to open this by explaining the meaning of the Lord's Supper, the Sufis remained silent. The subject had to be dropped as the meal was ready, and the moment it was over the guests rose to leave.

On 14 February 1812 the New Testament was completed, and three weeks later the translation of the book of Psalms was also finished. 'A sweet employment caused six weary moons that waxed and waned since the commencement to pass unnoticed.'

Scribes were employed to prepare two special volumes, one to be presented to the Shah and the other to his son, Prince Abbas Mirza. Three months later these two manuscripts were finished.

It was usual for a Persian writer to present his work to the Shah for his approval before being published. Henry not only felt it a matter of courtesy to follow the Persian custom but he also realised that the Shah's opinion could have a vital effect on the readers he was aiming for.

There was no one except Henry who could take charge of the precious books and deliver them to Tehran, so he decided to take them himself and present them in person.

All that remained for him to do in Shiraz was to supervise the making of several copies of the script. This left him free to spend time with Seid and Jaffir Ali, reading to them at their request portions of the Old Testament. Their interest and friendliness had been a great support during his stay in their city, and he was grateful.

On the last day together Seid Ali was given instructions what to do with the manuscripts in the event of Henry's death. Some were to be sent to India for printing by the Serampore Press. The two royal copies were wrapped carefully, ready to be taken by Henry for correction on his journey to Tehran.

Although Henry's health had improved since leaving the ferocious heat of the Indian summer, he was still troubled with chest pains, particularly after any long conversation or dispute. His will and determination to succeed in the work to which, under God, he had set his hand was far stronger then the frail frame in which it was housed.

He felt an increasing urgency to complete whatever tasks lay ahead in Persia, while realising that the wisest thing to do would be to go straight home to England to regain strength before returning to his work in India.

Had he been blessed with a wife at this stage it is likely she would have urged him to be reasonable and do just that. There were in fact days when he felt so unwell he almost decided to go back to Bushire and get a ship there. But his mind was set on personally handing over the precious Persian translation into the hands of the Shah. Only when that part of his mission was completed could he feel free to turn his face toward home and hopeful recovery.

Some may be inclined to call this pride, but a more charitable explanation would be that he feared, with robbers and bandits so prevalent, that his year's work might be destroyed.

In one of his long letters to Corrie, his friend in India, Henry wrote, 'I can conceive of no greater happiness than to be settled for life in India, superintending schools as we did.'

But for the moment it was necessary to prepare for the journey to Tehran. He was pleased that his party was to include the Rev William Canning, on his way to the British Embassy there as the new chaplain.

This time there was no trumpeter to announce his departure, and with mixed feelings Henry mounted his horse to ride north across the great Persian plateau toward Tehran.

24

Journey to Tehran

The travellers left Shiraz in the evening and were passing Persepolis, place of memories, about ten hours later. On 13 May they stopped for the day at a caravanserai, where Henry used the time to start correcting his manuscript until it was time to continue the journey.

The way led through mountainous country, bare except for heathers and broom, with little protection from the gusty cold wind. At one point there was a hoar frost and ice in the puddles, and away in the distance the high ridges were covered in snow.

It was 22 May when they arrived at Isfahan, a beautiful city of minarets, domes and pigeon towers, and sparkling fountains playing in the shade of many trees. Henry and Canning, as foreigners of some importance, were accommodated comfortably in one of the Shah's palaces. Here Henry was pleased to meet his old Shiraz scribe who willingly helped him go through the manuscript until they had finished the corrections. Now it was ready for presentation.

They left Isfahan at the end of the month, travelling

through most attractive countryside with many trees, cornfields and running streams. 'It was the first place I have seen in Asia which exhibited anything of the scenery of England. It was a mild moonlight night and a nightingale filled the whole valley with his notes.'

Night after night they pressed on, staying some days for rest, chatting with the villagers who gathered round in their eagerness to talk with the European in their midst who spoke to them so confidently of his faith in Jesus Christ.

The company neared Tehran on 8 June before the gates were open, so Henry put his bed down on the high road outside the walls and slept. He woke with the dawn and drew his coat closer round him, for the morning air was sharp. With half-closed eyes he looked at the wall against which he lay, wondering where he was until his thoughts cleared. This was Tehran, another step toward his goal, where he hoped to obtain an introduction from the British Ambassador, for without this he would not be allowed to approach the Shah.

But to his intense dismay Henry found that the Ambassador, Sir Gore Ouseley, was away at his home in Tabriz, about 400 miles further north. Desperately he began to consider what steps he could take for gaining an audience with the Shah and Prince. He was anxious to lose no time in presenting his book.

Henry learned that the Shah's Prime Minister, Mirza Shufi, was at the camp at Karaj, a night's journey further on. Fortunately Jaffir Ali had given him a letter of introduction to the Premier and it was decided that he should go on alone to Karaj and present it to Mirza Shufi, seeking his assistance in arranging a meeting with the Shah.

Henry waited till evening to set off and on arrival at a caravanserai near to the camp he sent a messenger to take Jaffir Ali's letter to the Premier. When Henry was sent for he found Mirza Shufi lying on the verandah of the Shah's tent of audience.

With him were two officials who took little notice of the newcomer, not rising as was their custom nor offering the usual water-pipe. But when they knew the object of his visit their tongues were loosened and they began a controversial discussion on religion and metaphysics that continued for two hours.

'He speaks good Persian,' was the final comment and Henry knew he was no nearer to gaining permission to meet the Shah than he had been before. In despair he returned to his lodging.

While he stayed on at Karaj, guarding his precious manuscript, hoping against hope that the Shah might come there and he would be given an audience, Henry was invited to attend the Premier's assembly and this time he took his book with him.

He found himself surrounded by a group of scholars intent on disproving his Christian faith. He sat alone among the hostile Mullahs. After a lengthy controversial and noisy dispute the Premier, who had set the whole thing in motion, said to the frail but valiant defender of the faith, 'You had better say God is God, and Muhammad is the prophet of God.'

Squaring his shoulders to meet the challenge he had anticipated, Henry replied, 'God is God, and Jesus is the Son of God'.

Immediately there was an angry tumult and one of them said, 'What will you say when your tongue is burnt out for this blasphemy?'

As Mirza Shufi rose to leave, followed by the rest of

the group, Henry saw his book lying on the floor where it was in danger of being trampled on. Quickly he went to retrieve it and wrapped it carefully in a towel, 'while they looked at me with supreme contempt. Thus I walked alone to my tent, to pass the rest of the day in heat and dirt.'

To complete the day of frustration and denouncement Henry received a message from the Premier that evening to the effect that he could not, or would not, arrange for the Englishman to meet the Shah or Prince Abbas Mirza.

The only thing to do now was to press on and try to reach the Ambassador at Tabriz. Mr Canning, the chaplain on his way to the Embassy, who had stayed behind at Tehran, now rejoined Henry and together they started on their journey, covering some forty miles before they stopped at a village.

'As I sat down in the dust on the shady side of a walled village and surveyed the plains over which our road lay, I sighed at the thoughts of my dear friends in India and England; of the vast regions I must travel before I can get to either, and of the various hindrances which present themselves to my going forward. I comfort myself with the hope that God has something for me to do by thus delaying my exit.'

Only someone who has found himself many difficult miles away from home and friends, with little prospect of a likely return, could appreciate the depth of Henry's feelings at this time.

They were further delayed by the sudden illness of Canning, and were unable to leave the village until 16 June. Then, warmly wrapped against the cold north wind blowing in from the Caspian Sea, they reached Zanjan. Here they were heartened by the sudden possibility of a cup of tea! For among the merchants bringing goods from Tehran were two Tartars carrying iron and tea for sale. Seeing the chance of a sale they approached Henry. 'Do you want tea of Cathay?' they asked. Indeed he did! But they found the merchants could talk nothing but Turkish and any negotiations with them proved so difficult that the blissful cup never materialised.

As they progressed the whole company were plagued with recurring bouts of fever, headaches and fatigue, with Henry relapsing several times and quite unable to move on. Lack of sleep, lack of refreshment, exposure to the sun and alternating cold winds drained his strength until, hardly able to sit his horse, Henry at last reached the gates of Tabriz. With his remaining breath he asked a man to take him to the Ambassador's house.

25

Convalescence

The list of ministerial duties of an ambassador is not likely to include that of taking into the embassy residence a sick missionary translator on his way to seek audience with the royal monarch. But to their lasting credit Sir Gore Ouseley and his wife took up the challenge facing them.

The man who had arrived on their doorstep in a state of collapse was the clergyman they had already met while staying at Shiraz; the one who had preached to their household and baptised their child. Now he was desperately ill and in need of all the love and care available, a servant of God to be nursed back to health.

For many days Henry was barely conscious as he lay in a raging fever, but in lucid moments he was acutely aware of the kind attention he was being given by the Ambassador and his wife.

It would seem like a touch of irony that during his illness the Prince Abbas Miraz came on a visit to the house. What an opportunity to present him with his copy of the manuscript—one of the main objects of Henry's fatal journey—but this was not possible. The sick man was delirious and unable to lift his head from the pillow.

Some weeks later the fever responded to the excellent nursing and gradually the invalid began to improve. And, once again, with recovery Henry's inherent good spirits revived. During convalescence his infectious laugh was heard again, this time throughout the Embassy, as he romped with the child of the house. She had quickly found a way into his heart.

He was reminded of the happy times he had spent with the orphan child who shared her treasures with him in the home of Mrs Sherwood in India; and the fun he had enjoyed with the children of David Brown on the lawn at Aldeen.

Like many people, he found that happiness and laughter can do more for a convalescent than strong medicine.

A letter from Lydia had at last reached Henry during his illness and now he was sufficiently recovered to be able to reply. In August he wrote, 'It has pleased God to restore me to life and health again. Not that I have recovered my former strength but I consider myself sufficiently restored to prosecute my journey. My daily prayer is that my late chastisement may have its intended effect, and make me all the rest of my days more humble and less self-confident... In prayer Christ appears to me my life and strength, but at other times I am as thoughtless and bold, as if I had all life and strength in myself... An account of all my discussions with these mystic philosophers must be reserved to the time of our meeting. Do I dream, that I venture to think and write of such an event as that? Is it possible that we shall ever meet again below? Though it is possible, I dare not indulge such a pleasing hope yet...'

At last Henry had been forced to realise it was essential for him to give up his plan of presenting his book to the Shah. His journey must now be homeward if he were ever to reach England. He discussed the matter with Sir Gore and Lady Ouseley, deeply regretting the fact that he had not been able to complete his mission. His disappointment was somewhat eased by the kindness of his host, who promised to take charge of the New Testament translation until he could hand it over personally to the Shah and the Prince. (When later this promise was fulfilled the Shah was delighted and publicly expressed his approval, commending it as a book to be read from beginning to end.)

While still at the Embassy, Henry wrote to his well-loved old friend and counsellor, Simeon at Cambridge. He told him of the proposed furlough, hoping he would understand how necessary this was.

He was still, of course, holding the position of a chaplain with the East India Company so, with his usual courteous attention to protocol, Henry sent a letter to Mr Charles Grant. He asked that the sick-leave should be extended in order that he could go home to England before returning once more to India.

The strings of home were beginning to pull stronger than ever and he determined to start on his long journey as soon as possible. From Tabriz he would need to travel across country, through Turkey, to Constantinople (modern Istanbul).

The Ouseleys were concerned that he should contemplate so soon the daunting prospect of travelling alone, except for servants, over 1300 miles of harsh and often hostile country. It was something even a robust person would view with apprehension, but they could see that their warnings were falling on deaf ears. Henry had become obsessed with the idea of returning to England by the shortest route, even though it was more hazardous for a sick man.

Not being able to persuade him to stay longer, the Ambassador and his wife did their best to send him on his way as well-prepared and equipped as possible. Sir Gore arranged for specially strong Chappar horses to be provided for the whole journey, and gave Henry letters of introduction to the various governors of the land over which he would travel. He also wrote one for the British Ambassador at Constantinople. He planned with Henry the route through Armenia and Turkey, knowing this would be the safest one and possibly less likely to be attacked by bandits.

Henry would need to take with him Armenian servants who knew both the Persian and Turkish languages and he managed to find one, Antoine, as a groom. Sergius, who professed to know Persian, Henry employed as an interpreter.

On 2 September 1812 Henry waved goodbye to his hosts and set his face westward toward the 'royal road' of ancient Persia, along which had passed many great kings from the past.

It was not long before he found that his interpreter's knowledge of Persian was 'rather scanty', so conversation was limited. Undaunted he records, 'We rode silently along. For my part, I could not have enjoyed any companion so much as I did my own feelings.' He had much to occupy his mind; fears, frustrated hopes, regrets and unfulfilled longings.

26

Towards Home

Once out of the city of Tabriz, with its many mosques, domes, lakes and its noisy bazaars, they came out on to the plain. This stretches for many miles; enclosed by remote, silent mountains whose summit merges with the blue heavens. After his long illness Henry appreciated more than ever the beauty and grandeur with a joyful sense of gratitude, as he and the silent Sergius rode along.

Toward the north-west of the plain they came to Sofian, and looked for their pre-arranged accommodation in the attractive garden village. They found the farmer in his corn-field directing his labourers, who were cutting straw into fine pieces ready to be made into fodder for the cattle. Henry watched with interest as they drew over the straw a cylinder fitted with triangular plates.

The farmer seemed too busy to pay attention to visitors but sent one of his men to show Henry the place where he was to sleep. The unsatisfactory room turned out to be one with only three walls. On requesting one with four, Henry was taken to a weaver's house where, 'notwithstanding the mosquitoes and other vermin, I passed the night comfortably enough.'

It was very hot next day as they went through a mountain pass but, to relieve the tediousness of the way, Henry was able to dismount. He sat thankfully beside a brook to eat his picnic of bread and raisins and, cupping his hands, took a cooling drink from the mountain stream.

His next bedroom was a corner in a stable, partitioned off for privacy but not from the strong smell of the horses. A healthy smell, he had always been told!

As he sat ruminating over the past day's happenings he reproached himself, feeling he had been too impatient with his servants over some trifling irritation.

'How much more noble and Godlike to bear with calmness and observe with pity, rather than anger, the failings and offences of others!'

But Henry had little pity for himself, undertaking what must have been a nightmare journey, with its lack of all comfort, enduring so many inconveniences and trials. In all his travels in various parts of the world his fastidious mind never lost its natural instinct for the cultured way of life; but this had been included in the sacrifice when, in Cambridge all those years before, he had given up the prospect of a professional academic career. It is difficult to appreciate what it cost him to do without even the most basic amenities.

Today the tourist sleeps in a comfortable room with hot and cold water, eats a substantial meal in a softly-lit dining-room, driving on next day in his high-powered car to the next smart hotel. He still finds an excuse to grumble! And should it be necessary he can board a plane to fly him straight home. But in 1812 there were no such luxuries.

By 6 September the company arrived at the banks of the Araxes, a river 'broad as the Isis, with a current as strong as that of the Ganges'. The ferry-boat, in appearance something like a large fish, was tied up on the opposite side so, not knowing how long it would be before it came across, Henry decided to catch up with his sleep.

But finding his servants had the same idea and that it was possible no one would be awake when the ferry-man came, he roused himself to keep on watch. In fact, it was dawn before the ferry came over, the man pushing it with a stick.

'I dare say he had never seen or heard of an oar, but we arrived safely on the other side in about two minutes.'

At Nackshan it was difficult to find a lodging but eventually one man, an important citizen, offered the use of his wash-house and a corner was cleaned and made ready for Henry's bedroom.

By this time it was almost noon and Henry's baggage had not yet caught up with them, so he had to go without breakfast. But he was so tired that, hungry as he was, he slept till the afternoon.

On the next lap Henry the linguist was hardly conscious of the miles, his mind completely taken up with a Hebrew word in the 16th Psalm which, he said, led him gradually into speculations on the eighth conjugation of the Arabic verb! 'I am glad that my philological curiosity is revived as my mind will be less liable to idleness.'

Next they came within sight of a high mountain and Henry was excited to learn that this was Ararat. Immediately his thoughts flew back to the Old Testament story, wondering on which spot Noah built his altar and offered his first thanksgiving sacrifice.

In the countryside just here there was abundant evidence of God's promise that seedtime and harvest should not cease. 'I had not seen such fertility in any part of the Shah's dominions.'

The next night the company lost their way, finding themselves in an area with many flooded ditches which in the darkness it was difficult to see and avoid. The horse carrying luggage sank in one so deep that the water soaked the contents of the bags, including Henry's books.

It was hopeless to try and find the next halting-place in the dark, so they tried to get help at a village they came across. For some time they wandered round without success, eventually knocking at the door of a house where they were greeted by two silver-haired elderly men. They invited Henry in and he explained that they were lost, travelling toward the Turkish border. Although it was late these good Samaritans lit a fire to dry their guest and his books, ordered hot coffee and a shelter for the rest of the night.

At daylight, with the help of a man from the village, they were guided through grass and mire to the mountain pass which they found led to country as dry as the last one was wet. They were now quite near to Mount Ararat, and soon arrived at Erivan.

27

Pomp and Ceremony

Henry made his way to the Governor's palatial residence at Erivan. Hosyn Khan, who commanded this highly important fortress on the frontier, was well aware of his own importance too. When the visitor was summoned to his presence Hosyn went on reading his Koran for several minutes before exchanging greetings. When the compliments were over he resumed his devotions, giving Henry the opportunity to admire the splendour of his surroundings.

The Governor was wearing a magnificent shawl dress but he ceremoniously exchanged this for a still richer pelisse, pretending to feel cold. He looked in good health but, seemingly to display the fact that he had a physician in residence, called for him to attend and feel his pulse. Once this had been done, the doctor took his place with the brightly-dressed servants standing to one side.

The letter of introduction Henry had brought had not been opened but lay on the floor until a moonshee was called to open and read it. Then Hosyn Khan became interested and attentive as he listened to what

Sir Gore Ouseley had written about the translations. His visitor was a man of more importance than he had supposed, and from then on one of the Governor's lieutenants was ordered to look after him.

During the afternoon Henry was asked to come again to the Governor's house and this time he found Hosyn reclining on a couch near a sparkling fountain, set in a basin of white marble containing grapes and melons. From far below the window came the pleasant murmur of a stream bubbling over stones and running on through the lovely gardens, behind which Henry caught sight of Ararat once again.

This time Hosyn Khan was entirely free of ceremony and although Henry tried to draw him into conversation, he seemed too languid even to talk. But at the end of the session he was not too fatigued to order a guard and fresh horses to be supplied for the journey which would eventually take Henry across Turkey.

The next calling-place was at Etschmiadzin, religious capital of the Armenians since 300 AD. Henry went with his letter of introduction to his lodging, an Armenian monastery where the monks take no vows but that of celibacy. One of the monks named Serope, a linguist who spoke French and Italian as well as English, took Henry to the room appointed for him, and was keen to tell him the fascinating story of his life. This monk was endeavouring to set up a college to teach the young Armenians logic, rhetoric and other sciences. With that accomplished he planned to retire to India and there write and print religious works in Armenian. 'I said all I could to encourage him in such a blessed work, promising him every aid from the English.' When the bells rang for Vespers they went together into the church.

Next day Henry had an interview with the Abbot, who welcomed him warmly and told him to consider himself completely at home in the monastery. The attention and kindness of the community had been so overwhelming and the grateful traveller was so happy to be there that, he said, duty permitting, he could almost be willing to become a monk himself. 'He smiled and, fearing perhaps that I was in earnest, said that they had quite enough!'

During Henry's stay the kind Serope proved to be the perfect host, doing all he could to make his guest comfortable. Then he helped Henry in his preparations for the journey ahead, advising him on the mode of travel in Turkey.

Much of the expensive equipment Henry had brought from Tabriz would have to be discarded, including a portable table and chair and a supply of sugar. Although this was in an age long before the advent of aeroplanes and airlines, there was nevertheless a restriction on the weight of luggage that could be carried. All the necessities had to be transferred from the heavy trunk and packed into bags, and a sword was bought for protection against robbers. Henry's servant was also armed.

The kindness and brotherly fellowship Henry had received at the monastery put new vigour into him, and sent him on his way with fresh hope of success in his struggle to reach first Constantinople, then his beloved Cornwall, and eventually back again to India, hopefully taking Lydia with him.

They left the monastery on 17 September and the first night the guard was able to find a comfortable lodging. At dawn Henry was ready to move on and after three hours' riding they had left the plain of

Ararat behind.

When they reached the Araxes again Henry let the company go on while he stayed to have a quick dip in the river, the last opportunity he would have of bathing in Persian waters. Soon afterwards they came to a village where the headman was sitting in a shed reading his Koran, with his sword, gun and pistol at his side. He was friendly and spoke to them in Persian, but chanted in Arabic with equal fluency.

The next stage of the journey took them along a dangerously steep road over the mountains leading to many miles of tedious tableland. It was hot and airless and nothing could be seen but bare rocks.

At last they came to an Armenian village in a hollow. The place looked strange with conical piles of peat everywhere, which the villagers used for their fires when they had no wood. All around were fields of growing corn.

The travellers were now over the border and had left Persia for the domains of the Sultan of Turkey. This was the first Turkish village. 'Not a Persian cap to be seen; the respectable people wore a red Turkish cap.'

28

The Last Ride

In the next village Henry found himself lodged in a
room that was a thoroughfare for horses, cows,
buffaloes and sheep. The animals took little notice of
the man in their midst, but most of the local people
came to stand and stare!

The guards were ever on the alert as they travelled
over the solitary plains, and when they came in sight of
a castle on a hilltop they moved with great caution. On
investigation it turned out to be quite empty; still and
silent as the grave, and they went on.

The next alarm came when they saw a company of
men in a valley and the guard again took their place in
front, guns at the ready. They realised there was
nothing to fear when they saw carts and oxen, but the
men in the valley were not so sure that Henry's party
were not bandits. They prepared to fire, but eventually
understood that there was no danger. They proved to
be an innocent group of Armenians carrying wood
from the town of Kars, to burn with peat on their home
fires.

When they reached Kars Henry was surprised to
see its European appearance; with houses of stone,

carts passing along the streets, a fort set high on a hill, and an enormous cemetery.

His groom took him at once to the Governor and an excellent room was provided for him in an Armenian's house, which had bow windows complete with cushioned seats, and a wide view of the fort and river. The Governor sent a message saying that he would be pleased for Henry to stay a few days and when he was ready to go on there would be horses and guards supplied.

In the event there was only one guard available, a Tartar who quickly displayed his fierce character by flogging the baggage-horse until it fell with its load. While this was being sorted out a crowd gathered—curiosity being the same the world over—and when the horse was once more on its feet they turned their attention on the stranger and his unusual clothing. But it appeared to be his Russian boots that interested them most of all!

The tuberculosis Henry had been fighting for so long was beginning to take its toll of his weakened body, and before they reached their next stopping place he was ill, with a high temperature. Hassan, the Tartar, went ahead and procured a room with a fire and here the invalid would have been comfortable had it not been that Hassan decided to share it with him.

Drawn by the warmth of the fire in contrast to the frost outside, other people joined them while waiting for the time of the meal. They were fascinated by Henry's watch and could not resist asking every few minutes 'Sir, what is your timer telling us now?'

The next day Henry was sufficiently recovered to be able to continue. The journey led through a beautiful forest of tall firs, with clear streams running in the valleys and lofty trees crowning the surrounding hills. Smooth paths led into the secret depths of the dark wood, and over all there was a solitude that tranquilised the mind. After nine hours of riding through these peaceful scenes they arrived at the post-house, where Henry found for himself quarters in the stable-room, thus avoiding the intrusion of Hassan, and at last being able to sleep in quiet.

The following morning the road brought them to a hot spring which ran into a pool set within four porches, beneath semi-circular arches, reminding Henry of the healing pool of Bethesda (John 5:2).

At this pleasant spot the company halted and stayed long enough for a bathe. Hassan, who knew well enough how to make life enjoyable for himself, smoked his calean (water-pipe) while up to his chin in water!

At Erzurum they found crowded streets and shops against a background of bougainvillaea and trailing vines. The crowds viewed with curiosity the strange assortment of newcomers, particularly the thin, frail rider with the white face. From his Persian attendants and the lower part of his clothing he would appear to be Persian, but there was something about him that stamped him as European.

When they realised that these were no more than peaceful travellers the natural Turkish generosity came to the fore. They brought melons and other food, offering them to the strangers with a dignified bow.

Everything emphasised for Henry the fact that he was in a Turkish town for the first time. 'The red cap, and stateliness, and rich dress and variety of turbans was realised as I had seen it in pictures.'

As they left Erzurum his temperature again rose. He was unable to eat or to drink anything but weak tea.

But even in his low state he recorded in his journal, 'My soul rests in Him who is as an anchor of the soul, sure and steadfast, which though not seen, keeps me fast.'

Mile after mile the hazardous journey continued, with Henry often near to collapse. Realising the serious state of his health he was desperate to complete it, but the merciless Hassan set the pace each day according to his own whim. Sometimes he would race the horses as if in a chariot contest, and another time delay procedure by refusing to get up until late in the day.

Sometimes he would not exert himself to find a room for Henry who had then to depend on his servant, Sergius.

In one stable-room Henry was so ill that he tried to get relief by laying his aching head down among the baggage on the damp floor before he lost consciousness. One can only wonder how he survived at all, yet he was able to write in his journal next morning, 'Preserving mercy made me see the light of another day. The sleep had refreshed me but I was feeble and shaken. Yet the merciless Hassan hurried me on.'

At one lodging there were two Persian fellow-travellers who saw Henry's distress and went to his assistance, while Hassan stood in complete indifference except to complain of the delay the illness would cause.

Then came the morning when there were no horses ready, giving a brief respite. 'I sat in the orchard and thought with sweet comfort and peace of my God; in solitude my company, my friend and comforter. When shall time give place to eternity? When shall appear that new heaven and new earth wherein dwelleth righteousness... none of those corruptions which add still more to the miseries of mortality shall be seen or heard of any more.'

For the last time the journal had recorded the thoughts of this dying man and the book was closed; to be opened only much later by his sorrowing friends in an atmosphere of reverent awe and wonder.

Henry Martyn had ridden himself to death. There is no record of the last ten days of his life but it is known that he reached Tokat, either still holding the reins of his horse, or more likely by being carried there. And in Tokat, on 16 October 1812, his old complaint, tuberculosis, possibly combined with the plague that was raging at the time, released his spirit from its battered shell. He was only thirty-one years old.

There may not have been a friendly hand for him to hold as he entered the valley of the shadow, but the trumpets must have sounded as the gates of the Celestial City swung open to receive this faithful servant of the God he worshipped.

He had left instructions with Sergius to take all the papers and personal belongings on with him to the British Embassy at Constantinople. In February of the following year Charles Simeon heard from the Ambassador's secretary, Isaac Morier, that an Armenian servant named Sergius had come into the office. He had brought the journal and other effects of his master, Henry Martyn, and reported that his master had died at Tokat on or about 16 October, and had been give Christian burial by the Armenians.

The sorrowing Simeon wrote to Calcutta to let his friends there know of Henry's death, and Lydia was also informed.

So the work of Henry Martyn was ended, and a humble grave in a foreign country was all the world could offer him.

29

To Whom Tribute Is Due

In every way Henry Martyn was outstanding. In his faith there was the simple trust of a child, the greatness of a giant, all enfolded in a meek humility and an awesome reverence. He was brilliant as a scholar, naïve as an individual, solemn in judgement but merry in laughter. He had a love for people and crowds, as well as a taste for solitude.

His writings have inspired many to aim for the highest standard in their work for God. Great men such as Murray McCheyne and Andrew Bonar, famous ministers of the Church of Scotland, read the memoirs of Martyn in the early part of their ministry, and recorded in their diaries the great impact this had on them.

But who can tell how many more have been influenced by his life and work? The mystics of Islam, his many friends and colleagues, and subsequent generations in many lands all owe him a tremendous debt.

Moreover, he was one of the Church's greatest linguists. He was responsible for translating the whole of the New Testament and the Prayer Book into Hindustani (Urdu), and the Psalms of David and the New Testament into Persian. Indeed, until recently his Urdu New Testament was the only major translation available, although it has been extensively revised over the years.

A present-day missionary to Urdu-speaking Muslims in Pakistan, Vivienne Stacey, quotes Canon W. J. Edmonds' tribute to Henry Martyn: 'I know no parallel to these achievements of Henry Martyn...the born translator. He masters grammar, observes idioms, accumulates vocabulary, reads and listens, corrects and even reconstructs. Above all, he prays. He lives in the Spirit, rises from his knees full of the mind of the Spirit.'

The papers and the first part of Henry's journal, which he had left with his friend Daniel Corrie in India, were sent to his executors, Charles Simeon and John Thornton. The latter section of the journal and the letters written when he was in Persia and Turkey were sent on by Morier from Constantinople. With a deepening sense of awe these were studied carefully in Simeon's room at Cambridge. In 1819 the journal and some letters were faithfully reproduced by John Sargeant.

The first edition of Henry Martyn's translation into Persian was printed in St Petersburg (today's Leningrad) in 1815 by the Russian Bible Society. For the second edition, printed by the Serampore Press, Seid Ali of Shiraz was invited to Calcutta in 1816 to supervise the actual printing.

Lydia, at last freed from the decision-making with which she seemed unable to cope, continued to live at Marazion for a further seventeen years, quietly mourning the memory of the man she had loved—but not enough to marry. She was ill for several years with cancer and died in 1829 at the age of fifty-four.

Henry Martyn is remembered in his native Cornwall and the baptistry in Truro Cathedral is regarded as his memorial. In Market Street, Cambridge stands the Henry Martyn Hall; next to Holy Trinity Church where Henry was at one time curate for Charles Simeon. Around the walls of the hall are the names of subsequent Cambridge graduates who followed Henry's example in taking the gospel overseas, and in the same building a library and an experienced adviser are on hand for the benefit of those considering the same step today.

The portrait of Henry, which was painted in Calcutta in 1810 before he left for Persia, was sent as a gift to Simeon and he received it in 1812. In 1836 it was bequeathed to Cambridge University Library, and the portrait is now on loan to the Henry Martyn Hall. There is a copy of it in St John's College Library, reminding today's students of the Cambridge man who in his day was winner of 1st Smith's prize and Senior Wrangler.

Above all his achievements, however, Henry Martyn was a man longing for God, always striving to enter in at the gate of every Christian experience, thirsting after righteousness, critical of his own weakness, deploring what he felt to be his lack of holy living.

Although Henry Martyn's life on earth had ended, the results of his faithful ministry continue through the years, and the memory of his courage, endurance and dedication must present a lasting challenge to all Christian people.

Bibliography

Bentley-Taylor, D., *My Love Must Wait*
Colebrooke, T. E., *Life of Mountstuart Elphinstone*
Cook, J. M., *The Persian Empire*
Dicks, Brian, *The Ancient Persians*
Loane, Marcus, *Cambridge and the Evangelical Succession*
Padwick, Constance, *Henry Martyn—Confessor of the Faith*
Sargeant, John, *The Life and Letters of Henry Martyn*
Smith, George, LLD, *Henry Martyn, Saint and Scholar*
Stacey, Vivienne, *Life of Henry Martyn*
Ure, John, *The Trail of Tamerlane*
Wood, Philip, *Touring Iran*

I am also indebted to:

the Very Rev D. J. Shearlock, Dean of Truro Cathedral,
Mr S. M. Mischler, former Headmaster at Cathedral School, Truro,
Mr H. L. Douch, BA, Curator of Truro Museum and Art Gallery,
the Library of St John's College, Cambridge,

Leicester University,
Leicester Reference Library,
the Church Missionary Society,
Serampore College, Calcutta,
the Rev John Kirkby BD, BSc, Rector of St Mary's
    Church, Byfleet, Surrey,
and the Rev Canon D. W. Gundry BD, MTh, Canon
    Chancellor of Leicester Cathedral.

"Be quiet and listen."

His chin tilted down. His brows rose. "Yes, Miss Cherroll?"

"I will not stay here."

He waited, his gaze locked on to hers.

"My s ... eeds me for the children," she said.

"I understand completely," he said, voice agreeing, and stepped to the door. "You can take my carriage to visit them as often as you wish." One stride and he would be out of her vision. "It is not a problem at all. Send your maid in Warrington's carriage for your things. The housekeeper will be with you shortly to help you select a room."

He was gone by the time she opened her mouth.

Author Note

Bellona's story formed while I was writing *A Captain and a Rogue.*

I envisioned her as wanting to be like the Grecian heroine Laskarina Bouboulina who owned a large warship and would have been active around 1822 of for *Forbidden to the Duke* begins. I also Bellona to be a bit of a Robin Hood in spirit. Her knife and archery skills could protect her from many dangers, except the most surprising ones.

But Bellona became a different character from the warrior I first imagined. When this story begins, she's on the path of separating from the security of her family and making her own way in the world.

The new hobby she finds at the end of the book wasn't planned until the words were being written, but I felt it truly expresses who she was meant to be, and the part of her she'd hidden from herself.

I hope you enjoy Bellona and Rhys's journey and see them as I do—two people who have to step out of the roles they were born into and rise to be the beginning of a new legacy.

Forbidden
to the Duke

Liz Tyner

HARLEQUINHISTORICAL

Recycling programs
for this product may
not exist in your area.

ISBN-13: 978-1-335-46768-3

Forbidden to the Duke

Printed in U.S.A.

www.Harlequin.com

Liz Tyner lives with her husband on an Oklahoma acreage she imagines is similar to the ones in the children's book *Where the Wild Things Are*. Her lifestyle is a blend of old and new, and is sometimes comparable to how people lived long ago. Liz is a member of various writing groups and has been writing since childhood. For more about her, visit liztyner.com.

Books by Liz Tyner

Harlequin Historical

The Notorious Countess
The Wallflower Duchess
Redeeming the Roguish Rake
Saying I Do to the Scoundrel
To Win a Wallflower

The Governess Tales

The Runaway Governess

English Rogues and Grecian Goddesses

Safe in the Earl's Arms
A Captain and a Rogue
Forbidden to the Duke

Visit the Author Profile page at Harlequin.com.

To Juanita Ballew, "Sis," a real heroine.

Chapter One

The pudgy-eyed gamekeeper pointed a flintlock straight at Bellona's chest. His eyebrows spiked into angry points. 'Drop the longbow.' His gun barrel emphasised his words and even without the weapon his size would have daunted her. He'd not looked so large or his stare so bloodless from a distance.

Noise crashed into her ears—the sound of her heart—and the beats tried to take over every part of her. She forced the blackness away and locked her stare with his. Charred hatred, roughened by the unshaven chin, slammed out from his face.

She nodded and tossed the bow into the twining berry thorns at the side of the path. The canopy of sycamore leaves covered him in green-hued shadows.

He put one hand to his mouth, thrust his fingers to his lips and whistled loud enough to be heard in Greece. The shrill sound jabbed her, alerting her that he wasn't alone. She'd never seen anyone else in the forest but this devil. She would be fighting two men and at least one weapon.

'…shoot at me…' He spoke again and the words snapped her back into understanding.

She cursed herself for not taking more care. She'd not heard him behind her—but she should have smelled his boiled-cabbage stench.

'I be bringing his lordship,' he said. 'Your toes be dangling and the tide be washing your face before they cut you down. You won't be shooting at me no more. You're nothing more'n a common wench and people in lofty places be wantin' you to hang.'

Her fingers stiffened, her mind unable to send them commands. She held her chin high. She'd thought she was in a safe land. She'd thought she'd escaped men who wanted to hurt her. Showing fear would be dangerous. 'You—' She couldn't have taken her eyes from his. 'I'm a guest of the Earl of Warrington and I have misplaced myself.'

The man's nose bunched up as he talked. 'But you ain't on the earl's land now, Miss Lady Nobody. You're no better'n me.' He waved the gun. 'You're a poacher and I've seen you here aplenty times before. I just niver could catch you.'

'The earl will be *thymomenos*, angered.'

He snorted. 'But this is the duke's land. His Grace don't lose no sleep over what an *earl* would think.'

She forced her fingers alert. 'You are the one who should think. You must know I live near.'

'But you ain't no real lady. I already told the duke all about you and how you been scattering my traps and he thinks I'm imaginin'. Your eyes is even uncommon dark like some witch borne you. I told him you're half-spirit. They hanged Mary Bateman. If they don't be hangin' you, you'll end up lyin' with vermin in gaol. Good 'nuff for you.'

He indicated the trail behind himself by swinging the barrel of the gun towards it. 'Don't move a feather.' The gamekeeper swaggered. 'His Grace be right behind me. I told him I set my traps near and this time I be catchin' somethin' big. You've ruined your last snare.'

Footsteps in the leaves signalled the approach of another. Bellona rested her left hand on the top of arrows tucked into the quiver strapped around her waist. 'You can go to the devil.'

The shoulders of another man came into view, and Bellona swallowed. She needed all of her strength. Two men to fight.

The gamekeeper stepped off the path so the other one could see her.

The duke stopped beside the gamekeeper and the scent of the air became clean. The newcomer examined her, not scowling or smiling.

She would not have thought this man a peer had she seen him without introduction, but she would have known him for a gentleman. His neckcloth looped in a simple, soft knot. His boots reached his knees and his dark riding coat had plain buttons. He wore every thread as if it had been woven to his own order. Sunlight dappled over lean cheeks. His eyes were the same colour as her own.

Her stomach clenched, but not with fear. She'd made a mistake. She'd looked into his eyes. For the first time in her life, she was afraid of something inside herself.

She stepped back.

'Your Grace, I caught the murderous culprit what's been stealing the hares from my traps and wishin' curses on us all. She be a common thief, a murderous woman and full of meanness, just like I said.' The gamekeeper's words spewed out, leaving even less air for Bellona to breathe. 'You want I should send the stable boy for the magistrate?'

The duke gave the slightest shake of his head. 'You are mistaken, Wicks. I will see her back to my estate safely and ensure that she is escorted on her way.'

'She be a thief, Your Grace, and a bewitched woman. Why, see how her eyes be puttin' evil my direction now. She be tryin' to burn me into ash right where I stand.'

'Miss—' the newcomer directed his words to Bellona and he leaned forward as he peered at her '—have you been poaching on my land?'

She sensed somehow that he jested with her. 'No. Never,' Bellona said, shaking her head. The knife was in her boot. But she didn't want to attack. She only wanted to flee.

The duke's lips firmed and he took in a small breath on his next words. 'Wicks…'

The gamekeeper's stance tightened and he rushed his words. 'She tossed her bow into the briars. She'd kill a man herself for blood sport. She'd cut out his heart and cook it.'

The duke's lips tightened at one side and his eyes dismissed the other man's words.

'I don't eat hearts,' Bellona inserted, directing a look straight into the vile man. 'Only brains. You are safe.'

'Your Grace,' the gamekeeper sputtered, outrage and fury mixed. 'She's—'

'Quiet.' The duke's words thrust into the air with the seriousness of a sword point held to the throat.

He stepped towards her, moving over the fallen log in the path, his hand out. 'The lady and I have not been introduced, but as this isn't a soirée, I think—'

Instinctively, she pulled an arrow from the quiver and held the tip against the duke's grey silk waist-coat—pressing.

His arm halted, frozen.

'Do not touch me.' Her words copied his in command.

His eyes widened and he straightened. 'I was going to take your arm. My pardon. It's usually received well, I assure you.'

She kept the arrow at his stomach, trying to keep the spirit around him from overtaking her.

The gamekeeper moved so the weapon again pointed at her. 'Just give me the word, Your Grace, I'll save you. She be tryin' to kill a peer. No sense wasting good rope round that boney neck.'

'Put the flintlock away, Wicks. Now.' The duke didn't take his eyes from Bellona. 'This woman and I have not finished introductions yet and, by my calcu-lation, the arrow tip isn't exceedingly sharp.'

'It's sharp enough,' she said.

'Miss…' He blinked. He smiled. But they were just outward movements. 'Most people get to know me a little better before they think of weapons. Perhaps you should consider that. It might make an attempt on my

life more enjoyable for you if there were some justi-
fication.'

She never saw his movement, but his hand clamped
around her wrist, securing her, not tight, but shackle-
strong.

'My property.' He stepped back from the arrow.
Then he extricated it from her fingers, the warm touch
of his hand capturing her in yet another way before
he released her. 'My rules, Huntress.' He studied her
face. 'Or if my observation is correct, should I refer
to you as goddess?'

As he examined the arrow, she took another step
back. She gave the merest head toss of dismissal and
readied her hand to the single arrow left in the quiver.

His eyes flickered to the sharpened tip of the pro-
jectile he held, but he wasn't truly examining it. He
twirled it around, tipped his head to her and held the
feathered end to her. 'I have met the lovely Countess
of Warrington and although you resemble her, I would
remember if I'd met you. That means you're the sister named for the goddess of war. The woman hardly
ever seen.'

'You may call me Miss Cherroll.' The rules she'd
studied fled from her, except the one about the curtsy
and she could not force herself to do it. She took the
arrow.

She only wanted to leave, but her limbs hadn't yet
recovered their strength. She controlled her voice, putting all the command in it she could muster. 'You're
not what I expected.'

'If you've been talking to Warrington, I suppose
not.' He tilted his head forward, as if he secluded them

from the rest of the world. 'What is he fed for breakfast? I fear it curdles his stomach—daily.'

'Only when mixed with entertainments not to his liking.'

'Well, that explains it. I can be quite entertaining.'

'He claims you can be quite…' She paused. His eyes waited for her to continue, but she didn't think it prudent, either to Warrington or the duke.

The duke continued, taking in the words she didn't say. 'Not many are above him, and, well, I might give him the tiniest reminder of my status, when it is needed.' He shrugged. 'Our fathers were like brothers. He thinks he has become the old earl and I have not attained the grandness of my sire. My father did limp— and that knee was the only thing that kept him from perfection. The injured leg was the price he paid for doing the right thing. He once thrust himself between someone and the hooves of an angry horse.'

'I would not be so certain of the earl's opinion.' She paused, softening her words. 'He says you are quite the perfect duke. A duke from heel to head.' Warrington had stared at the ceiling and grimaced when he spoke.

'A compliment. I'm certain. From Warrington.' He shrugged. 'Too many things distract me from perfection. I just trudge along, doing what I can. Hoping to honour the legacy my father left behind.'

He turned to the other man, sending him along. 'I'll see Miss Cherroll home.' Taking a step towards her, he paused when she moved the pointed tip the slightest bit in his direction. 'Assuming she doesn't do Warrington a boon and impale his favourite neighbour.'

When he stopped moving, she relaxed her hand.

'I will manage well enough on my own.' She turned, pulling the skirt's hem from a bramble, and moved closer to the bow. 'I know the way.' She heard her own words and turned back to the duke and leaned her head to the side. 'I have been lost here before.' She pulled the bow into her hand, freeing it from the thorny brambles clasping it.

'I would imagine so. Wicks claims you are here more than he is. I might call on you,' he said, 'later today to assure myself you arrived safely home.'

She shook her head. 'Please don't. Warrington is always claiming I bring home strange things from my walks.'

'My dear, I'm a duke. He won't be able to say a word. It's a rule of sorts.'

'You truly don't know him well, do you?'

'Well, perhaps he might grumble, but his good breeding would insist he appear welcoming. At least in your presence.'

She held the nock end of the arrow as if she were going to seat it against the bowstring. 'You're right in that my English father named me for the Roman goddess of war. And, it's said I'm completely lacking in the ways of a proper Englishwoman. But I do remember one phrase. "I am not at home."'

'Miss Cherroll. I would think you'd not mind sharing tea with me seeing as you have already shared my property.'

She shook her head. 'I have been called on before. I have not been at home.'

'Ever?'

She firmed her lips and shook her head.

'Why not?'

She didn't answer his question. She could not speak of her memories aloud. Putting them into words brought the feel of the rough fingertips to her neck.

His brows furrowed. Even though she knew a proper lady didn't scurry along the trail, she did, leaving the duke standing behind her.

Rhys Harling, Duke of Rolleston, sat at his desk, completely unmoving. Wicks stood in front of Rhys, repeating the same words he'd said two days ago and the two days before that. Rhys hoped the air would clear of the man's dank scent when he left.

Wicks waved the arrow like a sceptre. His lips didn't stop moving even when he paused to find new words.

Wicks rambled on, falling more in love with his discourse as he continued. If the gamekeeper were to be believed, the woman created more mischief than any demon.

It had been five days since Wicks had caught the woman. The gamekeeper had approached him twice to discuss the lands and could not keep from mentioning her.

Rhys interrupted, his voice direct. 'She did not try to impale me. Neither her teeth nor her eyes—which are not rimmed by devil's soot—show brighter than any other's in the dusk and she is not as tall as I am. You cannot claim her to be something she is not. I forbid it.'

'You can't be faultin' me for lookin' out for your lands, Your Grace.'

'I don't. But she's the earl's guest. You must cease talking at the tavern about the woman.'

'Who told you?' His chin dropped and he looked at the floor.

'Who didn't tell me?' Rhys fixed a stare at the man. 'Wicks, you should know that words travel from one set of ears to the next and the next and before long every person who has shared a meal with someone else has heard.'

'She does stick in my craw, Your Grace.'

He didn't blame the gamekeeper. Rhys couldn't remove her from his mind either. The quiver cinched her trim waist. A twig had poked from her mussed hair. The magical thing he'd noticed about her was the way her hair could stay in a knot on her head when most of it had escaped.

Rhys had known when the gamekeeper first mentioned the trespasser who it would most likely be. He'd wanted to see her for himself.

Wicks wasn't the first person to discuss her. Even the duchess, who talked only of family members who'd passed on, had varied from her melancholia once and spoke of the earl's sister-by-law Miss Cherroll. The foreign-born woman rarely let herself be seen by anyone outside the earl's household and that caused more talk than if she'd danced three dances with the same partner.

'Forget her,' the duke said. 'She's just an ordinary woman who likes to traipse the trails. I can't fault her for that.'

He couldn't. He'd travelled over those same trails countless times, trying to keep up with his brother, Geoff.

Looking for the woman had been the first time he'd

been in the woods since Geoff's death. The gnashing ache grinded inside him again, but the woman's face reminded him of unspoiled times.

But she was…a poacher of sorts. Nothing like her sister—a true countess if tales were to be believed. He wouldn't put it past Warrington to keep this bow-carrying family member in the shadows, afraid what would happen if the woman met with members of the *ton*.

'You didn't feel she could near strangle a man with one look from her eyes?' Wicks asked. 'I could feel that devil in her just trying to take my vicar's words right from mind. She still be trespassin' ever' day. Taunting me, like. She tears up my traps and she lurks out in the wood, waiting until I check them and then she tries to kill me.'

'I'm sure she's not trying to kill you.'

'This arrow weren't whipping by your head.' He pulled every muscle of his body into an indignant shudder. 'And since I caught her last time, she stays too far back for me to snatch her again.'

'You will not touch her.' Rhys met Wicks's stare. Rhys stood.

Wicks's lips pressed together.

'You will not touch her,' Rhys said again and waited.

'I don't want no part of that evil witch,' Wicks said finally. 'I looked at her and I saw the Jezebel spirit in her. I be sleepin' on the floor and not in my bed so she can't visit me in my night hours and have her way with me.'

Rhys put both palms flat on the desk and leaned forward. 'That is a good plan. However, if you sleep with your nightcap over your ears it will do the same.'

'You're sure?'

'Yes.' Rhys nodded.

Wicks's lips moved almost for a full minute before he spoke and his shoulders were pulled tight and he watched the arrow in his hand. 'Well, I'll be considerin' it. Floor's cold.'

'Do you think perhaps she is a normal kind-hearted woman, Wicks, and merely doesn't want little creatures harmed?'

'I wondered. But that seems odd to me. When I gave her my smile—' He bared perfect teeth except for one missing at the bottom. 'She didn't even note. Just raised her bow right towards me and let this arrow loose.'

Rhys rose, walked around the desk and held out his hand. Wicks slowly placed the arrow across Rhys's palm.

'If you see her again,' Rhys commanded, 'at any time at any place, you are not to give her one moment of anything but respect. You are not to smile at her or approach her, or you will answer to me in a way you will not like.'

'Not right,' Wicks said, his nose going up. 'Being shot at while doin' my work.'

'I will handle this. Do not forget my words. Leave her be.'

'I will,' Wicks said. 'I pity her. Has too many airs to settle into things right for a woman's place.'

Rhys glared.

'But I be keepin' it a secret.' He nodded. 'I ain't givin' her another one of my smiles. She missed her chance. And if she tries to have her way with me, I be turnin' my head and keepin' my nightcap tight.'

He used both hands to clamp his hat on his head as he shuffled out, grumbling.

Rhys studied the arrow and thought of his mother's melancholia. How she hardly left her room, even for meals. How she talked more of people who'd passed than of her own friends, and how she claimed illness rather than go to Sunday Services. His brother's death had taken the life from her as well. The one moment the duchess's thoughts had wavered into the present had been when she asked Rhys if he'd heard of the earl's guest, but by the time he'd answered, his mother's thoughts had wavered back into the shadows of the past.

He brushed his hand over the arrow fletching. Window light bounced over the feathers, almost startling him. Raising his eyes, he saw the sun's rays warming the room. He stood, walking to the sunlight, pausing to feel the heat on his face. He lifted the feathery end of the weapon, twirling it in the brightness.

Winter's chill had left the air, but he'd not noticed the green outside the window until now. The woman had also worn the colours of the forest, he remembered. She'd not looked like a warrior goddess, but a woodland nymph, bringing life into morning.

He snorted, amazed at the folly of his imagination. He'd not had such foolish thoughts in a long time. Nor had he longed for a woman's comfort overmuch in the past year. Now, he imagined the huntress and his body responded, sending reminders of pleasure throughout his being.

Leaning into the window frame, holding the arrow like a talisman, he tried to remember every single aspect of her. What she'd said and how she'd looked. Each word and moment that had transpired between them.

He pulled the soft end of the arrow up, looking at the feathers one last time before tapping the nock against the sill, staring at the reflections of sunlight.

This woman at the earl's estate, who was willing to fight for rabbits, but could keep the servants whispering about her, might be just the woman who could bring his mother back to life. She'd already reminded Rhys that he was still alive.

Within the hour, Rhys was in the Earl of Warrington's sitting room. The duke clasped an arrow at his side and waited as he expected he might. He moved to the window again, wanting to feel the heat from the sun streaming through the panes. Trees budded back to life. A heathen spirit might do the same for his own home.

The mantel sported a painting of three young girls playing while their mother watched. He wagered the painting was of Greece and one of the girls could have been the one on his property. Except for the single painting, the room seemed little different than Rhys's own library.

Rhys looked out over Warrington's snipped and clipped and trimmed and polished world, almost able to hear the laughter from years before.

Only, the laughter was not his, but directed at him.

Of course, both he and Warrington had matured now. They had left foolish prattle and childish games behind.

Warrington strode in. Rhys could still taste the medicinal the others had found in the apothecary jar and forced into Rhys's mouth when they were children. That had to be his earliest memory.

'Your *Grace*,' Warrington greeted. The earl moved to stand at the mantel. He glanced once at the painting above it before he asked, 'So what is the honour that brings you to Whitegate?'

Rhys held out the arrow. 'I found this on my property and heard that you have a guest who practises archery. I'd like to return it to her.'

Rhys had never seen Warrington's face twitch until that moment. He studied Rhys as if they'd just started a boxing match. 'You are interested in talking with *Bellona*?'

Warrington's eyes flickered. 'I'm sure whatever she did—' Warrington spoke quickly. 'She just doesn't understand our ways.' He paused and then sighed. 'What did she do now?'

'I just wish to meet with her,' Rhys said, 'and request that she refrain from shooting arrows on to my property—particularly near others.'

Warrington grimaced and then turned it into a smile. 'She does… Well…you know…' He held out a palm. 'Some women like jewellery. Flowers. Sharp things. She likes them.'

'Sharp things?'

Warrington shook his head. 'Never a dull moment around her.'

'Truly?'

'Beautiful voice—when she's not talking. Her sister forced her to attend the soirée at Riverton's, hoping Bellona would find something about society that suited her. Pottsworth wanted to be introduced. She'd not danced with anyone. I thought it a good idea even though he is—well, you know Potts. She smiled and answered him in Greek. Thankfully none of the ladies near her had our tutors. Riverton overheard and choked on his snuff. We left before he stopped sputtering. He still asks after her every time he sees me. "How is that retiring Miss Cherroll?"'

'Can't say as I blame her. You introduced *Pottsworth* to her?' Rhys asked drily.

'I'm sure she might wander too far afield from time to time,' Warrington murmured it away, 'but your land has joined mine since before our grandparents' time and we've shared it as one.' Warrington gave an encompassing gesture, then he toyed with what could have been a speck on the mantel. 'We're all like family. We grew up together. I know you and I don't have the very close bond of our fathers, but still, I count you much the same as a brother of my own.'

'Much like Cain and Abel?'

Warrington grinned. He waved the remark away. 'You've never taken a jest well.'

'The bull,' Rhys said, remembering the very incensed animal charging towards him, bellowing. Rhys was on the wrong side of the fence, his hands on the rails, and the older boys pushed at him, keeping him from climbing to safety. He'd felt the heat from the bull's nostrils when they'd finally hefted him through to the other side. Laughing.

He couldn't have been much more than five years old.

Warrington had instigated many of the unpleasant moments of Rhys's childhood. Actually, almost every disastrous circumstance could be traced back to War. Rhys had been lured into a carriage and then trapped when they wedged the door shut from the outside, and then he'd spent hours in the barn loft when they had removed the ladder. When they'd held him down and stained his cheeks with berries, he'd waited almost two years to return fresh manure to everyone involved. It had taken special planning and the assistance of the stable master's son to get manure put into Warrington's boots.

Rhys's mother and father had not been happy. The one time he had not minded disappointing his father.

War's face held camaraderie now—just like when the new puppy had been left in the carriage, supposedly.

'I must speak with your wife's sister,' Rhys said. 'I might have an idea which could help us both.'

'What?' The word darted from Warrington's lips.

'I thought Miss Cherroll might spend some time with the duchess. Perhaps speak of Greece or…' He shrugged. 'Whatever tales she might have learned.'

'I forbid—' Warrington's head snapped sideways. 'No. She is my family and she must stay with us.'

Rhys lips quirked up. 'But, War, we're like brothers. Your family is my family.'

Warrington grunted. 'You didn't believe that flop when I said it. Don't try to push it back in my direction.'

Rhys smiled. 'I suppose it is your decision to make, War. But remember. I am serious and I will not back down.'

'I assure you, Rhys, Miss Cherroll is not the gentle sort that the duchess is used to having tea with.'

Rhys gave a slight twitch of his shoulder in acknowledgement. Warrington had no idea his mother was only having tea with memories of death. She'd lost her will to live. With her gone, he would have no one. No one of his true family left. And he was not ready to lose the last one. 'Call Miss Cherroll. Let me decide.'

With a small cough of disagreement, Warrington shrugged. 'Speak with her and you'll see what I mean.' He reached for the pull. A child's laughing screech interrupted him. A blonde blur of a chit, hardly big enough to manage the stairs, hurtled into the room and crashed into Warrington's legs, hugging for dear life, and whirling so he stood between her and the door.

Bellona, brandishing a broom, charged in behind the little one and halted instantly at the sight of Warrington.

Rhys took in a breath and instantly understood Wicks's fascination with the woman. Her face, relaxed in laughter, caught his eyes. He couldn't look away— no man would consider it.

'Just sweeping the dust out of the nursery,' she said to Warrington, lowering the broom while she gingerly moved around him. The child used him as a shield.

Warrington's hand shot down on to the little girl's head, hair shining golden in the sunlight, stilling her.

Bellona's attention centred on the waif. 'Willa, we do not run in the house. We swim like fishes.'

The child laughed, pulled away from the silent admonishment of her father's hand on her head, puffed her cheeks out and left the room quickly, making motions of gliding through water.

Warrington cleared his throat before the chase began again. 'We have a guest, Bellona.'

Rhys saw the moment Bellona became aware of his presence. The broom tensed and for half a second he wondered if she would drop it or turn it into a weapon. Warrington was closer, and Rhys was completely willing to let her pummel him.

She lowered the bristles to the floor, but managed a faint curtsy and said, 'I did not know we had a visitor.' Her face became as stiff as the broom handle.

Warrington turned to Rhys.

'Bellona is… She gets on quite well with the children as you can tell.' His eyes glanced over to her. 'But she is not as entranced with tranquillity as her sister is.'

'I do like the English ways,' she said, shrugging. 'I just think my ways are also good.'

'But my children need to be well mannered at all times.' Warrington frowned after he spoke.

'I do adore the *paidi*. They are gold,' she said, voice prim and proper. 'But no little one is well mannered at all times. They have life. It is their treasure. They should spend it well.'

'They should also know the way to be proper and comport themselves in a lofty manner when they meet such a person as we are privileged to have in our presence.' He glanced at Rhys. 'His Grace, Duke of Rolleston. Rescuer of lost puppies, everywhere.' He turned to Bellona to complete the introduction. 'Miss Cherroll, my wife's kind and gentle-spirited youngest sister—' his brows bumped up as he looked back at

Rhys '—who has called me a few endearments in her native language that our tutor neglected to teach us, and when her sister translates I fear something is lost in the meaning.'

Her eyes blinked with innocence at Warrington for a moment before she acknowledged the introduction with a slight nod.

'I believe the duke wanted to speak with you.' Warrington walked to her, took the broom and looked at it as if might bite. 'And I should see about Willa.'

The earl took two long strides to the door. 'I won't send a chaperon.' He smiled at Rhys as he left. 'You're on your own.'

Chapter Two

Pleased Warrington had left them alone, Rhys's attention turned to Bellona. She'd moved a step back from him and stood close to an unlit lamp on a side table. Her eyes remained on the arrow in his hand.

Perhaps he'd been mistaken about her. She might be unsettled.

Bellona nodded towards the arrow. 'I believe that is mine.'

Rhys grasped the shaft with both hands and snapped the arrow across his knee, breaking the wood in two pieces. Then he held it in her direction.

The straight line of her lips softened. Her shoulders relaxed and she moved just close enough so that he could place the arrow in her hand. Exotic spices lingered in the air around her and he tried to discern if it was the same perfume from a rare plant he'd once noted in a botanist's collection.

'Thank you.' She took the splintered pieces and increased the distance between them. Examining the broken shaft, she said, 'I feared you would not be so kind as to return it.'

'You could have injured someone. My gamekeeper.'

She raised her eyes to Rhys. 'The arrow did what arrows do. I didn't want to hurt him, but he—' Bellona dismissed the words. 'His voice... You should speak with him about *glossa*—his words.'

'Leave the poor man alone. He has been on my estate his whole life and feels as much kinship to the land as I do.'

'A man cannot own land. It is a gift from the heavens to be shared.'

'For the time being, it is my gift and I control all on it. You upset the gamekeeper.'

She shrugged. 'He upsets rabbits.'

'They are invited. You are not. However...' His next words were about to change that, but he forgot he was speaking when her hand moved.

Flicking up the notched end of the arrow, she brushed the feathery fletching against her face. The arrow stroked her skin. One. Two. Three little brushes. Softness against softness.

His heart pounded blood everywhere around his body except his head.

He remembered where he was, but not what he'd been saying. He looked at her eyes, checking for artifice, wondering if she knew how he reacted to her.

'I do not know if this is a good idea.' He spoke barely above a whisper.

'The traps are a bad idea. Wrong. Thinking you own the earth is not correct.' She moved her hand to her side, the arrow tip pointed in his direction.

Traps? That problem was easily solved.

'At the soirée, what did you say to Pottsworth in Greek that was so shocking?' he asked.

She raised her brows.

'Never mind.' He turned away. Walking to the painting, he looked at it. An idyllic scene with a sea in the background. Waves lapped the sand and breezes brought the scent of moisture to him. 'Are you one of the little girls in the painting?' He raised his finger, almost touching the long-dried oils. She had to be the youngest one—the urchin had grown into the woman behind him.

'Miss Cherroll.' He turned back. 'Are you the little one in the picture?'

'It is just a painting. From my homeland.'

'Tell me about yourself.'

'No. You broke my arrow.'

'I beg your pardon.' He turned to her and locked his clasped hands behind his back. This intractable woman and his mother would not get on well at all. Such a foolish thought.

'You do not mean to beg my pardon,' she said. 'You just speak it because it is what you have always said.'

'I'll buy you a score of arrows to replace this one if you merely promise you will not shoot in the direction of a person. I was making a point.'

She waved a hand his direction. 'Keep your arrows. I have many of them.'

'Well, I must be going. You're not quite as I expected. Thank you for your time. I sincerely regret breaking your arrow.' He stopped. 'No, I don't. However, I will see that more are sent your way. Please be careful with them and do not practise archery on my land.'

She didn't speak.

He strode to the door. This woman could not reside with his mother. He did not know how he could have imagined such a thing. But he just did not know what to do. He turned back. He could not go out that door.

'You may visit my land whenever you wish.' He didn't recognise his own voice. His words sounded parched to his ears—the same as when he was little more than a youth and requested his first dance from a woman whose eyes glittered with sensual knowledge.

'I will not shoot near the gamekeeper any more unless he comes too close to me.' Her tone commanded, but underneath there might have been a waver in it. His thoughts raced ahead.

'But be aware he is not a nice man,' she continued. 'He has killed—he has killed them after taking them from the trap. With his foot.' Her voice dipped. 'It is—it is bad. He does not care.'

He turned away so he could concentrate and put his hand on the door frame, sorting his thoughts, listening with his whole body. 'He said you shot at him.'

'Yes. I was watching the traps to see if he'd caught anything. I was going to free the animals. But he was early. He knew. He saw me and he walked closer and I thought of the rabbits. The rabbits. What man could do that to another living creature? I could not let him near me. I shot at the ground between us. He stopped.'

'It is his job to watch for poachers.' He slid his hand from the wood and moved just enough to hold her in his line of vision.

'Nothing should be trapped like that.'

He asked the other question again. 'What did you say to Pottsworth?'

'The man at the soirée?'

'Yes.'

'I was in the gardens because I did not want to be with the people. I heard him speak to another man and say I was ripe for his hands. I only told him what would happen if he touched me, although I did not say it pleasantly. I knew he could understand my language. Warrington had told us that most men at the soirée had been tutored in Greek.'

'I have heard that your parents are no longer with us,' Rhys asked, tactfully changing the subject.

She touched a finger to the tip of the arrow. 'My *mana* is not alive. I miss her still. I miss her more now than when she died, because she has been gone from me longer.'

He stepped closer, into the whiff of her perfume—until he realised it wasn't only the exotic scent around her, but that of fresh bread. His eyes snapped to hers.

The arrow tip followed his movement, but he didn't care about that.

'Have you been in the...cooking area?' he asked.

She waved her palm the barest bit. 'The staff here works hard. They do not need me watching over them.'

He edged forward and she stepped back. 'You have a dusting of white on your face,' he said.

She reached up, brushing, but missed it.

A duke simply did not reach out and touch a woman's face, particularly upon their first proper introduction. But he did. Warm, buttery sensations flowed inside him. His midsection vibrated, but it was with

the outward pressure against his waistcoat. If he looked
down, he knew he'd see the tip of the arrow pressed
there again. But the broken arrow wasn't so long and it
connected their bodies too closely. His blood pounded
hot and fast. Blast. This was not good. He'd been too
long in the country where he had to take such care
because his movements were watched so closely. He
needed to get to London soon and find a woman.

She smiled. 'I use the arrows as my chaperon.'

'Perhaps a maid would be better instead?' He
reached the slightest bit to nudge the arrow away, but
stopped before connecting with the wood. If his hand
touched hers, that would be more than he wanted to
deal with.

He moved back, freeing himself in more ways than
one, and examined his fingers while rubbing the white
powder between thumb and forefinger. He was fairly
certain it was flour or some such. Something one
dusted on the top of cakes or used in producing meals.

'You *have* been in a kitchen.'

'I—' Her chin jutted. 'I do not...visit the kitchen.
Often.'

He shrugged. 'I do not mind. It just surprises me.'
He lowered his voice. 'You shot at my gamekeeper—
I don't see why you'd have a problem with going into
the servants' area.'

He wasn't in the mood to complain about her at
the moment. But he must keep his thoughts straight.
She had put a weapon against his waistcoat. She ran
through the woods, tormenting a gamekeeper. She'd
traipsed in the kitchen with the servants, chased a child
with a broom in the sitting room and probably would

not be able to respond quietly in the bedchamber as a decent woman should. He clamped his teeth together.

This woman was as untamed as the creatures she freed. She might be a relation of Warrington's, but one always had an errant relative who did not do as they should.

'I—' She stepped back. And now the broken arrow rested against her bodice. 'I cannot let the rabbits be trapped. I cannot.'

'I suppose I understand.' He did understand. More than she thought. She had a weakness for rabbits and right now his weakness was for soft curves and compassionate eyes. He must clear his head. No matter what it took, he must clear his head.

'I would like to reassure you,' he said, 'that the rabbits will soon be holding soirées among the parsnips and their smiling teeth will be green-stained from all the vegetables they harvest. The traps are to be removed. You do not have to check my lands. No more traps.'

'Thank you.' She nodded. 'It is a relief.'

'In return, I would like very much for you to have tea with my mother tomorrow,' he said. He heard the youth still in his voice. That strange sound. Too much sincerity for the simple question. 'Please consider it. My mother is very alone right now,' he quickly added.

She moved, still grasping the arrow pieces, but her hand rested on the spine of the sofa. She studied his face. 'I don't… The English customs…'

She was going to say no and he couldn't let her. He had to explain.

'My mother will not know you are arriving and I

will summon her once you are there. Otherwise she may not leave her room.' His chuckle was dry. 'She likely will not leave her chamber, unless I insist. But as you understand what it is like to miss a person you care for, I would appreciate your spending a few moments speaking with the duchess. Perhaps she will feel less alone.'

She didn't speak.

'My brother has passed recently. My father died almost two years ago, soon after my older sister and her new husband perished in a fire while visiting friends. My mother is becoming less herself with each passing day. She misses her family more with each hour.' He controlled his voice, removing all emotion. 'She is trapped—by memories—and only feels anger and self-pity.'

'I will visit your *mana*.' She spoke matter-of-factly. 'And if she does not wish to leave her chamber, I do not mind at all. I will visit her there.'

He turned, nodding, and with a jerk of his chin indicated the arrow in her hand.

'Would you really hurt me?' he asked.

Something flickered behind her eyes. Some memory he could never see.

'I hope I could,' she said. 'I tell myself every day that I will be strong enough.'

'You wish to kill someone?'

She shook her head, tousled hair falling softly, and for a moment she didn't look like the woman she was, but reminded him of a lost waif. 'No. I wish to be strong enough.'

'Have you ever…hurt anyone?'

She shook her head. 'No. I know of no woman who has ever killed a man, except my grandmother, Gigia.'

He waited.

'A man, from a *ploio*. A ship. He was not good. He killed one of the women from our island and hurt another one almost to her death. Gigia gave him drink. Much drink, and he fell asleep. He should not have fallen asleep. Gigia said it was no different than killing a goat, except the man was heavier. My *mana* and uncle were there and they buried him. I do not think the men from the ship cared about losing him. They did not hunt for him long. Gigia gave them wine and we helped them search.'

Rhys took a breath. He'd invited this woman into his home, where his mother would meet her. This woman who seemed no more civilised than the rabbits she wished to protect and yet, he wanted to bury his face against her skin and forget.

'I see.' He frowned, repressing his notice of her as a woman. He certainly did not need to be noting the insignificant things about her.

'From your face, I think you do.' Instantly, her eyes pinched into a tilted scowl, her nose wrinkled. She mocked him. His mouth opened the barest bit. Yes, she'd jested.

'Miss Cherroll,' he spoke, beginning his reprimand, holding himself to the starched demeanour his father had used, one strong enough that even a royal would take notice of it. 'Perhaps my mother could also be of some guidance to you.'

Lashes fluttered. A dash of sadness tinged her words, but the chin did not soften. 'I am beyond repair.'

Bits of words fluttered through his mind, but none found their way to his lips. He took a moment appraising her, then caught himself, tamping down the sparking embers.

This would not be acceptable. He had survived his sister's death. He had survived his father's death. Geoff was gone. The duchess was failing. Rhys's vision tunnelled around him, leaving only images from memory. He would take his own heart from his chest and wring it out with his two hands before he let it close to another person.

He turned his body from her with more command than he would ever unleash on the ribbons from a horse's bridle.

'I did not mean to anger you so…' Her voice barely rose above the drumming in his ears.

'I am merely thinking,' he said.

'You must stop, then. It's not agreeing with you.'

'I think you are the one not agreeing with me.'

'So it has never happened before?'

'Not recently.'

'An oversight?' Wide eyes.

'I can hardly believe you and the countess are sisters.'

'If you think we are brothers, then I do not know what to say.'

'You are—' He gave up. If she could use that same spirit to release his mother's mind from the memories snaring her, it would be worth the risk. He had no other options.

Chapter Three

Bellona took the carriage to the duke's house, frowning each time the vehicle jostled her. Darting through the woods would have been so much easier, but when the gamekeeper's eyes had rested on her the last time, a drop of spittle had escaped his lips when he'd smiled at her. The past had flooded back. She'd thought to put the memories behind her, but they'd returned like a wave, currents underneath tugging at her, trying to pull her to death.

Even now, looking out of the window, she could imagine a face peering at her from behind each tree. The eyes reflecting dark, evil thoughts, or no thoughts at all. Knowledge returned of looking into the pupils and seeing nothing human in a face she'd once seen innocently. Nothing behind those eyes which reasoned or thought, but only the same blankness from the face of an animal intent on devouring its prey.

She'd heard the tales of people being fed to lions. Telling the lion to think about the rightness of not clamping its teeth around her neck would do no good. Reminding the beast that she was merely wishing to live out her life wouldn't change anything. The lion might appear calm, but it would be thinking of only how to get a straighter lunge.

Bellona had known Stephanos before he killed— watched him dance and laugh and work as he'd grown older. Nothing had indicated how one day he would look at her with the harshness of death seeping from him like muck bubbling over the side of a pot left on the fire too long and too hot to pull away with bare hands.

The truth roiled inside her. She'd not escaped to a land where she could let her guard down. Men kept their power within themselves, behind their smiles and their laughter. Like a volcano, the fury could burst forth and take every being in its path.

The day her father had raged at her over a painting she'd accidentally knocked over, she'd known he would have preferred her to be the one broken in the dirt. If he could have traded her to have the painting back on the easel, he would have. He would have rejoiced if she could have been bruised and broken and his painting fresh and new.

Nothing had changed. She'd only lied to herself, hoping she'd be able to forget the past and sleep peacefully again, safe, in this new land.

Even the maid sitting across from her didn't give her the feeling of security she'd hoped. Moving her foot inside her boot, she felt the dagger sheath, reassuring herself.

She braced her feet as the carriage rolled to a stop. A lock of hair tickled Bellona's cheek as she opened the door and stepped out. Pushing the strand aside, she looked at the darkened eyes of the Harling House windows. Sunlight reflected off the glass and a bird flitted by, but the house looked no more alive than a crypt.

The entrance door opened before her foot cleared the top step.

The expanse of space between her and the stairway could have swallowed her former home. She could not blame the duchess for not wanting to leave her chamber. This part of the house, with all its shine and perfection, didn't look as if it allowed anyone to stop for a moment, but to only pass through.

The butler led her to a library which had more personality than she'd seen so far in the house. The pillow on the sofa had been propped perfectly, but one corner had lost its fluff. The scent of coals from the fireplace lingered in the air. The figurines on the mantel had been made at different times by different artists.

One alabaster shape had a translucency she could almost see through. One girl wore clothing Bellona had never seen before. A bird was half in flight. She noted a cracked wing on one angel. The hairline fracture had browned. This hadn't happened recently and been unnoticed. Someone had wanted to keep the memento even with the imperfection.

Then she studied the spines of the books lining the shelves. Some of the titles she could read, but the English letters her oldest sister, Melina, had taught her years ago were hard to remember. She asked the maid and the woman knew less about the words than Bellona did.

The open-window curtains let much light into the room and the view overlooked where her carriage had stopped. A book lay askew on the desk and another

one beside it, plus an uncorked ink bottle. The chair
was pulled out and sat slightly sideways. Someone had
been sitting there recently, able to see her arrive, and
had left a few papers scattered about.

She settled herself to wait, the maid beside her on
the sofa. The clock ticked, but other than that nothing
sounded. Bellona stood again and noticed the walls.
Framed canvases. These were not just paintings, but
works of art. When she looked at each piece, she could
see something else beyond it—either the thoughts of
the person depicted, the way the room had felt that day,
or the texture of the object painted.

They were nothing like her father's paintings. She'd
had no idea that such wonderful art existed.

Bellona was seated when the duke stepped into the
doorway. She'd not heard him, but the flicker of movement caught her eye.

He stood immobile for a minute, like the figurines,
but everything else about him contrasted with the gentle figures on the mantel.

She tightened her fingers on her reticule. When she
met his eyes, her senses responded, reminding her of
the times she and her sisters had build a fire outside at
night on Melos. Sitting, listening to waves and staring
at stars. Those nights made her feel alive and secure—
the strength of nature reminding her something was
bigger than the island.

Lines at the corners of his eyes took some of the
sternness from his face, and even though he looked
as immovable as the cliffs, she didn't fear him. Possibly because he seemed focused on his own thoughts
more than her presence. When he spoke, his lips turned

up, not in a smile, but in acknowledgment of his own words. 'I regret to say that my mother informs me she will not be able to join you. She is unwell today.'

Bellona stood, moving nearer to the duke. 'If she is unwell, then I cannot leave without seeing if I might be able to soothe her spirits as I did for my mother. I must see her. Only for a moment.'

The maid rose, but Bellona put out a halting hand and said, 'Wait here.'

A quick upwards flick of his head caused his hair to fall across his brow. He brushed it back. 'I may have erred in inviting you. Perhaps another day... Mother is fretful.'

'When my mother hurt, my sisters and I would take turns holding her hand or talking to her, even if she could not answer for the pain.'

'She's not ill in quite that way, but I think her pain is severe none the less.' Moving into the hallway, he swept his arm out, palm up, indicating the direction. 'The duchess is rather in a poor temper today. Please do not consider it a reflection of anything but her health.'

'My *mana* was very, very ill many days.' Bellona clasped the strap of her reticule, forcing away her memories. She raised the bag, bringing it to his attention. 'I brought some garden scents for Her Grace. I will give them to her. They heal the spirit.'

'If you could only coax a pleasant word from her, I would be grateful.'

Bellona followed Rhys into the room. He gave a quick bow of his head to his mother and the older woman's eyes showed puzzlement, then narrowed when she saw he was not alone. Her frail skin, along with the black dress and black cap, and her severe hairstyle, gave her an appearance which could have frightened a child. She pulled the spectacles from her face, slinging them on to the table beside her. She dropped a book to her lap. The pallor in her cheeks left, replaced with tinges of red.

'Rolleston, I thought I told you I did not want company.' The words snarled from her lips, lingering in the air. A reprimand simmering with anger.

Rhys gave his mother a respectful nod and looked no more disturbed than if her words had been soft. 'Miss Cherroll is concerned that you are unwell and believes she has a medicinal which can help.'

The duchess's fingers curled. 'I must speak with you alone.' She didn't take her eyes from her son. She lifted a hand the merest amount and then her fingers fluttered to the book. 'You may take whatever frippery she brings and then she can leave. I am not receiving visitors. Even the Prince, should he so enquire.'

Bellona stood firm, forgetting compassion. Her *mana* had been gentle even when she could not raise her hand from the bed or her head from the pillow. 'My own *mana* has passed and I have brought the herbs that made her feel better before she left us. And when their scent is in the air, I feel not so far from her. This will soothe your sleep.'

The duchess's brows tightened. 'I sleep well enough. It's being awake I have trouble with. Such as now. Leave.'

Bellona shrugged, looking more closely at the

woman's skin. She had no health in her face. Her eyes were red and puffed. 'Then give it to a servant.'

'I will,' she said. She examined Bellona and sniffed. 'Go away and take my son with you. I am not having callers today. Perhaps some time next year. Wait for my letter.'

'I will leave the herbs with you.' Bellona reached for her reticule, opened it and pulled the other knife out so she could reach the little pillow she'd made and stuffed with the dried plants.

'Good heavens,' the duchess gasped. Rhys tensed, his hand raised and alert.

'It is only a knife,' Bellona said, looking at her, flicking the blade both ways to show how small it was. 'After the pirates attacked our ship, I have always carried one.'

'Pirates?' the duchess asked, eyes widening.

'I am not truly supposed to call them that,' Bellona said. 'I did know them, so they did not feel like true pirates, only evil men, and Stephanos was...' She shook her head. 'I am not supposed to speak of that either.'

'You are the countess's sister?' The duchess's voice rose, becoming a brittle scratch. She sat taller, listening.

Bellona nodded. 'We're sisters. She's more English than I am. Our father was not on the island so much when I was older. I hardly knew him. My second sister, Thessa, wanted to go to London. I did not. I like it, but I had expected to always stay in my homeland. But my *mana* died. Melina—the countess—had left and started a new life with her husband here and with Thessa determined that we should leave Melos I had no choice. The evil *fidi* would have— I could not stay on my island without either being killed or killing someone else because I was not going to wed.'

'*You* are the *countess's* sister?'

Bellona smiled at the duchess's incredulous repetition.

'Does *she* carry a knife?'

Bellona shook her head. 'No. I do not understand Melina, but she has the children and she did not have the same ship journey I had. She did not see the things I saw. I really am not supposed to speak of them.' Bellona bunched the things in her hand together enough so she could pull the pillow out.

Rhys reached out. 'I'll hold that,' he said of the knife.

She slipped the blade back inside and pulled the strings of the closure tight. 'I'm fine.' She gripped the ties.

Walking to the duchess, she held out the bag of herbs. Rhys followed her step for step and her stare directed at him did not budge him.

The duchess took the pillow, keeping her eyes on Bellona. She pulled the packet to her nose. 'Different,' she remarked.

'At night, you are supposed to put them near your head and then your dreams are to be more pleasant. I have one. It doesn't work for me. But my *mana* promised it worked for her.'

'I do not think it will work for me either.' The duchess sighed, letting her hand rest in her lap.

'The dreams. The dreams are the worst part,' Bellona said.

The duchess looked at the cloth in her hand, squeezing it, crushing the centre, causing the herbs to rustle. 'I know.'

'Some nights,' Bellona admitted, 'I dream my mother is alive and for those moments she is. But I dream she is the one being attacked by the men and I cannot save her. Those dreams are the worst. And they only grow and grow. I cannot breathe when I wake.'

The duchess nodded, eyes downcast. 'Do not talk of this to me.'

'No one wishes to hear it,' Bellona said sadly. 'I cannot talk about it with anyone. And not to be able to talk with Mana makes it so bad. I did not think I would live when she died, but my sister Thessa started slapping me when I cried. That helped.'

The duchess stared at Bellona. 'How unkind.'

'Oh, no. No,' Bellona insisted. 'I would get angry and I would chase her and chase her and want to hurt her. I will always love her for that.'

The duchess looked thoughtful. 'Child. Perhaps a pat or hug would have been better?'

Bellona squinted. 'That would have done no good. I would have cried more.'

A chuckle burst from Rhys's lips. A light shone in his brown eyes that she'd never seen before in any man's gaze and she could feel the sunshine from it. Her cheeks warmed.

'You might as well sit,' the duchess said. 'You'll make my neck hurt looking up at you.'

While she stood there, unable for the moment to think of anything but the duke's sable eyes, he slipped the reticule from her hand.

'Find me in the library when you leave so I may return this to you,' he said. 'I have some work to finish and I will have tea sent your way.'

He strode out through the doorway.

'Do not dare slap me,' the duchess warned.

'If you need it, I will,' Bellona replied.

'Do not try it. I will not chase you,' the duchess added, studying her rings, before indicating Bellona sit beside her. 'I would send servants.'

Bellona shook her head. 'You've lost enough family members for many slaps…'

The duchess nodded. 'It was not supposed to be like that. My husband, I accepted he might die. He was much older than I. But my babies. My children. You don't know what it is like.'

'I know something of what it is like.'

'No. You don't.'

'Yes, I do.'

'You can't.'

'Then tell me.'

The duchess tossed the packet aside. 'My daughter had golden hair. I'd never seen a child so blessed…' She continued speaking of her past, taking tea when the maid brought it, and hardly pausing in her memories.

Finally, she looked at Bellona. 'You really must be on your way now. You've stayed much longer than a proper first visit lasts. One just doesn't act as you do.'

'I know. I do as I wish.'

'I can tell you have not had a mother about. You need someone to teach you how to act.'

'No. I do not. This is how I wish to be.'

'That is your first error.' She shut her eyes. 'Now go.'

Bellona rose. 'Thank you for telling me of your daughter.'

The duchess opened her eyes again and waved towards the door. 'I may send a note later requesting you to tea.'

Bellona left, hearing two rapid sniffs behind her. She shut the door, listening for the click. A dark hallway loomed, but she remembered her way to the library.

A few moments later, she found Rhys, sitting at his desk, leaning over papers. Her reticule lay at the side of his work.

'Where's the maid?' Bellona asked, walking into the room.

He twirled his pen between his fingertips as he stood. 'Below stairs speaking with the other servants. I think she is a cousin or sister or some relation to many of the women here.'

Bellona walked to the fabric bag, lifting it and feeling the weapon still inside.

He frowned and shook his head.

She ignored him and moved to the door.

'Wait,' he said. 'I'll send for someone to collect your maid.'

'I will find her. When I step below stairs and look around, servants will appear and the maid will rush to me. If it takes many moments, the housekeeper or butler are at my elbow, asking what I need. It works faster than the bell pull.'

'Perhaps you should leave them to do their jobs.'

'Yes. I should,' she agreed.

He smiled—the one that didn't reach his lips, but

made his eyes change in such a way that they became like dark jewels she couldn't take her own gaze from.

'Would you wait here whilst I see how my mother fares?' he said. The words were a question, but he was halfway from the room before she could answer.

'No. I'll be on my way.'

He took two more steps, stopped, and spun around. 'No?' He stood in the doorway, almost taking up the whole of the space.

'You will ask her what I said. How we got on and make sure she is well,' Bellona said. 'I know the answers to that. She mentioned having tea with me again, but she will change her mind.'

'With me, she cannot speak for crying and it has been a year,' he muttered. 'A year… I think the honeysuckle was in bloom when they were taking my brother from the house the last time.'

'It is not quite a year,' Bellona told him, shaking her head. 'Your mother knows the dates. All of them.'

His eyes snapped to her and he pushed his hair from his temple. 'Of my father's and sister's deaths, too?'

'Yes. And her own parents.'

'You must stay,' he said. 'You cannot keep the knife in case someone accidentally gets hurt. But you must stay. I have tried two companions for my mother and she shouted one from the room and refused to speak with the other.'

'No.'

'Miss Cherroll, I fear you do not understand how trapped my mother is in her thoughts and memories. You must stay and see if you can lift her spirits. Otherwise, I fear she will not live much longer.'

She moved, putting the desk between them. 'I cannot.' She had grown up with the myths of her ancestors and tales of men stronger than storms and compelling forces. But she'd experienced nothing beyond the world of her birth until the duke stood before her. He changed the way her heart beat, the way she breathed and even the way her skin felt.

He tensed his shoulders, drew in a breath and his arms relaxed. She looked into his eyes, but lowered her gaze back to his cravat. She could not stay in this house. Not and be near the duke. He held the danger of the pirates, but in a different way. She'd seen her mother's weakness. Not the one taking her body near death, but the one that had locked her into a man's power. The power you could not escape from because it stole a person from the inside.

He strode to the side of the desk, nearer her. 'I will pay you whatever you ask. You can go to the servants' quarters ten times a day if you wish. You can have your run of the grounds. The entire estate will be open to you.'

She held the bag close to her body. 'I will not stay in your house.'

He held his hands out, palms up. 'It's— There's none better.'

'It's not that.'

He continued. 'You can have whatever rooms you wish if you stay as my mother's companion. Take several chambers if you'd like. You can have two maids at your elbows all day. And two at theirs.'

'Be quiet and listen.'

His chin tilted down. His brows rose. 'Yes, Miss Cherroll?'

'I will not stay here.'

He waited, his gaze locked on to hers.

'My sister needs me for the children,' she said.

'I understand completely,' he said, voice agreeing, and stepped to the door. 'You can take my carriage to visit them as often as you wish.' One stride and he would be out of her vision. 'It is not a problem at all. Send your maid in Warrington's carriage for your things. The housekeeper will be with you shortly to help you select a room.'

He was gone by the time she opened her mouth.

She stared at the fireplace. Warrington's estate was not far. She could return to take tea with the duchess every day if she wished; she didn't need to live in this house. Bellona did not care what this man said even if he was a duke. She did not follow Warrington's orders and he was an earl *and* married to her sister.

Slipping the reticule ties over her wrist, she walked to the servants' stairs.

The maid from Warrington's estate was whispering to another woman, but immediately stopped when she saw Bellona and bustled to her, following as they left.

'My cousin did not believe you'd stay such a long time,' the maid murmured. 'My cousin says the duchess will follow her family to the grave before the year's gone. The woman won't leave her chair except to weep in the garden. She gets in such a state that her humours are all gobber'd up. The duke is the only one can settle her at all and even he can't be around all the time.'

Bellona remembered holding her own mother's hand

near the end. How cool her fingers were. So thin, and with no strength in them at all. The duchess's hands had felt the same.

'I will visit her again soon. Perhaps tomorrow. I am not certain. I am hopeful the herbs will help her.' She moved to exit the house.

'My cousin said the duke is right soured himself. Servants step wide of him since he became titled. Said he's wearing that coronet so tight it's mashed out everything not duke.'

'A man should take his duties to his heart.'

Her maid puffed a whistle from her lips. 'If he's got any heart left. My cousin says he don't care for nothing except for his duties.'

'He cares for his *mana*.'

'Simply another duty.'

They walked to the carriage. Bellona could feel eyes on her. She forced herself not to search the windows behind her to see if the duke watched her departure. But she knew he did.

She adjusted her bonnet and held the reticule so tightly she could not feel the cloth, but only the handle beneath. 'Tomorrow, when I return, I wish you to stay at my side.'

'What did you do to the duke?'

Bellona's oldest sister, Melina, stood in the very centre of the room. She tapped her slipper against the rug.

'I was nice to his *mana*,' Bellona said, adjusting the quiver at her waist. 'I am going to practise.'

'The duke is here, demanding to see Warrington.'

'Truly?' Bellona asked.

'But War is in London. So the butler said Rolleston demands to see you.'

'I am not at home.'

'I told the butler to tell him we will speak with him. The duke is our neighbour and War's parents and his parents were very close.' She frowned. 'Bellona. You just cannot tell a duke to go away, particularly this one.'

'Warrington does not like him.'

'They are quite fond of each other, in the way men are.'

'I am quite fond of the duke in much the same way,' Bellona said darkly.

'You can't be. You have to pretend to like him. We are ladies—as I must remind you as often as I remind Willa.'

'He wishes for me to move to his estate.'

Her sister's foot stilled. 'You are—imagining that, surely?'

Bellona shook her head. 'He thinks I can help the duchess. His Grace told me I would be her companion. I will visit her, but that is as much as I can do.'

Melina stepped near Bellona. 'She will see no one. It is said she is dying. How ill do you think she is?'

'I do not know. Bones covered in black clothes, with her face peering out. I would not think she would make it through a hard winter or a heavy wash day.' She forced her next words. 'Almost like Mana at the end.'

Melina's hand fluttered to her cheek. 'You must move in with her. It is the thing Mana would want.'

'I do not even want to visit her every day,' Bellona said, shuddering. 'She doesn't have the gentle ways of Mana.'

'You must. Besides, to live at the duke's house…'
Melina put a hand at her waist. 'He might have friends
visit. And you might meet them. You could learn a lot.
The duchess is a true duchess. She could help you. You
are not as wild as you pretend. Her Grace could teach
you so much if you just watch and learn.'

'I already know how to say *I am not at home*.'

'Sister. A woman. Her husband gone. Her daughter
and her oldest son gone, too, and you are asked to help
her and you will not. Mana would weep.'

'I will help her. I just do not want to live in the
duke's house.' Bellona turned to leave the room, but
her sister's quiet voice stopped her.

'You do not like living here, either,' Melina said.

She couldn't tell Melina what she felt about the
duke. Stone and towering and dark eyes. She remembered standing at the edge of the cliffs and looking at
the ground far beneath, and knowing if she swooned
she would fall—feeling brave and scared at the same
time. The duke made her want to step closer and yet, if
she did, the ground might crumble away. He reminded
her so much of the stones she'd seen jutting from the
sea and the cliffs.

'I wish to be here with the children. And you.' Bellona pleaded with her sister. 'I do not want to leave
the little ones.'

'You'll never have your own babies if you do not
learn how to mix with society. A footman will not do
for you and you know that. The duchess could introduce you to someone suitable.'

'I went to the soirée. The men smelled like flowers.'

'Pretend you are a bee. You can sting them after you're wed. Not before.'

'I will not pretend to be anything other than what I am.'

'You cannot go back to the way we lived. You must go forward and the duchess could help. She could ease your way into society in a way that I cannot. They hardly accept me.'

Bellona hit her own chest with her fingertip. 'That is where we are different. I do not want to be in society. Bonnets pull my hair. Slippers pinch and corsets squeeze. The flowery world has nothing for me.'

'A husband helps if you want children of your own— and it is best for the child to be born within a true marriage, one with love. You know that as well as I.'

'Even children are not worth a husband. I have a niece and two nephews. They are my babies.'

'You are hiding. From everything. From the past and the future. The duchess needs you. You know how long the nights can be after a death and we had each other. We had the three of us, you, me and Thessa. You are just like our *pateras*, our father.' Melina crossed her arms.

'That is an evil thing to say. I am surprised your tongue does not choke you for forcing those words past it.'

'You are like Father. Of the three of us, you are the most like him,' her sister continued, pacing the room. 'Even Mana said so, just not where you could hear her.'

Bellona raised her voice. 'I am not like him.'

'When we angered him, he would go paint.' Melina swaggered with her shoulders as she walked. 'When he did not want to do something, he would paint.' She stopped and mused. 'Did you ever notice how paint brushes are shaped almost like little arrows?'

'You're wrong to speak so. I practise archery. I do not live for it.'

'Even the way you stick out your chin. Just like him.' She jutted out her jaw in an exaggerated pose.

'You always say that when you have no better words to fight with.'

Melina returned her stance to normal. 'I cannot believe my own sister has no kindness in her heart for a woman with no daughters or sisters.'

Bellona raised her chin. 'I will tell the duke I will stay a short time with his mother. It will be better than listening to you. *You* are the one like Father, insisting on having your way.'

'Only when I am right.' She examined Bellona. 'Please arrange your hair before you see the duke.'

'Of course.' Bellona patted both sides of her head, achieving nothing.

'Much better.' Melina paused. 'I expected you to pull a strand loose.'

'I thought of it.' Bellona sighed. But the duke probably wouldn't appreciate it.

Melina reached to Bellona and pushed her youngest sister's hair up at the sides, moving the pins around. 'There. Now you look as well as me.'

Bellona walked past her. 'Now you see why I do not show my face in society.'

Melina's chuckle followed Bellona from the room out into the hallway.

When Bellona reached the sitting room, the duke's gaze swept over her. The rock stood, unyielding.

Even with a scowl on his face, she still wanted to look at him. The thought irritated her.

'I will return to your house,' she said curtly.

The flicker behind his eyes—the intake of breath. She would have imagined he'd just been hit, except his face softened much the same as Warrington's did when her sister walked into the room. The duke inclined his head in acknowledgment. 'It will mean a lot. To the duchess.'

Chapter Four

Bellona arrived at Harling House the next morning and the housekeeper appeared at her side almost instantly. The woman had a sideways gait, but moved forward so fast Bellona hurried to follow.

After being shown a chamber whose ceiling would need a heavy ladder to reach, she mused, 'I could put an archery target in here and practise without leaving the room.'

'We have no targets which are suitable for use inside.' The woman's face pinched into a glare that would stop any servant.

Bellona gave the woman the same look Warrington had given her countless times. 'I suppose if I asked the duke, he would arrange something.'

'Of course,' the housekeeper said. 'This was his childhood room. Let me know if you need anything.' Then she darted away.

The room had the same scent of the storage rooms in Warrington's house and made her miss the sea air. No flounces and lace adorned it. Instead there were walls the colour of sand and darker curtains that required strength to move. She wondered if every trace of the boy had been removed, or if the room had never had anything of him in it.

The huge chamber didn't feel like home, but she was tired of looking for Melos in everything she saw and not finding it.

She placed her bow in the corner. Her mother would not have believed such a large room existed for one person to sleep in.

Someone knocked at the door. A maid, who looked almost the same as the one from Warrington's house, suggested Bellona go to the library to meet with His Grace. Curiosity and the desire to see more of the house pulled her straight to him.

'Miss Cherroll. Welcome,' the duke greeted her. Quiet words, almost cold, but his quick turn from the window, and one step in her direction, caused a flutter in her stomach.

The last year of his life might have been no easier than the duchess's, she realised. If Bellona had lost either of her sisters to death, the world would have become dark and bleak and suffocating.

He surprised her by the merest corner of his lips turning up at the edge. 'The maid who is unpacking for you will store your arrows and knives in a safe place. She will direct the footman to bring them to you each time you need to practise marksmanship and he will take them when you return to the house and make sure they are properly cared for.'

'You are most thoughtful of my property,' she said, thankful he did not know of the knife in her boot.

'Of course.'

'Then let us discuss payment for my stay.'

'Certainly.'

'I want another two score of arrows. The best that can be made. I also require a dagger perfectly balanced. And I must have a pistol that will fit my hand and someone to show me how to clean, load and shoot it. I have heard there is a Belgian hidden-trigger boot pistol in which the trigger does not fall down until it is cocked. I would like to see one of those. You can have someone bring selections of these things for me to choose from.'

'Ah.' The word wasn't clearly formed from his lips, but was more of a sound. 'No duelling swords? Fencing lessons? Cannons?' he asked, blinking once each time he named a weapon.

'Cannons are heavy, and—' she touched the bridge of her nose '—so are swords. A man with long reach can best me any day. I could not practise enough.'

'Miss Cherroll. Any necessities will be furnished to you and they do not include guns, knives, arrows or swords. You will accept the usual payment from me—enough to buy all the armaments you need and Warrington can help you choose the weapons after you leave. I will refrain from paying you until then because I realise what you might do with the funds. Since you do not like to see game injured, I fear what you might plan to do with any weaponry. You will not have such items in my home.' He stood with feet planted firm. 'I myself do not even keep them at hand.'

'No duelling pistols?' She raised a brow.

He looked aside and absently moved the pen at his

desk on to the blotter. 'Yes, I have them, but they were gifted to my father and they are locked away. There is not even powder for them.'

'Swords?'

'Fencing is something we all had to learn.'

'Where are the swords?'

'I believe they are locked in a case in the portrait gallery. The butler has the keys and he will not be sharing them. With anyone.' His voice rumbled from his chest. 'I think you forget you are here to see my mother, a woman of trifling size who is stronger with her glares than most people are with their body.'

'Do you have daggers? Arrows? Flintlocks?'

His head moved enough so she couldn't see his eyes, then, before she could protect herself, he directed his full attention at her, consuming her with it. 'What do you fear?'

'Not having weapons.'

He shook his head. 'I am sure there is a bow and arrows somewhere. I don't think the bow has a string any more. No daggers.' Still standing alongside the desk, he splayed his fingers and gave the top several hard raps. 'Miss Cherroll, you do not have to concern yourself that someone will attack you in my home. I have footmen and stablemen no one would dare confront. I have had no violence on my estate, ever. That will not change while you are here. I realise you had a harrowing experience on your ship journey here and not a pleasant meeting with my gamekeeper, but you are now in what is the safest place in the world. My home.' For a second, he spoke with his expression. Relief. Thankfulness. 'I must let you know I was pleased to see you arrive.'

She didn't think any man, ever, had looked at her with so much hope on his face.

'You are in more danger from a fall on the stairs than anything else,' he added.

Or a fall from a cliff.

'I am exceedingly angry at the duke for bringing you here,' the duchess said to Bellona.

The duchess wore a fichu tucked into her bodice and the sleeves of her obsidian gown almost swallowed her hands.

The older woman had a maid at her side, holding a stack of four books. 'You must know that I cannot take my anger out on him, so it will land about your ears.' She pulled out one book and waved the servant away.

'I am not happy with him either.' Bellona sat in the matching chair. 'I will probably share that with both of you.'

The duchess frowned. 'Why are you not pleased with him?'

'He took my bow and a small dagger.'

'Your mother should have taught you better.'

'Why? I did not need to be better on Melos and I am fine enough to sit in a duke's home.'

She duchess snorted, just as Bellona's own mother might have. She held out the book. 'You may read to me.'

'I would rather talk.'

'I would rather hear what someone else wrote.' The woman thumped the book and held it out again.

'I am not going to read to you.'

'You have no choice. I have asked you to. I am your elder.'

This was not going to get any better. Perhaps his mother would summon the duke to complain about Bellona. That would tip his tea kettle over.

Bellona saw no reason to explain her struggle to read the English language to the duchess.

'It would indeed be an honour for you to read to me,' the duchess said, changing her methods, 'and might dispose me more kindly towards you.'

'I do not mind if you are not nice to me.'

'Well, I do. My prayer book is the only thing that gives me hope. My eyes hurt from reading it and the letters blur. The maid cannot read and I do not wish to replace her, though I might be forced to because I need someone who can see better than I.'

'You may replace me,' Bellona said. 'I do not read English words.'

'But your sister is a countess. And everyone knows she is from the best society in your home country.' The duchess looked at the book. 'So do not feed me such nonsense that you cannot read. Your family would not educate one sister and leave another unschooled. I have received notes from your sister several times. One she wrote when she visited me and I could not see her, so she must write them herself.'

'I am not my sister.'

The duchess shook her head. 'You do not read?'

'I know the English letters. Melina read our father's letters to Thessa and me many times and I could understand most of the written words. It has been a long time since I have looked at words, though. I do not like them on paper. I prefer a person's lies when I can see their face.'

'I do beg your pardon.' Words spoken from training. 'I cannot begin to imagine what my son was thinking to enlist a companion who could not read to me.'

'I do not dance or do any of the other things society women do, except archery. It is my favourite thing next to my niece and nephews. I sew, but only because one must have clothes. I do not like the nice stitches to make flowers. I like the strong sewing. I am from my *mana's* world.'

'I am from my mother's world as well,' the duchess said. 'Every day we had our hair dressed to perfection, our skin just so. We could not move if it might disturb our clothing. I sometimes hated it, but now I see the value of it. One must give others something to aspire to.' She leaned towards Bellona. 'Take a note of that. Because you are a companion only and from some foreign land, I will tolerate some folly on your part.'

'I am thankful I will not have to tolerate any on your part.'

'Child, I say again that I do not know what the duke was thinking to ask you to stay with me.'

'He was thinking I would be a slap for you.'

The duchess showed no outward reaction. 'Rolleston is making a good duke. He has always been a good son. Although he might have erred this one time.'

'He might have.'

'Do not be so quick to agree with me. Surely you have some accomplishments? What entertainments are you versed in? Recitations? Music? Song?'

Bellona smiled, tilted her head to the side and said, 'Would you like to hear a song the English sailors taught me? I am not sure of its meaning.'

The duchess's neck moved like a snake rising to eye prey, trying to get situated for the closest tender spot. 'Oh, my dear, I think you know full well whatever that song meant and I am not daft enough to fall for that one.'

'I already told you that I have no accomplishments,' Bellona insisted flatly.

'How do you spend your days?'

'Archery. The forest. I spend hours with my niece— I miss the little one. Her joy makes me laugh.'

The duchess opened the book. 'I know what it is like to miss someone.'

'You spend too much time with books,' Bellona said. 'If they make your eyes hurt it is not good for you. Poison in the stomach makes it hurt. The head is the same. Your eyes are telling you that you must not read.'

'Oh. Thank you for informing me.' The duchess digested the words.

Rhys walked into the room, greeting them both, a book under his arm. His eyes had a faraway look, but he settled into a chair and asked them to continue as they'd been because he needed to study the accounts.

But even though he stared at the volume in his hands, Bellona felt his thoughts were on her much the same as a governess might have her back to the children, but be aware of their every move. She felt the need to test her idea and knew she would before the conversation was over.

The duchess leaned towards Bellona. 'How did you learn to speak English?'

'My father was English.' Her father was alive, but he was dead as far as she was concerned. 'He insisted we only speak English when he was home. He made us recite to him. Yet he knew Greek well and if we spoke Greek in anger, we were punished. He is... It is hard to talk of him.' She sniffed and lowered her face. That would discourage any questions of him.

'At least you speak two languages.'

'Some French, too.'

The older woman nodded. She appraised Bellona. 'Did you leave behind family in Greece?'

'None close,' Bellona said. 'I have never wed. Marriage. It makes a woman change. And cry. Men are only good for lifting and carrying, much like the bigger animals that do not think well.'

The duke didn't respond to her deliberate prod.

'Well, yes, some of them can be,' the duchess admitted. 'But marriage is not all bad. Children make you change and cry, too. I do not know what I would have done without my own.' A wisp of a smile landed on the duchess's face. 'My three children were the best things that ever happened to me.' Then her expression changed with the memory and she began to sniff.

Bellona searched her mind for a distraction. 'At least I will not have to marry—like His Grace will have to before he gets much older.'

His mother's sniffle turned into a splutter. Bellona didn't have to turn her head to know where the duke was looking. She pretended to look like her own thoughts were far away.

'Yes. He will marry. Of course,' the duchess said. 'But that is not for you to discuss, Miss Cherroll.'

'I hoped that you would call me Bellona.'

'That is a strange name.'

'I was named for the Roman goddess of war. I remember that every day.'

'Perhaps you should put it from your mind. She doesn't sound like someone appropriate to be named after.'

Bellona shook her head. 'I'm proud of it. To get to England, I had to flee in the night. Thessa's suitor chased us.' She had slept though the final confrontation, unaware of all about her. Earlier, she'd fallen asleep with the rhythm of the ship and woken when her sister had shaken her awake. Thessa's rapid voice had fallen back into the Greek language while she'd told Bellona how the pirates from their homeland had followed the ship, planning to force the women into marriage.

She thought of what Melina had told her of Almack's—a marriage mart, her sister had said.

'Have you ever been pursued, Your Grace?' She turned to Rhys. He did have her direct in his vision, watching her without censure, but as if she were a very interesting…bee, and he wasn't afraid of getting stung.

'Not by a pirate,' he said. 'Only by a very unhappy bull.'

'I'm sure you could escape.'

'I have managed thus far.' He glanced at the book again, but even with his eyes averted, she could still feel his attention on her.

'My poor Geoff,' the duchess said, 'he was once

chased by an angry dog and I thought—' Her lip quivered and she reached for a handkerchief.

Bellona did not want the discussion to return to sadness. A slap with words worked as well as one across the face. 'Reading does appear a good way to waste time. A way for people with no chores to be idle.'

The duchess's sniff turned into a choke.

She had the older woman's full attention and Rhys's book looked to have turned humorous. For little more than a blink, their eyes met. Sunshine suffused her and didn't go away when he examined the book again.

After his morning ride, Rhys heard the clock as he strode into his home—the same peals he'd heard his whole life. The sounds didn't change, but if they clanked about in his ears, he knew the world felt dark. For the first time in a long time, the peals were musical.

His mother had spoken to him repeatedly about the *heathen*, informing him that the miss was beyond help. Each time she'd recounted the discussion between the two, her voice rose in anger. Not the bare mewl it had been before.

Finally, she'd left her room of her own volition to come and find him to complain with exasperation of having to deal with this motherless child who'd been left too long to her own devices. She'd wondered how he could possibly expect his own mother to correct such a tremendous neglect of education in the woman. 'It would take years, years,' she'd explained as she walked away, shaking her head.

He'd quashed his immediate urge to go to Bellona

and pull her into his arms, celebrating with her the re-
birth of his mother's life.

Thoughts of Bellona always caused his mind to
catch, wait and peruse every action or word concerning her a little longer. The miss did something inside
him. Like a flint sparking against steel. Made him
realise that his heart still beat, his life still continued
and that some day he'd be able to walk into a room
and not be aware of all that was missing, but see what
was actually there.

He turned, moving towards the archery target that
now stood in the garden beneath the library window.

Disappointment edged into him when he did not
find her near the targets she'd had placed about. He
went inside the house, thinking of her hair and the way
she reminded him of pleasures he did not need to be
focusing on right now. As he passed the library door,
he heard pages rustling.

He stepped into the library. Stopped. Stared.

She was lying on his sofa. Around her face, her hair
haloed her like a frazzled mess, more having escaped
from her bun than remained. This was the moment he
would have walked to her, splayed his fingers, held her
cheeks in both hands and kissed her if…

Ifs were not for dukes, he reminded himself.

She rested stockinged feet on the sofa. Her knees
were bent and her skirt raised to her calves while she
frowned into a book. His mind tumbled in a hundred
directions at once, all of them landing on various places
of her body. The woman should not be displaying herself in such a way.

Courtesans did not act so…relaxed and improper.

Even the women he'd visited in London—ones without modesty—would have remained much more sedate in daylight hours.

But he remembered his manners. Perhaps he'd erred, not she. She had not heard him enter the room. He took a quiet step back because he did not want to mortify her by letting her know he'd seen her sprawled so indelicately.

But then he saw the books. A good dozen of *his* most precious books scattered about her. One was even on the carpet. How could she? It was one thing to trespass, another to shoot an arrow at a man, but...the books...

Books were to be treated as fine jewels—no—jewels could be tossed about here and there without concern—books were to be treasured, removed from the shelves one at a time, carefully perused and immediately returned to their place of honour. They were made of delicate materials. A nursemaid would not toss a baby here or there and books deserved the same care.

She looked up, swung her stockinged feet to the floor as she sat, dropped the book at her side. Her foot now sat on top of a boot, her skirt hem covering it, as she lowered her hand towards the remaining footwear.

Modesty. Finally. 'You may dress.' He turned his back on her slightly, so he would not see if her skirt flipped up while she put on those worn boots. He would have thought Warrington would have done better by her. He would put in a word to see that she had decent indoor shoes.

He heard a thump and the sound of pages fluttering. 'I cannot read this—this—'

From the corner of his eye, he saw the title of one

of his father's favourite volumes disgracefully on the floor. He pressed his lips together and gave himself a moment. 'Why are you in the library since you disregard reading?' he finally asked.

'Your mother has insisted I pick a book, study it,' she muttered, 'and be able to speak about it. She is punishing me.'

He heard the sound of her fidgeting about and then silence. He turned.

She glared at him, but she only had one boot on and she held the other in her lap, her right hand resting on it.

'I do not think I like your mother,' she continued. 'The duchess told the servant who stores my bow I am not to have it. The servants are afraid to disobey her.' She stared at him. 'The duchess said it is good for me to learn to read English. That I should not be *unleashed on society* until I have better ways. I am fine with that, as long as they are my ways. I told her I do not wish to be *unleashed on society*.'

'The books?' With his hand, he indicated the floor.

'They have too many pages and not enough drawings.' She frowned. 'Melina taught me the words when I was a child and when I discovered I was not reading Greek, but English, I hid the books. I have only read a few letters since then and they are never more than three pages long. This—' she stared at him as if he had written the offending length '—this has so many words I do not know how the man did not run out of them.'

She picked up the book, holding it in her left hand and shaking it in his direction. For a moment he forgot to be outraged. Her bodice bounced enticingly.

He pushed his thoughts in a safer direction.

He remembered how she'd helped his mother. He took a breath. He must remind himself that the duchess's health was more important than any book that had been in the family for near a century. Even one with hand-inked illustrations which Miss Cherroll had just waved about without any care.

He switched to a ruse she had used, turning it in her direction. 'Books are actually only meant for the upper classes. Only peers should have them. They are too much for the common folk to appreciate.'

'I agree. Only peers. Common folk have no time for reading. I sold both our books to a sailor,' she said. 'He knew how to read. It did not make him smarter, though, because he paid a good price for nothing.'

Her eyes sparked with a challenge that bolted inside his stomach.

She perched on the sofa like a preening bird and let the books rest about her like so many twigs.

'I suspect his purchase was not as much—' he eyed the books '—as my father and grandfather and I spent for those.' He walked to the sofa and picked up a tome from the floor. 'So when you are not casting jabs about the books, what do you really think of them?'

'They are too much to read. But very dear to sell. I was so happy when I discovered that.' Lifting one volume, she put it atop another. 'I would not damage such costly items.'

'That almost reassures me.' Rhys kept his face unmoved. 'What books did you sell?'

She held her chin high. 'I do not remember. But I remember the necklace we bought for our *mana*. She had it on when she died. We claimed our father sent it with a ship.'

Rhys imagined the three girls giving the gift to their mother.

'Your mother,' she continued, 'says I have been addled because I lost my own *mana* so young. She said I misled her about the pirates trying to capture our ship. She thought I lied about everything.' Bellona's lips firmed and she shook her head precisely.

'So I sang the sailors' song to her. She believes me now.' She lowered her eyes. 'I should not have done it. I do not like that song. It is *erotikos*.'

Damn. The song had probably singed the pages of his mother's prayer book and he would be hearing about it the rest of his life and on into eternity if he made it that far. He waved a palm about. 'You do not sing improperly—not to a duchess. My *mother*. Miss Cherroll, you are to be a companion, not—'

She sighed, shut her eyes and shook her head. 'I do not think she truly minded. I only wish I did not do it because it gave her a reason to trick me into looking at these infernal books.'

Dark eyes, more like some woodland pet than a woman's, took him in. She didn't say one word, but argument was in that gaze. He'd never seen eyes like those. His midsection jolted again and he looked at the floor to push his attention elsewhere.

In one stride he picked up a book and held it in both hands. 'This is Alexander Pope.'

'Well, that tells me nothing.'

Then he saw her eyes turn to the book at her feet. He gasped, and pulled it from the floor. 'You cannot place *The Life and Adventures of Robinson Crusoe* on the rug. I have read it three times.'

'I didn't like the first page. Warrington has a copy. My sister read the first words and I left the room.'

His head twitched to indicate the book. 'You simply cannot judge it by the—'

She contradicted him with her eyes. 'Why not? The first page of the book is about the rest of the story.'

'This one is about a man who lives on an island and learns to make do with what he has, and he is very happy because no women are about. Just cannibals.'

She snorted. 'I do not see how that makes fine reading. My sisters and I lived on an island.'

'He was marooned.'

'You mean he could not leave if he wanted. How sad...' She smiled. 'And is England not an island? I cannot return to Melos, which is also an island. Melina and Warrington refuse to let me go back home because of the Greek war for independence and they fear pirates.' She snorted again. 'And then there is the man on Melos who wished to marry me, but...one of us would not have survived the wedding night.'

'You were asked to wed?' He studied her, and, yes, he could see how a man might say anything to get her into his bed. She sat, wiggling that one stocking-clad foot, like an asp, tempting him to partake of forbidden fruit.

'If I had not hated him,' she said. 'I might have thought of it. I did not care for him and he had the mean eyes.'

'Marriage is an honourable state.'

'Your mother would be surprised to hear that from

your lips. You should have married long before now. She has feared many times you would do as your father did and near destroy everything dear.'

'My father?' Rhys struggled over the words. 'My mother held my father in the highest esteem.'

Bellona nodded. 'Of course. But it was hard for her to love him at first.' She grimaced. 'When your brother was born and your mother became ill, your father stayed in London while she remained here. When he left, he told her he was a duke first, a man second and a father third. He did not mention being a husband.'

He heard her words. He saw her lips moving.

'Do not joust at me. My father is dead,' he said. 'His memory is sacred. I will not have you disgrace him.'

'Your mother said everyone knew. She felt abandoned. When she became strong again, she went to London and reminded him she was his wife.'

He picked up the volumes and placed them back on the shelf while he controlled his temper. Once the books were shelved he turned to her.

The rumours said Bellona's father had died young and left a wife behind who'd been descended from the Greek upper classes. Perhaps the sister Warrington had married was descended from some Aphrodite-like ancestor, but this one was from the wrong side of the clouds. It did not matter to him if she had been born on a gilded mountain-top. Once he discussed her with his mother and repeated what false tales Bellona had just spread about his father, the woman would be gone. He would have the carriage readied and escort her to it himself. A woman could not disparage the duke's father in his own home and expect to remain.

'Nothing my father ever did was disrespectful to my mother.'

Her eyes widened. Pity directed at him. He frowned.

'I must have misheard,' she said finally.

'I am certain you did.'

She glanced away. 'I am certain I did, too. Perhaps I do not understand English as well as I think.'

When she turned her head, he saw a flash of gold at her ears. His mother's earrings. He swallowed. He had unleashed the worst sort of woman into his very home.

'Your mother fears leaving her rooms,' she said. 'She knows when she does you will think she can manage on her own and abandon her for London just as your father did.'

'I would not *abandon* my mother.'

She looked down. 'She knows you would not mean to. It is your duty. She understands.'

'You are… I am… That is unacceptable. You are a liar of the worst sort. You will return to Whitegate.'

Perhaps that would be safest for them all. For her— because if she discovered how society would truly perceive her, she might be crushed. For his mother— because she did not need a woman near who would take her jewels while spreading lies. And himself—for a reason he did not wish to consider.

Bellona's jaw clenched. She jumped to her feet, and moved to the bell-pull, her boot under one arm. 'I will send for a carriage. I will not have to read at Warrington's house.'

He could *not* believe it. His bell-pull. In his house!

'Cease,' he commanded, hand out in a halting gesture. No one except he or his mother touched this bell-pull. And he would not let this thief leave with his mother's jewellery.

She stopped, still clutching the boot. 'I'm leaving. Even the walls are sad here. No one laughs. No one plays. It is all reading and embroidery and dressing of hair and clothes.' Her nose went up.

'I will see that you do leave. A carriage will be readied.' He waved an arm. 'Come with me. I want my mother to know what you have said about my father.'

'You first,' she said impudently.

He did not want her to dart away with the earrings. 'I insist. You first. I am a gentleman.'

'Then do as I wish.'

He would not stand and argue with her. 'Do not dare run for the door.'

'You tell me to leave and then tell me not to go.'

He stepped forward, but kept an awareness of her and held out his arm for her to precede him. She rolled her eyes, but flounced from the room.

He gave a quick rap on his mother's door and strode inside. She sat in her chair, but instead of the prayer book... He stepped closer. Fashion plates.

She glanced up at the two of them, but then returned to the books. 'Oh, Rhys. I do not know how this poor child will ever be saved from herself and I have such a short time to mend her because I am going to send her packing any day now. She does not listen. She is worse than you are and I never thought anyone could be worse than you...'

He stared at her.

She clucked her tongue, examining the engravings. 'I send her a maid to fix her hair and she complains. I gave her gold earrings and had to insist she wear them. Gold. What woman thinks gold is unsuitable?' She held up a plate so he could see. 'Child…' She held the drawing so Bellona could see. 'This is the gown I had made for me in blue to match my eyes. I don't want yellow for you, but I cannot decide.'

'I do not need any new clothing.' Bellona's words were clipped. 'I am leaving.'

'Nonsense,' his mother commanded. Then his mother's eyes caught on Bellona's boots. She gasped, eyes wide. 'Un-for-giv-able. Where are the slippers I found for you?'

'I hate them. They pinch. I cannot wear them.'

Rhys watched. He just watched.

His mother's fingers shook so that the papers in her hands made a fluttery sound. 'Your stockings are *dirty*. Were you raised in a stable?'

'Above one.' That goddess nose tilted up. Rhys thought she might not have any of the society airs about her, but her nose and eyes could manage well enough and needed no lessons.

'Now. Go. Put on fresh stockings and get those slippers and return to me. I wish to see you wearing them now.'

'You are just like Gigia.' Bellona frowned. She looked at Rhys. 'She is just like Gigia. I will never drink too much around her.'

'Then you were very lucky if you knew someone like me, but obviously you did not pay her enough heed,' his mother said. Her eyes tightened on Bellona. 'And you are just like my daughter was—may the angels hold her tight in their embrace. I thought never to get her wed to the right man.'

Bellona pursed her lips and blew. 'I do not need anyone to find a husband for me.'

'Bellona. I cannot believe it.' The duchess sat, closing her eyes. 'What did I tell you about being a lady?' She shook the paper towards Rhys. 'And you are in the company of a male.'

'But he is only the duke and has already tossed me out.' She shook her head. 'I must return to Whitegate. You must give me my bow and arrows so I can leave.'

Only the duke? Rhys tried not to be offended. That was a phrase he had never heard in his life.

'I forbid it,' the duchess said firmly. 'You are running amok and you have no mother to train you. You cannot leave until I tell you to. You will never have that bow and arrows if you do not do as I say.' His mother turned to him. 'Rhys. She cannot leave until I tell her.'

'I am not running amok,' Bellona said. 'I am doing as I please.'

'Exactly the same thing.' His mother turned to him. 'Tell her, Rhys. Tell her she cannot leave.'

'I believe she should,' he said stiffly.

'Nonsense. Why, no man of any higher level than a nightsoil collector would give her a glance as she is. And she has good skin and rather a startlingly good singing voice. I am teaching her a hymn.'

Rhys took in a breath. 'Is that what she sings to you, Mother?'

'Why, yes.' Her voice calmed and her shoulders relaxed. 'Along with a few old songs from her country.' She looked at Bellona. 'Run along and change those stockings, and hurry back because I want you to decide on a colour.'

'I will not hurry,' Bellona said, leaving.

He cleared his throat, giving the wench a chance to pull the door shut behind her.

He must inform his mother about the tales. Then he would explain to this miss the repercussions of disrespecting a duke's household—*only a duke*—and send her packing that very day.

Rhys forced himself to soften his words. He did not want his mother upset more than she must be. 'She is a talebearer.'

'Nonsense,' her mother said. 'I am quite sure she is honest. She told me the brocade in the sitting room is quite the wrong colour.'

'I am not talking of fashion. I am talking of the deeper qualities of a person.'

His mother's eyes widened. 'She has some deep qualities. They are just deeply common.'

'She has said—things about Father. Even suggesting he might have not seen you for a time after Geoff's birth when you were ill.'

This time his mother put her hand over her open mouth. Her eyes fluttered.

Rhys knew right where this was heading. Bellona would soon be waiting at the door for the carriage to be pulled around.

The duchess clasped her fingertips as if her hands were cold and then whispered, 'I do not know how I am going to teach her what is proper to speak of and what is to remain behind closed doors. A servant could have overheard. Not that I'm sure they… Well, you know how things get remembered like that.'

Rhys drew in a deep breath, studying the truth on his mother's face. His father? His father had behaved so callously? 'Mother. Did my father…?'

'Well… Rhys, I thought perhaps your father had mentioned it to you before his death, or even Geoff. I know Geoff and your father spoke of it. I heard them. So I assumed you knew as well.' She wilted against the sofa back. 'I have just had so much on my mind. It is hard to think of everything.'

His mouth opened. Bellona had moved into his house and discovered family truths even *he* did not know of. And his mother was discussing these things with her instead of with him.

He took the matching chair.

Then his mother straightened and pulled her handkerchief from inside her sleeve and refolded the fabric, her eyes on the cloth.

'Rhys, you understand…' She looked up. 'Geoff had just been born and it was a difficult birth. He was… I was… He cried so much and the nursemaids didn't know what to do. My baby was small and didn't want to grow at first. I felt I'd failed my husband. Your father and I did not always get on well. I may have… been harsh in some of the things I said. Your father was angry because I could not think of anything but the babe, so he left me. But then, Geoff started getting bigger and I became better and your father returned home, after a nudge.'

She daubed the handkerchief to her eyes. 'That was

a difficult time. And to think I would eventually lose them both… So near to each other.'

Rhys didn't speak.

'I had all a woman could hope for.' Her eyes filled with tears.

'My father…' He shook his head.

'Rhys, please do not tell me you are such an innocent. Sometimes, things happen.'

He stood again. 'I am not an innocent, Mother.' He straightened the sleeves of his coat. 'I am just surprised that I never knew of this. That no one told me. It's… You know how Father was. He was the perfect duke. Always.'

'Yes.' She straightened her shoulders. 'He was. And you know, Rhys—in some respects—nothing is forbidden to a duke.'

'Miss Cherroll—a woman we hardly know tells me of this.' He shook his head in disbelief. 'How could you share this with her and not with me?'

'She lost her own mother and has had so many trials. I understood much of the pain she felt and I told her. The words just escaped my lips.'

Since Bellona had been correct about that, perhaps she had spoken truth on one other thing, too. 'You do not have to worry about my abandoning you, Mother, even when you become hale and hearty once more.'

'I know, Rhys. I understand completely. I know you would never wish to leave me.' She exchanged the fashion plates for the prayer book on the table beside her chair. Running her fingers over the lettering on the cover, she sighed. 'But, Rhys, if you do not… If you do not go to London and find a wife, you will be abandon-

ing your title. Your duty to your family. Your brother's
heritage. You have no choice.'

She raised her face. 'I understand you must go. I
do not want you to marry a wife only to make her unhappy. Togetherness in marriage, I believe, is formed
by people who have the same background and the same
interests. You must marry a woman you have something in common with. One who shares your dreams
for the dukedom and can be at your side, a helpmate. I
wish the same marriage for you that your father and I
had, except, of course, for the one year when we could
not stand the sight of each other.'

'I know what I have to do.' He did. A wife. House
of Lords. A son to pass the title to. It did not have to
be written in stone to be engraved in his head. Geoff's
heritage.

'It's harder for a duke with all his duties and responsibilities and the stewardship of the estate,' she
said. 'And women notice the duke, Rhys, rather than
the man, as I am sure you are aware.'

Rhys remembered the last soirée he had attended
with Geoff. The women had fluttered around Geoff,
and the brothers had jested privately afterward about
the peerage being far more handsome than any visage.
The next event Rhys attended after Geoff's death, the
perfume had choked him, the expanse of pale flesh
had burned his eyes and the high laughter had been
like spears in his ears.

Without Geoff, it was not humorous any more.

The door opened and Bellona walked in, wearing
both boots and carrying the slippers. 'They bite my
toes,' she insisted. 'I cannot wear them.'

'I know you must have slippers at Warrington's estate,' the duchess said. 'Send for them or trim off a few toes.'

Bellona put the shoes on the floor beside her. 'I will be considering which toes I can spare.'

'Of course,' the duchess murmured, 'you do want your little niece, Willa, to be proud of her aunt…'

The tousled head darted up and her eyes could have flailed the duchess. 'I do have some slippers my sister gave me. I suppose I could send for them and a gown that matches.'

'I have a tutor planned for you tomorrow in the ballroom. Do not be late. He will not.'

'I will not dance. I have a pain in my foot.'

The duchess spoke to Rhys. 'She can practise archery for hours. A few moments' dancing will not hurt her.'

'I will not,' Bellona said again, calling the duchess's attention back to her.

'It would mean a lot to your sister to know you are settled with a nice vicar or man of affairs. Perhaps a soldier who has returned and needs a wife to care for him? Your sister might even wish for a niece or nephew of her own. Someone her own little ones can call cousin. If you do not dance with a suitor… He will see you as thinking yourself above him and dance with someone more…pleasant.'

She held her fingers up as if dusting crumbs from them.

'I will dance the country dance if you insist.'

'Send a servant to me and I will give the order for your bow to be returned,' the duchess said.

'My foot is hurting more now and the pains are moving up to my head,' Bellona said, turned and left.

Rhys saw the jutting chin as she stepped his way, but as she passed by him, the tiny wink nearly did him in.

The door crashed behind her.

The wench would be the death of him.

'I would not say this in front of her, but if she carries on like this, that heathen child will never even be worthy of a tradesman as a wife. It's just…she did lose her mother, as she is *constantly* reminding me,' the duchess grumbled to Rhys. 'I cringe to think what would have become of your sister had it not been for my firm hand.' The duchess stared ahead. 'This one is more like your father's mother.' She nodded and her lips firmed. 'No one ever took that woman in hand and I will certainly not let this motherless child be so unruly.'

'You gave her the gold earrings.'

'Yes, and the matching necklace. I never really liked them. I'm trying to make a female out of her, Rhys. No man will ever give her a second glance if she does not present herself as a lady.'

Rhys turned to the door. He did not correct his mother on that point. But she was very, very wrong.

Bellona grabbed her cape, shaking it in her frustration. She had to escape the house for a few minutes and practise her archery. The first dancing lessons with the tutor had gone well, but today he had insisted on a much more difficult dance. Bellona had refused. She was determined the man would not touch her.

The maid returned and slipped into the room. 'Please, miss, the duchess is distressed.'

'She must get over her temper fit.'

'She is crying.'

Bellona stopped. 'Tears of anger?'

'Quiet tears.'

Bellona slipped the cape from her shoulders and tossed it on the bed. 'I'll speak with her.'

'Thank you, miss,' the maid said, backing away.

Bellona knocked on the duchess's door and walked inside. The woman sniffled, but didn't look at Bellona.

'You know I don't wish to dance.' Bellona shut the door.

'I know.' The duchess stared at the embroidered bit of linen in her hands. 'If you wish to be a heathen, then you may be a heathen. I wash my hands of you. My daughter. She loved to dance. Loved the dresses. The laughter. I just thought… I just thought you would, too.'

Bellona sighed. 'If you will help me, I will try.'

The duchess dotted her eyes dry. 'The tutor is waiting.'

'No. You must help me. I cannot do it without you. I *cannot*.'

'You are being ridiculous.'

'I am asking for no more than you are from me.'

'Very well.' The duchess stood. 'I am too old and tired to fight you any more.'

Chapter Five

Muffled pianoforte music wafted down the hallways. Rhys stopped, listening. That wasn't his mother playing. She'd long ago ceased, claiming her fingers hurt if she even looked at the pianoforte, though she wasn't above persuading someone else to play for her.

Rhys trekked to the ballroom and then stared.

His mother sat in a high-backed chair similar to a queen's throne. She held her arm out and hummed above the sound of the music, as she grasped a fan like a sceptre and let it bounce in time with her hums. A man at the pianoforte had the music before him, but his eyes were closed as his fingers moved.

Rhys recognised the other man, the dancing master who had tutored every child from every estate in the area. The man danced, his lips in a grim line as he held Bellona and led her through the steps around the room. His hair was smooth at one side and the other stood out as if someone had tugged him around by the white locks. The wench had a disastrous effect on hair. Rhys's own was beginning to grey since he had met her. Only the duchess's hair stayed locked in place.

But when he looked closer, his mother's eyes were red-rimmed and he wasn't sure Bellona's didn't follow suit.

'Shoulders back,' his mother commanded, between hums, her voice reaching a crescendo. 'Bellona, the hand. Stop pulling your fingers from his. You are causing the tutor to miss his steps to keep you close. Hum-hum-hum. Hum-hum-hum. One-two-three. Feet. Feet. Feet. Remember the— Stop. Stop. Stop!' Her voice rose and her fan-tip jumped up.

Bellona immediately stepped back from the man.

Standing, the duchess moved to Bellona and the dance instructor. 'Bellona, you must simply refrain from pulling away from him. You were doing so well in the country dance, but you cannot manage one step of this dance.' She walked behind the man and straightened his back. He winced.

'Mr Mathers, you must, must, must pay attention as well. You do not have quite the grasp of the dance as I had hoped or Bellona would be able to do better. I will demonstrate for her. Dance with me, Mr Mathers...' She raised her hand and stepped into his grasp.

The dance continued, with his mother and the tutor.

Bellona stood at the side. Her eyes showed dark against wan skin.

The duchess and the tutor danced round the room. Bellona breathed deeply.

'It's not truly difficult,' Rhys said, walking to her side. 'Perhaps I could show you since the instructor is lacking.'

He would hold her only for a moment. That would

not cause any problems within him. He could not even remember all the women he had danced with.

Her head jerked around, as if she'd not known he was in the room. She moved back, increasing the distance between them. 'I know. But I hate this dance. I hate it.'

'It's so elegant and the music is beautiful.'

'This dance is… Your mother said some people think it improper. They are wise. To be in a man's grasp like that…' She shuddered.

Rhys talked softly, leaning towards her. 'Has the tutor behaved badly to you?'

'Just in the same terrible way he is with the duchess.'

Rhys's head darted and he watched the couple swirl, his mother's voice slightly louder than the music as she instructed the tutor.

'They're just dancing,' Rhys said. 'If anything, Mother is holding him too close.'

'I cannot.' She shook her head slowly. 'I will tell her that I cannot do this…unsuitable dance.'

He studied Bellona's face and he reconsidered where his eyes had roamed on some of his dance partners. He raised his chin and slowly nodded downward. He moved his view over her shoulder and kept his eyes away from her breasts, but spoke in an undertone. 'I am sure, if you tell my mother, she will see that you have someone to fashion a gown for you with an adequate…bodice.'

She looked at him, studying his deliberately neutral expression. 'I don't understand?'

He furrowed his brows. 'Wasn't that what you were talking about?'

Her lids dropped a bit and her face changed. The eyes narrowed. 'What is wrong with my bodice?'

'Nothing.' It was the truth. He spoke dismissively and assumed the privileged bearing that usually stopped all questions. Whoever had fashioned her close-fitting garment should have been well paid.

Her gaze widened, and he could see the thoughts working away behind her eyes. She grumbled a word he could not make out.

'I thought,' he emphasised, 'you might prefer a more concealing dress—because you think the dance improper. A thicker fabric might give more of a feeling of distance—propriety—of all those things—important things—necessary for a dance. I am just trying to assist.' He heard the soothing tone of his voice and reminded himself he had meant no offence. He did not need to grovel to her.

One of her feathers unruffled. 'I will consider what you said.' She crossed her arms, and patted one hand just at the top of her capped sleeve. Her arm now draped over her chest. 'I will never, ever dance in this dress now.'

'Just wear a dress that's more—less fashionable.'

Her eyes, if they could, became even more lustrous with disapproval. 'I was not speaking of that, although I will certainly take what you say into account when I choose my clothing.'

'Miss Cherroll... You must accept the norms of societal behaviour if you are to live in England.'

Her face didn't lighten. 'No. He holds my hand and around my waist and I cannot... In a moment he could clasp me tightly. I could not pull away if I wished.'

He looked at his mother and the instructor. 'The tutor did not hold you closer than that?'

'It was still too close.'

Oh, this woman was surely unsuitable for any man's wife. He felt sorry for her and the man she might wed, assuming she didn't geld him with an arrow first.

'I've held women in that manner and none seemed to mind.'

She shuddered. 'I cannot speak for them. But I cannot tolerate any more lessons.' The intake of her breath spoke of her determination.

She grasped her dress, lifted the hem enough to show those unsightly boots and darted from the room.

His mother must have been watching. She stopped in mid-step and shouted a command to the man at the piano. The music ceased. The two men and his mother were both looking at him.

'What did you say to send her away?' His mother stepped away from the tutor. She waved a hand. 'You would not believe how much effort this day has taken to organise.'

This was not the place to mention the bodice discussion. 'I may have made her...doubt her...ability to learn the dance.'

His mother's fingers splayed and her hands went up. 'Rolleston, I cannot believe...' She caught her words. 'I had to near drag her from her room just to get her here at all.' She pointed a finger at the ceiling. 'Just one moment.'

The tutor dropped his head, and a small moan fell from his lips. 'I so must beg your pardon, but I have another appointment, and I do not think I will be able to continue… With the greatest of regrets and sadness. Not today or tomorrow.'

'See what you've caused…' She looked at Rhys. 'We had made an improvement.'

Before she'd finished the sentence, the tutor was out through the door. The musician stood and tucked his music under his arm, turning to leave.

The duchess raised her ringed fingers, stopping his departure. 'Stay. We will try again. Do not think to tell me you also have another meeting.' She turned to Rhys, her eyes showing the little lines at the side which could grow into quite huge ones depending on her temper. 'Rolleston, you do not realise how very important this is. Wait here,' she muttered. 'I will get Bellona and we will continue and, Rhys, you will show her that she is quite the dancer.'

Bellona sat in her room. She had taken country dance lessons at Whitegate with her sister and no one had ever minded that she did not participate in other dances. She'd merely taken the lessons to appease Melina and the women always practised together. Sometimes even the children partnered them.

The duchess didn't understand, and when she'd mentioned dancing to Bellona, Bellona expected no more attention to the matter than she'd given with her sister.

When the man touched her, she could not think of feet or music or dance. All she could remember was the feel of hands clasping her neck on the ship—all the more terrifying as it had happened after they had escaped Stephanos and his men, and the captain had promised her her safety. Or the night she and Thessa had escaped Greece—when Stephanos and his men had stolen her from her home.

She had made a promise to Melina not to speak of it. She said the things people whispered about, they over-looked. But if their suspicions were publicly confirmed and indiscretions admitted openly, then the *ton* could no longer ignore them. Nobody wanted to be seen as approving an open scandal as everyone wanted to up-hold their place in society.

Bellona thought of a gasping fish lying in the sand, eyes wide, breathing air, but not truly breathing. That was how the dance instructor's hands made her feel. That was how she always felt when a man stood close enough that his hands could seize her neck.

Three quick raps on the door sounded.

Bellona forced herself to her feet, knowing the duch-ess would be on the other side.

The duchess stood there. 'I do not blame you for this, Bellona. I have explained to Rhys that he must mind his ways. The dancing master—I do not think he has even read Thomas Wilson's book or looked at the drawings. He does not know the correct method of dancing. He's left now and I'm sure—'

'He's left?' Bellona interrupted.

The older woman nodded. 'No loss. His posture was not good. Return and I will see that you learn properly.'

Bellona did not ever wish to attend another soirée—she hated them. Even the country dances caused her insides to ache when many people were together. Ev-eryone moved this way and that and anyone could grasp her from behind. Breathing became impossible.

Almost before her thought was completed, the duchess fastened her hand on Bellona's arm and marched her out through the door. 'You must do this. Mothers need children. You must marry in order to have babies. You must attend soirées and dinner parties to meet the men. Even a vicar will expect a dance with his wife on occasion.'

Bellona walked back into the ballroom. Movement caught her eye. The duke stood at the side, talking quietly with the musician.

His gaze locked on her. He studied her—just a blink, but all the same, he'd already had too many thoughts she couldn't decipher. Too much intensity in his gaze.

The touch of the duchess's hand on Bellona's arm freed her to move again. 'Now, dear, don't be awed that you'll be dancing with a duke.'

Bellona paused, unable to take another step forward. He did not make her fear him as the other men did, but when his eyes raked over her, her strength waned.

Bellona spoke to the duchess. 'You must show me.'

She could feel the duke thinking about her, watching her.

'Nonsense,' the duchess said, waving Bellona's words away. 'Rolleston is a wonderful dancer. He knows what he's doing. With his height you might think his legs would get in the way or his feet would crush you, but he's quite graceful.'

Bellona moved her head sideways in refusal, as he stepped forward, movements slow.

'Miss Cherroll.' His words, rumbling just louder than a murmur, barely reached her ears above the sound of her heart beating. He stopped two arm lengths in front of her. His hands were at his side. 'I would be pleased if you would give me the honour of a dance.'

She could not speak.

'Child.' The duchess, all smiles, reached out to nudge Bellona forward. 'Do not be afraid you will step on his feet. He's quite able to withstand it, I assure you.'

'Mother.' Rhys raised his arm the slightest bit. His voice was quiet. 'I can help her. Why don't you ring for tea? Or some wine, perhaps? I'm parched.'

'That would be lovely.' She turned, signalling the musician to begin, before she moved to summon the tea.

'Listen to the music,' the duke said to Bellona. 'Just listen for a bit. Let it get into your thoughts.'

She nodded, unable to move her eyes from his and trying to slow the roar in her ears. His mother stood near. The duchess. All was safe. Bellona knew it. But her body did not feel safe.

He raised one hand into the dance pose, but the other remained at his side. 'Step forward and put your hand in mine.'

She drew another breath into her lungs and looked into his eyes. They were not harsh or threatening or angry. They had softened at the edges, guiding her, and his head leaned forward the merest amount. Now she couldn't escape. She was trapped. But the snare was the velvety hue of his eyes and the rumble of his voice curling into her with the richness of a covering being wrapped around her on a cold day after the cloth had been warmed by the fire.

She moved towards him and put her fingertips in his palm, waiting for the moment when his hand would

tighten over hers. The movement in his hand signalled
to her that his fingers had flexed, but he didn't close
them against her. He hadn't realised she wasn't scared
by him, but was trying to keep from letting her life be
changed in a way she'd never believed possible. This
weakness she'd fought against because she'd seen her
mother deserted by the man she'd loved.

'Now put your hand on my shoulder and I will rest
my arm at your back, but I will not hold or clasp you
tightly. It will be just the barest bit of my hand resting against you.'

Her throat tightened, and she tried to keep her
breathing calm and the world from fading so that the
only remaining thing was him.

'You will be safer than you've ever been before. I
will let nothing hurt you. Mother is here. She's looking
at the music and she is telling the man how she wishes
to hear him play the piece.'

He stood, as if he were the one who couldn't move.

Bellona put her hand at his shoulder—wool soft beneath her fingers. The scent of shaving soap touched
her nose.

He hadn't moved. 'Are you ready?' he asked.

She nodded.

She felt the flex of his shoulders and the slightest
touch of his hand near her back.

'Pretend I'm not even here.' His words barely
reached her ears over the tune the pianist just started
playing. 'It will be simple as a stroll around the room.'

She nodded and he took the first step of the dance.

Bellona stumbled, managing to find Rhys's feet.

He tensed his arms, but he didn't try to right her or gasp at her.

When she moved back into the dance, he looked beyond her and hummed a rich, soothing sound.

She listened to his voice, and thought of the music. She could still move. His eyes weren't on her and his thoughts looked far away. She forced herself not to move closer to him. The distance would save her.

The pianoforte music wafted inside her body and it was the same as being in the forest, free and alone—the moment of the leaves in the trees brushing the air over her and being safe, held by the forest.

Her arm barely contacted with his coat—a mountain of man moved beneath her touch, but instead of causing cold breaths inside her, the world invited her. She tightened the fingers of her raised hand, feeling his palm, and he responded with the merest pressure, silent reassurance passing between them.

She wanted to see his face, but she didn't dare raise her eyes. She didn't want to ruin anything about this moment.

The music stopped and their feet ceased at the same step. He did not move at all until he spoke to the duchess. 'I think she has the grasp of it.'

Then he ushered her to his mother and left the room.

'You did well enough,' the duchess said. 'I knew you could learn. Rhys is a much better dancer than the tutor, if I do say so myself. You should see the ladies at soirées beam when he asks them to dance. I'm sure it quite goes to his head, but it doesn't show. The dance is not so hard, is it?'

'No.'

She appraised Bellona's face. 'You need not concern yourself about the dance again. All it took was for Rhys to show you. Don't expect your next dancing partner to be like my son, though.'

Bellona nodded, and left the room. She didn't expect any man to ever be like him.

Chapter Six

Rhys stood just inside the open window. He'd had one of the servants move Bellona's target closer to the library window again. He suspected she'd lugged them away before because they'd slowly migrated from under the windows. He'd just wanted the arrows going away from the direction of the fields. *True*, he told himself, and the *thwack* of the arrow both irritated him and pulled him like a siren's song. *Liar*, he admitted.

A carriage rolled up. Warrington's.

The door opened, and Warrington stepped out, then turned to help Bellona's sister from the vehicle. His hand lingered in his wife's until a blonde bundle jumped from the opening and both parents turned to her in caution.

The little one dodged her parents and ran screeching to Bellona. Warrington reprimanded her, but his wife placed a gloved hand on his arm and then Warrington moved from view.

Bellona's bow and arrow slid to the ground and Willa bounded into her aunt's arms. The dark head and the light one bumped together. Bellona moved, hugging the little one in a swirling movement.

'Willa insisted her aunt is out with her bow and arrows slaying dragons. She claims you are doing so to rescue her.' Melina's voice carried through the open window.

'Only six dragons.' Bellona's excited voice was no quieter than her sister's.

'You killed six,' the little one insisted. 'But I killed ten for you.'

'What with?' Bellona asked.

The girl laughed, jumping back from her aunt. 'I stomped on them. They squished.'

'That is ugly, Willa,' her mother said.

'Yes,' Bellona agreed. Her hair had half-fallen from its pins. 'You must save them whole so we can have a feast. Dragon's meat is very tasty and is already cooked from the dragon's breath.'

'Bellona, stop adding to her imagination,' Melina said.

Willa shot an imaginary arrow into her aunt and Bellona was putting more drama into the play than any actress he'd ever seen at Drury Lane.

He wanted to join them. He wanted to hear the laugher around him, especially Bellona's.

'Sir,' a voice behind him interrupted. 'The Earl of Warrington did not bring a card, but suggested I tell you—'

'—To roll yourself out of bed—' Warrington stepped behind the servant '—because you are so tired from staying up late looking at your face in the mirror and wondering why the heavens have been so cruel to you.'

Rhys's quiet response would have earned him a fortnight of prayers from the vicar. The butler's lips quirked and he slipped out through the door.

Warrington walked to the other side of the window and looked out, viewing the same scene Rhys saw.

'Have you gambled away the inheritance yet?' Warrington asked.

'No.' Rhys turned to the earl. 'Do you need me to lend you some funds?'

'Like hell.'

'If you throw the first punch, you should be prepared with another one.'

'So how is the duke?'

Rhys tapped his boot toe at the base of the wall. 'It's been difficult managing the properties around London through my man of affairs instead of seeing for myself. I have had to depend on Simpson completely because the duties are so new to me and the duchess has been so distraught. I believe Simpson quite capable, but I need to take responsibility myself at some point.'

'It gets easier,' Warrington said. 'I was fortunate to have my brother Dane to help me after my father died. If you need anything, just ask. I'll send him.'

'Much better than having you around, I'm sure.'

'True,' Warrington said.

Both men stayed at the widow. All three females chattered and seemed to be having no trouble following every word spoken, mostly in Greek.

'So how are things here?' Warrington said. 'The duchess?'

'Mother is better.'

Warrington nodded, his voice soft. 'Bellona doesn't

like quiet. My wife, fortunately, does. Hard to believe they are sisters sometimes.'

Rhys didn't speak, just watched the gestures down below. Bellona unstrung the bow. The little girl wore the quiver. The women moved with each word they spoke.

'You'd think it's been years since they've seen each other,' Warrington said, moving away from the window.

Rhys still watched the scene. 'At least they get along.'

'They do. For the most part.'

Rhys stepped nearer the bookshelves, and considered his words while he looked at Warrington. 'Is Bellona truly nothing like her sister?' He waited for the response.

Warrington chuckled. 'Night and day. It's odd how they disagree on things, but never seem to argue. My brothers and I argued even when we agreed.'

'How did their father die?'

Warrington walked away from the window, and stood at the unlit fireplace. 'He's actually alive and I would prefer that to remain between us. I've been concerned word would get out concerning the pompous goat. That's what they disagree over. Melina wishes to keep him from all aspects of her life. Bellona has visited his wife secretly several times, though she doesn't like the man either.'

'Where does he live—in Greece?' Rhys knew her mother was dead and he'd thought her father was, too.

'On St James's Street in London. He's actually Lord Hawkins.'

Rhys relived the words in his mind. Yes, he'd heard correctly. Bellona's father was an English peer.

Warrington gave the smallest nod and studied Rhys. 'In his youth, he visited the island, married their mother and forgot to tell her he had a wife here. The second marriage was probably a farce to him, but still, the women didn't know of each other. Two families. Two sets of children. He sailed back and forth a few times. The children's ages are near the same.'

'Lord Hawkins?' Rhys could hardly stand to be in the same room with the man. His voice usually carried to all corners when he talked of the great art of the past and no one else's opinion on any painting came close to Hawkins's self-professed judgement skills.

'It's best that people think Melina's father is dead,' Warrington said. 'Better than the truth and having to acknowledge him. Better for the women. For everyone.'

'I can see how that would be.' Rhys watched the women laughing. He could not connect them in his mind to Hawkins.

'My wife thinks Bellona wants so much to be different from her father that she almost becomes him. Hawkins has that nose up in the air, thinking he is above society's ways. Bellona can be uppity, too, around society. Can you imagine Bellona making morning calls or indulging in polite conversation at a house party? She's more likely to be asking the servants how many eggs a day the chickens are laying.'

'She's been a boon with the duchess, though. They have even looked at fashion plates together.'

'Bellona? That is not her normal way. My wife finally reached an agreement with Bellona so that at least her gowns are acceptable. I'm fortunate Hawkins spent more time with his eldest daughter. He insisted Melina act like a lady. When Bellona was growing into a young woman and should have been learning the same skills, Hawkins returned to England for several years. Probably hoped they would starve. I doubt he cared much either way as long as he didn't have to think of them. It's a wonder they survived into adulthood. I saw how they lived when I went to the island. I saw how hard it was for Melina to leave her two sisters behind, believing coming here was the only way to save her family.'

'Bellona has helped Mother think of something besides her grief.'

'That really doesn't surprise me.' Warrington stepped back to the window. 'One day, I smelled a stench in the hallway, but I ignored it, thinking a chamber pot had been dropped. Then I heard a strange noise and discovered Bellona had been keeping an orphaned pig in her chamber because she thought no one else could keep it alive. A pig. In the family quarters. Willa cried when I said little Snowdrop had to be removed. It was not leaving *snowdrops* in its wake. I was the only one in the entire household who didn't know of the creature.'

'Still, Bellona has something that…'

Her laughter trickled in through the window. Rhys head turned towards the sound.

'You need to watch yourself Rhys.' Warrington shrewdly studied the duke's face. 'Don't make an error which might cause us to kill each other.'

Rhys didn't answer. London. He would have to go to

London immediately. If even Warrington could sense his interest in Bellona…

Rhys couldn't even step away from the window.

Homesick. Heartsick. Bellona touched her stomach, before resting her hand on the fabric of the chair in the library. Seasick on land. She missed Melos, but she could not return. She missed her sisters, but they both had wed—Melina to the earl and Thessa to Warrington's brother, Captain Ben.

In the past, Willa and her brothers had always taken Bellona's mind from the feelings of sadness. Today, seeing her niece again had only heightened her loss. Her *mana* and sisters had laughed together so many times. Mana was gone for ever.

Now, instead of having her peaceful mother, she was sitting every day with a woman who could have tackled Zeus and made him leave the heavens. Bellona could not go back into the duchess's chambers right now. She had told the maid so—twice—when the duchess summoned her.

Bellona had chosen to sit in the library because it had the largest windows, but now the evening shadows lengthened in the room, darkening everything. The duchess was suffering a fit of irritation. The older woman always became more cross as the sun set. She could sit it out alone this time.

Rhys walked into the library. He held a half-full glass of amber liquid. He sat it on a table, but his eyes met hers. 'My mother has asked me to collect you.'

Her chest constricted. She didn't know why she did

not have the strength to make her body unaware of him whenever he walked into the room.

She was in the duke's chair. The arms of the chair seemed to grow bigger and the back taller. She rose. She had to free herself from the confines. 'Your chair.'

His head moved only an inch to each side as he shook it, but his eyes didn't move at all. They remained locked on her. 'Miss Cherroll. Please be comfortable. I am just as at ease wherever I sit.'

She raised her chin in acknowledgement of his words. 'I have been here too long. When I saw my family today, I realised how much I miss them. I...' She moved back, planning to tell him she would have to leave.

'My mother just stormed into the dining room where I was eating,' he said. 'She insists you are being contrary.'

'I would not say I am the contrary one,' she said.

He turned to her, eyes shining, lips upturned. 'I would say you are, but with a definite purpose. You annoy her to keep her mind from dwelling on other things.'

'I suppose I must go see how she is faring.' But her feet didn't move.

'Please,' he said. 'Sit for a moment with me. I think you owe me,' he said. 'I soothed my mother and kept her from searching you out. She checked your room, by the way.'

She sat, but kept her back straight. 'I think you are contrary, too.'

'Very.' He sat on the sofa, legs stretched in front of him, one booted foot rocking back and forth on its heel. 'But you do not need to go to my mother right now. She is currently looking for my valet. I have told her when I go to London next, I am going to purchase a waistcoat and cannot decide on the right colour to go with yellow stripes. She is hoping to convince my valet of the proper garments I should buy so I do not look like I have lost my wits.'

'She tires me. All the sadness. It just reminds me of my own. I sit with her and have to remember that I am alive today. All of yesterday is gone. I must be alive for today or I will have nothing.'

'I just study the ledgers or read when I am lost in sad memories.'

'Or ride your horse, or check on the stablemen or write letters to your man of affairs.'

He stared at her. 'How do you know all that?'

'I wake many times in the night and it is too silent. My sisters were always with me when I was young. My mother near. Now I wake up and the room is so large and I am alone in it, so I move about the house. I was— I see you writing at night. I have been in the hallway many times and noticed the light from the open library door. I hear the shuffle of your papers and your sighs.'

'I do not sigh.'

She took in a deep breath, looked at him, parted her lips and imitated the sound of a weary sigh.

He shook his head in disagreement.

'And you grumble. I do not even have to be near the door to hear you complaining to the paper.'

'Next time, just walk into the room.'

She settled back into the chair and let her fingers

rest on the arms. 'You must have many sad memories if you spend so much time working not to think of them.'

'A few. Mainly of my brother. We pretended to be jousting knights. We had fencing duels. We took our lessons together. He never was as robust as I, but I never expected him to die, even when he got very sick. I wasn't even here at the time. Now I ask myself, how could I have not known?'

'I hate sadness. Sometimes the duchess's melancholy almost swallows me.'

'She was not this way before. Not always gentle, but never was she like this. She's not the same person.' He raised a brow. 'I understand quite well. If you need someone to make you angry to take your mind from your sadness, search me out. I will do my best.' He gave a definitive nod of his head.

'That is kind of you.' She smiled. 'But I don't wish to be angry.'

'How does a person slap you with their words?'

'By criticising my clothes or my hair. Telling me how I should act. Disparaging my boots.' She kicked out her hem of her dress. 'I like my boots even if no one else does.'

Her chest flooded with warmth. His eyes. He appraised her with something she recognised as laughter, but it was also mixed with the same look Warrington often gave her sister. In this moment, she could look at the duke directly and feel cosseted by his eyes.

'I cannot understand why your boots aren't revered. It's quite interesting how one even appears bigger than the other.' His voice flowed smoothly. 'And the toe appears to have a chunk out of it.'

'I disarmed a trap with it.'

'Perhaps you should have used a stick.' He studied her and, even as he commented on her footwear, he complimented her with his eyes and voice.

'I did the next time.'

'I will be happy to have those beautiful boots replaced for you with an even more lovely pair.'

'No. But thank you, Your Grace.'

'I assure you, I can have someone fashion such suitable, extraordinary footwear that your toes will sing.'

'You cannot have more *suitable* boots made for me because these are perfect. And I hope you do find a yellow-silk waistcoat with something fashionable painted on it. Perhaps blue slippers.' She lowered her chin. 'You would like to discuss my hair next?'

'Hair like that…' His eyes wandered away. 'A man does not want to discuss it.'

She tightened her jaw.

But when he looked back at her, his eyes had changed. He'd lost the look that made her feel she knew him. 'I'm sure Byron could find something to say about your hair much better than I could.'

She wanted to bring back the feeling of companionship between them. 'Try,' she challenged.

He frowned. 'No. I am no poet.'

'You are every moment the duke?'

He gazed at her hair and his voice dropped to a whisper before his gaze took control of her. 'I do not have to touch it to feel it against my skin. A caress. Unequalled by any other woman's fingertips.'

The explosions in her body took her breath. 'I forgive you for what you said about my boots.'

'I am fond of your half-boots.' The seriousness left his face. 'They are quite serviceable, you do not have to have a valet to care for them and they do cover your feet well.'

She looked at her feet. 'That is the first nice thing anyone has ever said about them and I do think it might be the worst as well.'

He shook his head. 'It might be. But you find them comfortable and you wear them and you do not care if they are not quite the thing. You like them and so they are on your feet. That is all that matters.'

She half-nodded. They also held her knife. 'They are indeed serviceable.' But most importantly, they made her feel safe.

Only even with the knife hidden in her boot, she'd still not recovered her ability to sleep well after the attacks she experienced on the ship from Greece to England—first from Stephanos and his men and then later from the crewman who had tried to strangle her.

She'd been asleep when the pirate, Stephanos, had attacked the ship and she'd only woken when Thessa had burst into the room after everything had ended and Captain Ben had secured their safety. Realising she could have awakened to find her sister gone for ever had terrified her.

Stephanos had always watched every move Thessa made when he saw her and when she and Bellona had fled Melos by swimming to the ship of Captain Ben—whose brother, Warrington, had taken Melina from the island—Stephanos and his men had followed them. The group had included the man who had wanted to marry Bellona… He had the demon's eyes. Eyes that darkened to a soulless pit. All the demons in her dreams had devouring eyes. And they always, always had the same scent of rotted eggs, while jagged-edged black earth crunched under her feet when she ran from a man with eyes growing darker and darker as he came closer and closer.

Captain Ben and his men had fought off the invaders and defeated Stephanos. The pirates had had no choice but to retreat and allow the Englishmen to leave with Thessa and Bellona on board.

'I must keep my boots nearby me at all times.' She studied Rhys's face.

'I feel the same about mine.'

She looked at his feet. 'Your valet is quite good.'

'I surround myself with the best.'

She gave the merest nod of acknowledgment and let the thoughts rummage around in her head. She chose something safer to mention.

'Your mother still says I must leave and when I agree with her, she becomes even more angry. She doesn't want me to go, but she doesn't want me to stay.'

Nothing about him moved, except the rocking of his boot, until he spoke. 'Before you came here, countless times, every day, my mother said she prayed to die.'

He stood, towering up, but she did not feel frightened. 'I would like you to stay. You have no notion how much better she is today than the day before you came. She has not summoned anyone but me since Geoff died. She has not looked at fashion plates since my sister died. You have roused her spirit.'

His eyes stayed on hers. 'You've been a boon to me in so many ways.'

Looking up, she could only nod.

'If she becomes too much for you to bear, seek me out. Any time of the day or night.'

He left. The glass remained along with the lingering scent of shaving soap and leather from the chair. She'd not noticed it before. It had the same earthiness of the duke and it surrounded her on three sides—an embrace.

Chapter Seven

Bellona shut the duchess's door with the lightest of clicks and stood in the hallway. Then she made a gesture she'd seen the sailors use.

The older woman deserved respect, but certainly did not earn it. She'd called Bellona an ungrateful bumble-knot. A foreign muddle-mind. A featherhead.

The woman had been unwilling to accept that Bellona did not want to learn to read English, had managed just fine so far without such a habit, and the letters did not all stick in her head.

Bellona had explained she couldn't read that much in Melos as she hadn't had books and with so much work to do there hadn't really been time. Then she'd been told she was not in Melos now and discovered that the duchess and Bellona's own father had a similar way of expressing their ire. They waged a war on her ears.

Bellona had promised to search out a book and study it—because that was the only way to finally quiet the woman and escape.

The library was empty. Bellona pulled out the first book she saw, opened it, shuddered and, with a thunk, slid it back on to the shelf. That one was not even in English. She did not know the language at all.

Poetry might be ideal, she mused. That was why people liked poems. A poem did not require as much reading.

If she memorised a verse of a poem that she could recite in a mournful voice and become too carried away to finish... She could honestly claim it to be her favourite verse and favourite book and perhaps that would satisfy the duchess.

Bellona searched until she found a volume of poetry with a long introductory section at the beginning. She skipped that.

Bellona sat in the library with the book, staring at the few bits of words she recognised and the pleasant white space, knowing she would have to study the dribs of ink in more detail.

Pages. Pages and pages. Whoever invented paper must have hated everyone. Whoever decided to put words into sentences should have had to sit in a room with nothing else but paper and ink and a pen and write for the rest of his life.

But this family placed importance on books and if books meant something to them then Bellona would try to read. Especially if it might make the long stretches of night move more quickly.

She tried to sound out the first word. *E. X. P. O. S. T.* The next letter, *U,* she did not recall at all. *L. A. T. I. O. N.* She did not remember enough to read even the first word. She groaned at the fifth line. Books. That word she could read. This poem had books in it, which made no sense at all.

The duke strode into the room. He still wore the clothes of the day, but had discarded his coat. His sleeves would have been out of place on Melos, too much cloth and very white. The waistcoat, obsidian, and the night, took the lightness from his face, creating a cold look which reminded her of the marble pieces she'd seen on her island. They were all crushed and broken, though, and he didn't appear possible to shatter.

His face showed the beard trying to poke through for morning. He raked his fingers through his hair.

'I thought you did not like books.'

She could not make out the first word of the title. She held it up so he could see. 'I don't. This *biblio*…'

He walked closer, bringing all the pleasant scents of the outside with him. He'd been riding. Leather and wool blended into the air.

'Lyrical Ballads,' he read aloud.

She gave a sideways turn of her head. 'I have read enough of it.'

His eyebrows rose in question.

Nodding, she admitted, 'One word was enough. I even like embroidery better than reading. At least when you finish sewing you have something to show for it. When you finish a book, you still have the same pages you started with and tired eyes.'

'You've not read the right story.'

'I've not read any book.' She stood. 'I do not have to eat a tree to know if I would like how it tastes.'

'Sit for a moment,' he said, indicating the sofa. He walked to the shelves behind the sofa.

'Do not try to make me read.'

He tugged a book out and held it so she could see

the title. 'This is a tale you cannot help but enjoy. I'll give you a primer on it.'

'Does your *mana* like the story?'

His jaw dropped. 'Of course Mother likes the book. Everyone does.'

'She expects me to read to her. She said when she holds out the book far enough to read the letters, her arms collapse.'

'She has spectacles. She refuses to wear them when anyone is near.'

'Spectacles? Then I will not worry about reading. If she wishes to read badly enough, she will do it herself.'

He rested the book against the top of the sofa back. 'Perhaps you could just read some *Robinson Crusoe* to her. If you do not like it, then you can truly say you do not like books.'

'If I do not like him, then you will believe me?'

'Yes.'

She settled into the edge of the sofa, her back straight. A crease appeared between his brows, but then his attention returned to the book in his hand.

Letting him worry about the words would be so much easier than doing it herself.

He moved to the chair across from her, whisking the lamp along with him and setting it at the side. He took up much more of the area than she'd believed possible. 'Listen.'

He read aloud for a few moments and his voice became like a soft thunder off in the distance when rain was needed. Something pleasant and hopeful. Her thoughts were pulled along with his words.

'Wait,' she interrupted.

He looked up from the words, his brows knit again, and that caused her own face to tighten.

'You are reading about a man who is being told to be happy he is not of higher birth—that to be born in a situation of middling life, not poor, not wealthy, is the best. Is that how you feel?'

'Of course not.' He turned back to the book, reading again. 'The writer was correct for Crusoe, but not for everyone.'

'Wait,' she interrupted a second time. 'The older man is crying. You cannot like that.'

'Perhaps you should not really listen,' he said, not raising his eyes. 'But only sit there and pretend—to please me.' He took a breath, frowned and said, softly, 'Imagine I am enjoying reading the book and would like to have your company while I do so.'

He continued reading aloud.

Her company, she mused. What an odd thing to say. She intended to tell him she did not want to listen, but when she opened her mouth to speak, his voice increased and his words filled the air. She leaned back in her chair and his tone returned to normal.

She crossed her arms in annoyance, but the story wasn't so terrible. After a few moments she relaxed. If reading made him happy, she could pretend to listen.

The duke read of the man's age. He was only a few years younger than Bellona's age of twenty-two and he was planning to go on a sea voyage. Bellona shut her eyes and leaned back with a sigh the duke could not have missed. She'd been on a ship. If one liked bland sea biscuits and ale—in a gaol surrounded by water— then sailing was the best place of all to be.

Now, the tale told of the young man's *mana* trying to dissuade him from travelling. She nodded in agreement. If her own mother had lived, Bellona would never have stepped on the ship and left her.

Bellona shut her eyes and listened, letting her arms relax. His voice could make even the tale of sailing sound pleasant.

He paused a moment, but she didn't look at him and he continued reading.

She listened to every word and time vanished.

When his voice stopped, her eyes opened.

'See, reading isn't bad.' He handed her the book still warm from his hands. 'Finish the story and then tell me you don't like it.'

She challenged him with her eyes, and smiled. 'I really cannot read English.' She'd been so determined to forget every word of English her sister had taught her. Forced it from her mind, but now she wished she'd kept the knowledge. Not that she wanted to open a book any more than she wanted her skin scraped with thorns, but perhaps her mind might change.

'No matter.' He tossed the words aside. 'As a gift to you for spending your time with my mother, I will have a tutor installed here.'

'The dancing master didn't work out.' A tutor. She shuddered. Brambles in human form.

The duke's lids flickered just a bit. 'I am sure I can find someone you get on well with.'

'I am not educated. Warrington saw no reason for me to be taught if I did not wish it.'

'I do not care if that is how Warrington feels. It is a

gift. From me to you.' He spoke as if the words were straight from some ecclesiastical scribe.

'I will consider it,' she said finally. It would not take her long.

'Yes. I am sure you will. In the meantime, I will have someone go to London tomorrow to collect a tutor for you.'

Bellona shook her head, eyes never leaving the duke.

'Miss Cherroll, if you are to move among society with your sister's family it would be an asset for you to be able to read. You may wish to look at the caption under an engraving to see what the ladies are laughing about in a shop. Or, like my mother, read your prayer book.'

She nodded. 'You are right. When that happens, I will learn.'

Three blinks of his eyes.

She smiled. 'Your Grace.'

'Miss Cherroll.' His shoulders relaxed and he leaned back into the chair. 'You did enjoy Mr Crusoe. I promise you would not need a tutor for very long before you would be reading for yourself.' He held out *Robinson Crusoe* to Bellona. She hesitated.

Rolleston leaned forward enough to put it in her hand.

She stared at the lettering and handed it back to him. 'I know most letters. I know some words.'

He turned the book around. 'Then why do you resist so much?'

'You have never met the first mate of the ship that brought me to England,' she said. 'I liked him. He does not read. He said he carries his knowledge here—' she pointed to her head. 'He does not have time to keep turning pages.'

'Some of us cannot carry all the required knowledge and would prefer to have more than is allowed in such a small space.'

'And you see what happened to your sailor,' she muttered. 'Crusoe.'

Rhys acknowledged her words with the merest smile. 'What would it take to convince you that you need this?'

'I don't believe you truly care if I read or not,' she challenged.

'Of course I do. You've helped my mother. I wish to return the gift.'

'Then—if it is so easy, teach me yourself.'

He coughed. 'I do not have time. I have duties. Tenants. Ledgers.'

'Then it is not important.'

She stood and moved to the door.

'I will do it.' His voice rumbled. Strong. Irritated.

She turned. His eyes did not match his face. For a passing second, the boy he'd been peeked out from his expression. Then he became the duke again.

'I must be daft.' He stood and *Robinson Crusoe* slammed back into the bookcase before Rhys stared her way again.

'You do not have to do it,' she said quickly. 'I don't wish to. You punish both of us for doing no wrong.'

'An unwilling teacher and an unwilling student should make a tiresome combination, so we will start tomorrow to finish all the sooner.'

She could change her mind. She could insist on a

tutor. But the image of the boy behind his eyes flashed in her memory and tumbled about her body. He'd mentioned she was a boon in so many ways and she'd wondered about those words. He could be just as alone, in his own way, as the duchess. He'd even wanted to begin teaching her the very next day.

'The day after,' she asked, checking his response.

'Oh, no. Miss Cherroll. Tomorrow. I accepted your challenge. I dare say you will be reading quite quickly with me as a tutor.' He took the volume of poetry and walked to her, placing it in her hands. 'Look over this one, too. Mother can recite a bit of it from memory. She might like speaking it while you follow along with the words. It might help her as well.'

'You wish for your mother not to be alone because it will be good for her…'

'Yes.'

'You wish for me to read because it will be good for me…'

'Yes.'

'Have you thought about what you should do because it will be good for yourself?'

'Most certainly.' He stepped back. 'To be a son my father would be proud of. To continue his legacy.'

She shook her head. 'You have only considered what your father's needs would be. Not your own.'

'My needs were formed the moment Geoff died. I cannot let him or my father down. That is what I am doing. And I thank you for reminding me that I should be about my duties. The most important thing I can do is have a son, because if I don't marry and produce a child, everything my father and grandfather did will pass out of their direct family line.'

She pressed the books together. 'Does that not feel as if you are being commanded to do something?'

'No. It is simply another duty. If a tenant's roof blows away, I must replace it. Now I must put another heir at the table.'

'I am fortunate that I do not have to consider such a thing. I was almost forced into marriage once. I did not like it.'

'A lot of women would wish to be a duchess.'

'I am sure they will also find you tolerable as well.'

Chapter Eight

The poems were mountains and crevasses of words. She could not make sense of them. She'd forgotten almost all of what Melina had taught her. She tried for hours to remember and not enough had returned to her memory.

The only good thing about this situation was that it gave her something to do in the long hours before dawn. She could not have read into the night on Melos, though. They only had the one good lamp.

After studying, she'd fallen asleep and dreamed of being chased. Again she'd awoken breathing fast, her throat hurting and her heart pounding. She'd sat in bed, clasping her knife. When the shadows in the room were replaced by sunlight, she felt herself nodding off.

The next thing she knew, someone knocked.

'Miss,' she heard a woman's voice call through the door.

'Enter.'

A maid, mob cap snug, walked inside. 'His Grace wishes that you might meet with him in the library.'

Bellona pushed herself up. The knife handle showed

from underneath a fold in the counterpane. She swept the covers back over the blade. She closed her eyes and wiped her eyelashes with her fingertips, and yawned.

She could not learn the words when she was this tired. The duke would think her the same bumble-head his mother did.

'I believe I will sleep longer.'

'His Grace,' the maid said softly, as if the words should stand alone in the room, 'wishes you to see you in the library.'

'Please tell him I would be pleased to...' She looked back at the bed. 'But I cannot meet him now.'

The maid didn't move.

'Could you bring chocolate— several hours from now?' Bellona asked.

'If you are certain,' the maid said finally.

Bellona crawled back into bed and covered a yawn before speaking. She didn't know how she would inform the duke she could not read—ever—but she was too tired to tell him now. She could not even remember the letters of her own name, and could barely hold her eyes open. 'I am certain. I cannot see him now. I must sleep.'

The maid nodded. 'I will tell His Grace your head pains you.'

Rhys sat in the overstuffed chair in the library, a stack of unread newspapers on the table beside him. He'd changed from his riding clothes after he'd seen the maid, eyes averted, rush by the door with a tray. His mother had eaten. He had eaten. The tray could only be for one person who was not in his mother's room, nor in any of the common areas of the house.

He would not go to her chamber and find her. She would have to leave it some time. The woman did not sit about in her room with books or sewing or staring out of the window as his mother did. She flitted around the house and the gardens—a bird moving from one berry to the next with a flight of fancy behind her eyes.

He'd worked the ledgers and made notes for Simpson and now Rhys started with the oldest newspaper, more aware of the sounds of the house than the print before him. He tended to let them gather before he read them. Perusing them in the carriage on his trips to and from London didn't work out well. His eyes could not adjust to the jostling. He'd tried. Now he used the travelling time to review things in his head. On occasion he'd had his man of affairs ride with him so they could plan. The trip certainly went faster, but he didn't like to take Simpson from his home because he knew the man preferred staying near his wife.

The clock chimed one note.

He turned the page. The library had been both his mother and father's favourite place. To be allowed to sit there with his parents and older siblings had been a treat when he was a child. Whoever sat in the library could tell most of the movements about the residents on this side of the house.

He did not think he could have missed seeing Miss Cherroll if she had left her bedchamber. He snapped the paper straight. Five times servants had whisked by the door, certainly having been summoned by his mother or Bellona. The staff was well trained to stay invisible otherwise.

Even the paper didn't look to have been ironed properly. He'd smudged a word with his hand, and the smear vastly irritated him.

Something creaked. A door softly shut. No footsteps sounded, but he could almost feel her movements. He lowered the print enough so he could look over it.

'Miss Cherroll,' he said before she even appeared at the opening.

A rap sounded at the wall. He would wager that was a bow bumping wood.

She stepped to the threshold.

When she met his eyes, the bow was held in both hands, flat to her chest. The quiver cinched the dull fabric of her dress.

'Oh, Miss Cherroll,' he continued, 'I see you have arrived to practise your reading.'

He stood, folding the paper. Shadows rested under her eyes and her hair was more mussed than usual. Compassion touched him. Perhaps the maid had told the truth. Perhaps Bellona had really been feeling ill.

'Do you need a medicinal prepared?' he asked.

Puzzlement. He saw it. Puzzlement in her eyes and then the memory washing over her. The wench had forgotten she was supposed to be unwell.

'I am fine. Now,' she added. Her shoulders dropped and her chin weakened.

He looked at her the same way he'd reprimanded the gamekeeper. 'Wonderful. Then we will read.'

'I must practise my archery.'

'I am rushed for time. I think it would be best if we worked together first.'

'I should have a tutor,' she said. 'I cannot take you from your duties.'

He placed the paper on the desk as she spoke. Now he put a hand on his heart. 'I cannot think of any duty more important than your education, Miss Cherroll.'

'I have changed my mind.'

'I have not.'

'I cannot learn.' She shook her head. 'I have no mind for it.'

'Nonsense. You and I will have hours and hours of nothing but lessons until you learn.'

'You will be wasting your time.' The chin went up. 'I cannot even remember all the letters.'

'Then we will start there.'

She shook her head. 'I have already tried. I have tried and I have tried.'

'Last night?'

She nodded.

If the paleness of her face told the truth, then perhaps she had worried over it. He wanted to reassure her. But he could think of only one way to do that. 'You will be reading in no time.'

'I know you have more important things to do,' she said. 'I will have the tutor.'

'I suspect you will not make progress with a tutor,' he said. 'I think you will somehow manage to convince the man to quit his post. I have seen no dancing tutor of late.'

'You do not trust me?' Her brows rose.

'Should I?' he responded in kind.

The brows lowered. 'You do not know what you ask for.'

His eyes didn't leave hers, but he managed to take in her whole body. Warmth flooded him, and he felt he could conquer the world, but perhaps not stand upright any longer. 'I know what I am up against. I will fight the challenge.'

She glanced at the book he opened and the ink swirled into the dreaded confusing shapes. The duke stood, watching her. His hair curled the slightest bit at the end, brushing his ears. Some rested at the collar of his shirt, and some hid behind the cloth.

The currents in her stomach increased. How could she learn with the duke near her?

'I would prefer to stand,' she said. 'If you sit at the desk, I will watch.'

'You only want to be able to leave quickly if you can think of an excuse. You are scared of the words.'

No. His words flamed a challenge inside of her. She had survived far worse than this. 'We must start with the letters first.'

After putting the book away, he moved to one of the overstuffed chairs, grasping the back to move it near the desk.

'I will stand.' She shook her head.

He dropped the back of the chair. 'Very well.' He moved to the desk, shuffled the ledgers aside and pulled out a paper and dipped the pen in ink.

As he wrote the alphabet, she spoke the letters she knew. When she didn't remember, he marked it and went to another one. Then he asked her to pick out her name and she did.

'You knew all but four of the letters,' he said, glancing at her. No smile. No frown. 'Memorising them should be easy. You also know your name. I'd say you're more than halfway there already.'

Then he sketched short, quick strokes on the page.

She leaned towards him, watching the movements he made and noting the scent of his hair, bringing back memories of the mornings by the sea, causing a stab of homesickness and a curling reassurance of home.

'And this is a pig,' he said of the drawing, jarring her mind back into the room.

He wrote the letters under it and spoke them aloud. She'd not remembered the G.

'We will name him Snowdrop.' He glanced up at her and she saw sparkling brown eyes and strong lips, half-upturned, and with a private laugh hidden behind them. Then he returned to his mission. He wrote the letters and called them out as he put them down. 'This is the W.' He tapped it with the pen, leaving a drop of ink. 'And Snowdrop wasn't quiet. So we'll have the Q and U.'

'How did you know of Snowdrop?'

'Warrington told me.'

'The earl was wrong. Snowdrop wasn't unpleasant. I kept her in a soapbox with oilcloth under her because the sow didn't like her. The stable boy could not have kept her alive, but I did.'

He digested her words. 'You must not only learn to read—you must let the servants do their jobs. Do you wish to live among the staff or with the people who employ them? If you do not keep your station, your children will not have the same opportunities they could have. The legacy you create for them will follow for centuries. You do not want your children considered less than they could be. If you ignore society's ways, they will ignore you.'

She stepped back. 'I do not think they will ignore me. I think they will banish me. How terrible. No more dancing. No more maid putting her hands around my hair and pulling it tightly, trying to put a stinking mixture on it to make it stay in place. I do not want to anger people, but I do not like their discomforting ways.'

She lifted the hem of her skirt slightly as she retreated so he could see. 'These are my boots. I wear them comfortably in the house. And you spoke to me about them because they are not slippers. The more beautiful my clothes, then the more people will note my boots and talk of them. So I wear the plain dresses.'

'I noted your gown in spite of its plainness,' he said, almost under his breath, as he drew another line on the page.

'Without looking,' she asked, 'what colour is it?'

'Lighter than your eyes. Softer than your hair.'

Seconds passed. She spoke again. 'Brown. So my boots do not appear so different.'

'If you are saying you chose that gown so you would not be noticed so much…' He barely looked over his shoulder at her, but his lips caught her attention. 'You failed miserably. I hope you do better at reading or you won't learn a word.'

'My dress is the colour of leather.' She moved forward again, standing more at his back.

'Leather. Yes. Exactly the colour I meant. Just couldn't think of the word.' He turned sideways in the chair. 'But you did succeed. I did not think of your boots.'

She touched his shoulder, pressing him to turn back to the paper, not wanting him to see the heat she felt in her cheeks.

He didn't continue writing. 'I cannot help jesting with you, Bellona. You need some escape from the sadness at Harling House. So do I.'

She made a light fist and rested the knuckles of her hand against his collar, just brushing at the end of his hair. 'You don't seem sad...'

His shoulders moved under her hand when he breathed out. 'I know. But perhaps I am. And perhaps I am not enough. You are right in what you said. My life is all planned for me now. I no longer have to think what I should do—I only have to think how I should go about doing it. Generations of people have decided it for me and how could they all be wrong?'

'Perhaps.'

'No. I have lived in this world my whole life. I have seen what has happened to those who do not see the failures of others and who do not learn. A person's mistakes are his legacy, too. His children can be lifted by their father's past or have to fight it.'

'I know that well.' She looked at him and let her breath flutter past her lips. 'If the wishes of others are so important to you, then you will have to marry soon. It is what you are supposed to do.'

His gaze looked through her. 'I, too, know that well.'

She tilted her chin. 'All you must do is seek out

a woman who is fond of society. You have all that a woman might wish for and can put it at her feet.'

He frowned, but the words weren't from his title but from him. 'It is true, a woman may wish to wed me for the world I can give her, but how is that different from you?'

'My dowry is not so large it will choke a man.' She twitched her shoulders. 'But he may cough,' she admitted.

'I was not talking of funds. You could wed well without a dowry if you would just accept our ways. It is not much for a man to ask.'

'No. It is not much. It is everything. For my sister, she flutters about like a butterfly when people are about. For me, the eyes on me make my stomach feel seasick. The clatter at the soirée made my head hurt. Sitting with others with tea in my cup, pretending to like it, pretending to care about the brim of a bonnet, knowing I cannot even think of the right word to say something pleasant. I feel the same as a speck in the bottom of the teacup.'

Her hand fell from his back and she stepped closer so his gaze met hers. This time her chin tilted down and her eyes levelled at him. 'Would you give up all that you care for to sit and pretend to like the taste of a foreign tea that tastes like weeds on your tongue, while you discuss the brim of a bonnet, and only wear boots that do not fit? For the rest of your life?'

'Most women like bonnets and tea and those things.'

'Then they can enjoy them. I do not wish to take theirs. I am quite sincere in that.'

'Why do you not try?'

'I have. I have sat in my sister's house and I have seen her life. For the two years since I arrived in England.' She held up her fingers. 'I have travelled to London and made morning calls and walked in her steps. We returned home again. She flutters about there and her face shows that she has been in a garden of nothing but flowers. She says I can be a bee, too, and I understand, but her garden is wrong for me. And you—' Her voice slowed. 'You have not truly taken on your new duties. You have stayed in the country rather than go to town to find a wife. Do you not feel trapped?'

'Do not put words in my mouth.' He moved. His shoulders turned. He still sat, but his body faced her. 'There is nothing I want more than to accept my duties. Nothing.'

'You have not wed—'

'I merely have not had the time.'

'You are well over thirty. You've had more than ten years to look for a wife.' She waved an arm. 'Not enough time?'

'Apparently not.' His lips turned down. 'And I am not *well over thirty*. I am thirty-one. At *first*, I was the second son and Geoff was the shining star in the heavens. Every woman I thought fascinating only met me in order to speak with my brother. I could see where their attention went. I remember that well. I decided marriage was not for me—until I met one woman at a soirée and I thought she was the one.'

'Did she reject you?' Her voice wisped away at the last words.

'Not really. I have not asked her yet because… Geoff has not been dead a year. A respectful period of time should be waited. He is—was my brother. And truth be known, I pursued her before he died. Geoff just did not know it. He never missed a soirée where she attended that he did not ask her to dance. He told me he would win her some day—but that she thought him too rakish and said she could not imagine him forsaking his mistresses for a wife.'

Winter's chill settled in her bones, even though the temperature was warm. 'You and Geoff pursued the same woman and he did not know?'

'I have not had a woman in my bed since Louisa said a man must give up his mistress for her.' He picked up the paper with the alphabet and handed it to her. 'Geoff had told me what she'd said to him. I mentioned to Louisa, later, that I had made certain conclusions and that I wished Geoff understood my unwillingness to traipse about with him—to disreputable places. She certainly had to know what I meant.' He made a loose fist and tapped it on the table. 'I pursued her with more determination than Geoff. I selected every word before I said it to her. Now that he is gone, I don't know what I think any more. Except I do not like what I did to my brother. When he died, I received the message at her father's house.'

She looked at the page of letters and wanted to crumple it up, but she didn't. 'I believe I have met Louisa. She is one of my sister's closest friends. We went to the shops. She chose slippers with pink rosettes. When she laughs, no one near can frown.'

'That would be Louisa.' Rhys turned away, suddenly fascinated by the unlit lamp. 'When my brother left the room, I often talked with her. I made her laugh. I did whatever it took to get those smiles. I thought her worth the risk.'

'The risk of hurting your brother?'

She thought his silence meant he would not answer. He didn't need to. He'd not wanted to pursue the same woman as Geoff.

'The risk of—more than that. By then my sister had died. To lose her had been so unfair. I imagined the fire taking her. The pain of it. We'd all loved her so much. I still cannot dwell on it. I did not want to repeat such a thing, and if I married Louisa, how could I keep her safe? But I eventually pushed those fears aside. And then my brother died. And now that I am the duke...' He tailed off.

'You should always be a person before you are a title,' she said, then turned to leave. She'd reached the door when he responded.

'That is not how it works.'

The quiet emphasis of the words rang in her ears and when she looked back, he still gazed at the lamp.

She wondered if he imagined Geoff's face or Louisa's smile.

Chapter Nine

After his morning ride, Rhys walked to the library. A rustle in the room alerted him that someone stood inside.

Entering, he felt a surge of disappointment that Bellona wasn't there. Guilt replaced the displeasure, but then he truly felt pleased. His mother fussed with a curtain. She'd not shown any care of the house in a very long time and to have her standing with the sunshine about her brightened his own heart.

'You would think the maids would have learned by now how to arrange the folds.' She moved them this way and that, frowning.

'Now I am crushed.' He moved beside her. 'I thought you were here to see me and it is only the windows you wish to inspect.'

'Well, I might inspect you a bit, too. Now that I see you in the light, it appears your valet does not know how to keep a man's hair properly trimmed. Or you have been leading him a merry dance again.'

'Guilty.'

She reached up and patted his cheek. 'Rhys. I am

not here to merely note how you have let yourself go because it is possibly a good thing.'

He chuckled. 'How's that, Mother?'

'When you are truly well groomed, it would be so hard for a young woman to keep from losing her heart to you.'

'You must be sure to tell the young women this. I don't think they are able to realise it on their own.'

'Nonsense.' She frowned and fussed with the curtains again. 'I think we have one under our very roof who is becoming rather taken with you.'

'I am certain she might be a bit fond of me, Mother, but I believe she is also fond of the stable master as he has secured archery targets for her. She's also had Cook prepare a poultice for one of the footmen.'

'Your valet talks too much of the other servants.'

'Just as a lady's maid talks too much to the mistress of the house. You should not believe idle talk when someone suggests Miss Cherroll is taken with me.'

'This is not idle talk. It's from her own mouth.'

'Miss Cherroll?' He studied his mother's face, uncertain he heard correctly.

'Yes.' She nodded her head. 'She does not exactly say it in words, but a mother knows. A mother definitely notices when a woman's eyes change if the son's name is mentioned. If she speaks differently when he is discussed. It's obvious.'

'I've seen none of it.'

'I am not surprised. Only concerned. But please do not encourage this woman, Rhys. Such heathenish ways. But she does make the days bearable and she has a heart of gold underneath all that rubbish she spouts. I don't want more unhappiness for her. She's had enough. No parents. Not settled like her sister. I see a poor future for her and I don't wish more unpleasantness on her, especially not under my roof.'

'You have nothing to worry about.'

Her eyes batted his words back at him. 'If you say so. She's not right for society. You should hear the tales of her life. She is of a different world. If it were not for the earl, she'd be making her way at the docks.'

The image of Bellona walking among the toughs and cutpurses jabbed at him.

He pulled open a desk drawer, searching, for what he did not know, but he would know if he saw it. 'I am aware of the role I have to fulfil. I know how uncomfortable a woman as spirited as Bellona would be living this life.'

'How uncomfortable *she* would feel? The whole of the *ton* will be watching whom you choose as a wife, Rhys. They would not be pleased that you have turned your back on their daughters and sisters. They will think you married beneath yourself. And you will have. Remember your father's last request. He counselled all his children on the importance of marriage. He asked for his name to be carried on. He wanted the family to continue. *Wed a suitable duchess*, he said. He said that many times. It was one of the last things he asked for.'

'Those were not his final words to me. They were to Geoff.' His breaths were quick. Taking out a pen, he put it by the first one. He stared at them and then put one back inside the desk.

She walked to the window. 'I worry. I can't help it. I know how easily you could be taken from me. Everything has changed so much. Not quite a year ago, Geoff was here. A year before that, your father was here. He started failing soon after he told me of your sister's death.' She looked into the rain. 'It was like he died on purpose, so he wouldn't have to...'

'Mother. He was seventy-eight. I don't think he had a lot of choice in the matter.'

'Did you notice the honeysuckle blooming when Geoff died? I'd been in the garden with him the day before and we'd talked about how he loved the scent of them. So do I. His passing was so cruel—taking him in the spring when so much life began around him.'

She pushed back the curtains and didn't speak for a moment. 'He loved honeysuckle. When he was a boy, he'd pick the little flowers and bring them to me and I'd sniff them and exclaim to make him happy, but I truly was the most pleased. The two of you grew up so fast, Rhys. I remember how he felt as a babe in my arms. So many of the things I'd forgotten about while he was here, but after he died I remembered them all so plainly. The best children a mother could have. And the three of you so close. You and Geoff always watched out for each other and your sister. No rivalry at all. I couldn't have been more proud of my children.'

'Geoff was my only brother.' The words sounded normal enough—at least to her.

She turned. 'I wish for the family every hour. Every day I hear myself thinking about how I wish they would return. It's not asking much. To have my family. They were given to me once, but whisked away. Even the grandchildren they would have given me were taken from me. A home of this size should be filled with family. Instead we have servants and more servants and no one for them to take care of.'

Walking towards him, she smiled. 'I don't want you to think you're amiss. You're doing a fine job of managing things since they left, Rhys. I appreciate everything you've done to take over where your father and Geoff left off. I know how much you cared for them, too. How much you loved your sister. They would all be so proud of you. I am proud of you. I want you to know that.'

'Thank you.'

A maid crossed by the doorway with a tray, certainly taking it to Bellona's room. His mother's attention wavered and she waited until the woman could not possibly hear the conversation. 'Bellona must leave or you must go to London.'

He let out a loud breath of disagreement.

'Rhys. I am your mother. It is not only her acting differently. You are too aware of her. You understand quite well what I am really saying. A man's nature is such as it is. You could ruin her. She does not deserve that. You would hurt her. It is not the best situation for either one of you and you know it. She has told me how she is more comfortable with the servants at the earl's house than the guests. She has been there two years.' She paused. 'Think of her.'

His mother glanced at the statues. 'They're just bits of pottery. I don't know why we thought them anything else. Meant to hold memories of the past. They do. Soot left after the fire is gone.' She made a motion of sweeping them away before fixing her eyes on him. 'I don't know why I kept them.'

She stopped at his side, and reached to the loop of his cravat, straightening it. 'Think of *her*,' the duchess said again.

She left, skirts fluttering at her ankles. The maid moved by the doorway again, tray empty. Rhys called, stopping her.

'Inform the stable master to be ready to journey to London at a moment's notice.'

Rhys finished his meal, surrounded by empty chairs. The lamps lit the room as brightly as they always had. He sat at the same place he'd always sat.

He lifted his wine glass, sipped and put it down. Echoes of his sister's laughter, Geoff's jests and his father's half-hearted grumbles bounced in Rhys's memory. His mother, one brow raised in feigned dismay, or lips pressed to hide her smile, had presided over them all.

An infinite world at the time.

If he had known what was to happen, how could he have enjoyed the moments, knowing they were to end? But if he had known the future, the time with his family would have meant so much more.

Nothing could change one second of the time before or since. No oath was strong enough. He'd tried them all.

He stood, took the glass and finished it, sitting it back in the place it had always been and left the room.

No oath was strong enough.

Walking along the hallway, he stepped into the library and picked up one of the statuettes, turning it in his hand before putting it back on the mantel. His grandmother had owned one. His mother had added to the collection and his sister had given one to his mother. The women had thought them precious and he'd seen no value in them at all. None. Except now they'd somehow begun to matter a great deal to him.

Once he'd had to grab his mother's wrists to keep her from smashing them to the floor. They were supposed to have been passed to a daughter's daughter.

'What are you thinking of?' The question jarred him from his thoughts. He turned. Bellona stood in the doorway, staring at him. Yesterday, the message she'd sent to him had begged off reading practice because she said the duchess insisted on helping her. He knew why his mother kept Bellona at her side. He also knew just how long it had been since he'd been alone with Bellona. Two days. That he had kept count disturbed him. That his senses came alive when he saw her concerned him even more. His mother was right.

He watched her study his face. 'I was thinking of the statues on the mantel. How long they've been there. Most of them, my whole life.'

She walked into the room with the assurance of someone who'd never seen a cloudy day, but her eyes belied her steps.

'Your mother. I am concerned about her.'

'She is more demanding?'

Bellona shook her head. 'No. She's more pleasant, but still…'

'The woman you have met is not the woman she was before. She wasn't gentle, but she wasn't the same as she's been. The grief took over. Her worries surrounded her.'

'I run from mine.' She only touched her skirt long enough to hitch it up on one side, before letting it flutter into place. 'Sturdy boots, remember.'

'You can't always escape the things that trouble you.'

'If you say so.' She stepped to the books, grimaced and began to study the spines. 'I am thankful I ran from Melos. I am also making certain I do not have to stay in London if I don't wish it. If I cannot be in my own country, then I have no place to bind me to it. That is why I have decided to learn to read. Your mother said it might be needed some day to write to my sisters.'

'A good reason.'

She tugged at a book, looked at it and put it back.

'Where would you go?' he asked. He hadn't thought beyond the moment.

'I have a friend who thinks of me as a daughter, I believe. And she knows a woman who married well, but is lonely. They have written to each other and the woman says I might visit and, if we get on well, I can stay with her.'

'But you are already a companion to my mother. You must agree you take her mind from her grief.'

'I do. But she tells me she is so much better already and she is.'

She studied the books. 'Your mother said you had another book by the man who wrote *Crusoe*. I thought I might like it better. What was that man's name?'

'Defoe,' he said, not letting her divert his attention.

'I do not know how *Crusoe* ends,' she said. 'But he could not return to the same world. When a year passes. Two. So much changes if you do not see the people often. You cannot return to the same world as before. And neither can I. So I will move somewhere else. Somewhere smaller. While I have the chance to make a new life. I want children. But there are many motherless children. Many. I might gather some about me.'

'You could have your own. Marry.'

'Marriage.' She shook her head. 'Look at the grief that marriage has caused your mother. A husband and two children lost.' She paused. 'My mother did not truly have a husband. He was gone most of the time.' She took another book as she spoke. 'The woman who thinks of me as a daughter, her husband did not do right by her either. Marriage—' She shrugged. 'The pigs and goats and chickens do not marry. And yet women do. They think they can change—' she looked at him '—nature. Yet the males of the species do not seem that particular.'

'I will be loyal to my wife. A vow is a vow.'

'You say that.'

'I know that,' he said. 'I have— I made no vow yet to Louisa. But for her I gave up other women…to prove to myself I could do it…' He had not thought it possible to go so long without a woman. 'I assure you it has not been easy, but I make no idle promise. I can be a true husband.'

'I am proud for you.' She looked at the book she'd taken out and her mouth formed letters, before she stopped, watching him. 'But I do not know if I can make such a vow.'

'You jest.'

She shook her head and held the volume towards him, letting it rest in the air between them. 'Sows.

Ewes. Hens. They do not seem particular about their mates. Women, too, change their affections. Widows remarry. Women on Melos… I saw their hearts change. My mother's did not after she married my father, but I could see that did her no good either.'

'I pity the man who you might marry.' His fingers clasped over the leather, but she didn't release it and he didn't pull it away.

'That is why I should not wed. I wish to be happy. I like to smile.'

'I think you would like giving a man grief, too.' He looked at the book they held. Defoe. *Roxana.*

'Ochi.' A definite no. 'I do not want a man close enough to give him any sorrow. It would rebound double on me.'

'Your choice.' He slipped the book into his control and put it back on the shelf.

This woman was no society miss. The *ton* would certainly not accept someone so different, so free of restraints. He spoke his thoughts aloud, puzzled. 'Your sister cannot encourage your folly. She surely wants you to follow her example. I may not always agree with Warrington, but I believe he treats her well. Theirs is a good union.'

'Warrington is kind to her. Her heart is filled with him and the children. They are of such a similar mind.' Her eyes flicked up. 'Similar to yours. I have considered this life in England for two years, and after being at Harling House I know I may be wrong for others, but I am right for me.'

'You met me and decided marriage and society was not for you?'

'I would not say that.' He lips curved into a smile. 'I have been away from my sister and the children. I have missed them, but it is them I miss. Not just any baby or child. I see your mother and I see the damage even good love can cause in a person.'

'Your father. You are letting his actions rule yours. All your thoughts of marriage are coloured by the way he left you all.'

'No.' Her chin tilted and her lips thinned. She ducked her head, but not before he could read her face. Her next words didn't match her expression. 'I hardly knew him. I remember my mother crying more than I remember him. My uncle did what he could do to help when I was very young. But he died—killed for no reason. We had so little. I do remember that when my father came home, the food was better. Everything. But inside the house was not always better. Our life was a calm sea when he was gone even though my mother struggled so hard. But when he returned there was a storm inside our home. I only wanted the goods he brought. I did not care for him at all.'

Then she made a gesture with her hand. He didn't know what it meant, but he was certain it was not a suitable action for a lady. He'd noticed it before. Her wrist would turn quickly and her lips firmed and words formed in her mind, but her fingers executed the phrase he didn't know.

'You should not say such,' he said, testing his theory.

'A society woman would not,' she agreed. 'Another reason to remain as I am.'

'I surrender,' he said, moving to the desk. He caught her gaze and smiled. 'I have a surprise for you.'

He did not want to argue with her, but he did want to hear her voice. He had lost his mind somewhere among the pins in her hair, but as long as no one else knew and he recovered soon, all would be fine. He hoped.

He opened the desk drawer and pulled out a book, holding it aloft. *Cobwebs to Catch Flies.* He brushed a hand across the leather cover. 'I don't know where it was or which servant found it, but they have all been rewarded.' He smiled. 'Geoff, my sister and I all read this.' For a moment he was held by memories, all good. 'Sit near me.' He waved the book towards the cushions. '*This* one will have you reading.' He opened it, moving to the section with the three-letter words.

Bellona settled on to the sofa and he put the book in her hands and sat beside her. Spices flowed into the air. The memories and scent of Christmas around her made the present feel as good as the best of the past did. He could hardly wait for her to begin.

She took the tome and her lips moved the barest bit, saying the words silently while she studied the page.

Her mouth. He watched it, willing her to repeat the action. She didn't, but she still held the book.

A weakness plunged into him. He relived a memory that kept him strong.

He'd written some bit of fluff to the girl who'd given him his first kiss. The moment had been…a surprise.

He'd not really thought much about what a kiss could feel like. And he hadn't meant to be alone with the girl. They'd happened upon each other by chance. She'd rounded a corner and he'd caught her just as she stepped into him and then she'd trounced his boot and he'd been worried about his boot being scuffed. She'd purposefully rested her foot on his other boot and he'd meant to remove her, but her waist had felt more important than any new boot had ever felt in his life and he'd not been able to budge the little wisp of her. He didn't remember the conversation or how long they'd stayed there, but she'd reached up and kissed him.

His world had changed.

Later, he'd written to her about how her lips tasted—but the letter had been stolen from his chamber before he could give it to her and it had somehow ended up in his father's hands—thank you, Geoff—and his father had called Rhys into the library, told him to shut the door and they had had another talk. The letter had been returned to Rhys and his father said it was Rhys's choice whether he gave the letter to the chit or not, but to remember that words written could never be changed. He should consider how a wife might feel some day to read something which might concern her. Or how their servants might snicker to learn of such a thing about their master.

Rhys's father gave him the letter. Rhys threw it in the fire. He'd disappointed his father.

Just as his father would be disappointed now if he'd walked into the room. Rhys shoved the thought aside.

'Why don't you read aloud?' Rhys suggested, and she did.

Initially, she stumbled over the words, but she could understand them, slowly at first and then more easily.

She closed the book, but held the place with one finger. 'I did not know books were like this. Cats and rats and dogs.' She looked at him. 'I would wager there will be a pig in it, too.'

'I do not want to give away the ending.' He leaned closer, pretending to look at the pages. 'Keep reading. It is good for you.'

'I do not like to hear something is good for me. That usually means I won't like it.' But she wiggled a bit, reminding him of a hen settling into her nest.

Again she read the words aloud.

He watched, half his vision on the book and half on her. The only other noise in the room besides her voice was the occasional sound of the page turning. He listened and then forgot everything else as her fingertips touched the paper.

His thoughts were much safer when he imagined only her hair. Now he watched her hands, heard her voice and could not stop his fascination from growing.

She reminded him of childhood and innocent times, and then she'd turn the page and he'd be ever so thankful to have left all that behind him and be alone with her. She made his chest feel broad and his skin vibrate just because her voice moved towards him through the air.

Her head dropped a bit to the side and her words wearied.

He wanted these moments. They were harmless. Nothing to be concerned about. Nothing he would remember later and feel guilty for, even when he was married to his duchess. No one would know that his mind wandered to places where it shouldn't. This was just a simple moment between two people who happened to be in the same room.

'I am tired of reading,' she said, closing the book.

He took it from her hands and put it on the other side

of himself, causing him to move so close their sides brushed. Without her voice, it felt as if the whole world had ceased to have sound.

Rhys spoke softly, not wanting to disturb even a dust mote in the air. 'Tell me why you cannot tolerate dancing. Not the dance itself, but the holding.'

'It has always been this way.' The words were slow and barely reached his ears. She'd closed her eyes for a moment and she opened them when she answered. 'Or at least for a long time.'

'When did it start?'

'I'm not sure. But I know the dreams started on the ship to England. The first night I slept afterward.'

Her eyes flicked to his face. He didn't move, waiting.

'I told you that when I was on Melos…' The purr of sleepiness left her voice, but her lids dropped again. 'Men woke my sister Thessa and me during the night. They forced us from our rooms and one was going to wed my sister Thessa whether she wished it or not, and the other was going to—wed me, and I…could not have survived marriage to him. Or he could not have survived marriage to me. Snake. *Fidi.*'

'And…' he said, barely speaking.

'And Thessa and I swam to the English ship in the harbour. It left. We sailed here.'

He didn't want her to open her eyes, afraid if she did she'd pull back, taking him from this shared moment. He gave a soft sound of acknowledgement, looking at the shape of her face, and the skin, so delicate he feared even brushing his fingertip against it might be too rough.

He slid further from her on the sofa so he could put his hand along the back. His fingertips could have easily held her shoulder or dipped a bit lower and touched the bare skin where her sleeve ended. In his mind, he could feel her. Perhaps he truly did because the warmth of her body flowed outward. He was so close it had to be wafting to him.

'The island men pursued us, but the captain and his crew fought them off. I thought we were safe, but later on our voyage a man decided I was bad fortune.' She touched her throat, slender fingers resting against her skin. 'He tried to toss me overboard to drown in the seas. I couldn't breathe I was so frightened. Thessa pulled him from me.'

Spears of rage hit his midsection. Those words changed everything. They slammed into him as if his own body had been thrust hard against a wooden fortress. His temple pounded. He pulled back, not wanting her to sense the violence inside him.

How dare someone touch her so? He would have killed him without hesitation. He forced his voice to be calm, but it took a moment. 'I am pleased you were unhurt.'

Her lips turned up, not so much in a smile, but in some sort of inner amusement. 'I have a sword. I thought it would protect me, but I almost cut off my own nose.' Her eyes opened and she looked at him. In that second, he felt the same intimacy he might when looking across bedcovers at a woman, only it wasn't the same. This was more intense, deeper—something he hadn't known existed. It was as if she'd just taken over his whole body. As if her spirit was twice his size and had wrapped itself around him, cradling him. He never wanted to lose this feeling.

She leaned towards him, touching, perhaps not touching but brushing, just at the top of her nose, and he almost felt the sensation of her fingertips. The trail of her hand lingering against his skin in the same way she swept her hand above her own nose. 'Can you see the scar?' she asked, voice husky. She slid more towards him. He could not move.

A tiny white line rested just at the bridge. 'How did you do that? Was it that man?'

'It wasn't him. This was when I was living in England. I was taking the weapon from the shelf where I had put it to keep it from my niece. It fell.' She shut her eyes again, only for a moment. 'I didn't know how I was going to tell my sister, since she'd already complained about the sword. But luckily, her babe chose that moment to be born and no one noticed my hand—' she rested her palm over her nose and peered out at him from around it '—covering my face. By the time my nephew was safely tucked into the family, the scratch hardly showed.'

She took her hand from her face. 'He was so tiny. I did not see why her *stomachi* needed to grow so big to have such a little babe.'

He studied her face.

'Your nose is rather a pleasant nose.' The words slipped from his mouth, sounding like a caress. If he raised his forearm just the slightest bit and moved just the merest bit forward, he could be holding her.

'I didn't expect to like the babe.' She grimaced. 'He'd caused my sister such discomfort already and he wasn't a girl. Warrington already had a son and daughter, and I hoped the little girl would have a sister. I wanted another small Willa in the house.'

She pulled herself straight on the couch. 'I told Melina just a few days ago…about the mark. She thought it humorous that I could manage to sail from Greece to here, sleep when the pirates boarded the ship trying to take our other sister before being defeated in their efforts and have no marks to show for it. Then I wounded myself with the weapon I kept for protection.'

She looked at him. 'Let me try reading again. I like it much better when the words are small and the story is about children.'

He moved, securing the tome without looking at it. Holding it in her direction. Her hands skimmed over his as she took the volume, slowly, from him.

She turned the pages to the spot where she'd left off. 'The words are getting harder, though.'

His arm rested at her shoulders. 'Just hold your finger to the word and I'll help you.'

She began to read, and at the first stumble she moved into the cradle of his arm and pointed for him to read the word aloud.

She stayed where she was, and when she paused again he let go of the breath he'd been holding and helped her.

The book wavered because she pointed to another word. He took hold of the other side of the cover and held it.

As the words became longer and longer, he never realised when he became the speaker and she became the listener. His words lingered, so she could follow easily, and he read to her about the happy family of eight children and the merry-go-round.

He read more slowly as he neared the conclusion, and when the story finished they closed the book together, then he pulled back and she straightened.

'I did not want the story to end,' she said. 'I quite liked it.'

'I did as well.'

'A good tale,' she said. 'Better than *Crusoe*.'

He nodded, holding it with one hand. 'Though I enjoyed it as a child, I had not realised before how much interest it has.'

'Sometimes things more scholarly are not always the most enjoyable.'

'They are good for onc, though.'

The flicker of her eyes when she heard the words acknowledged his jest.

'So true.' She stood and leaned towards him again, taking the book. 'Do you mind if I keep this in my room for a time?'

He looked up at pale skin, a long neck, a wilful chin and lips that he wanted to touch in all the ways that he could.

'As long as you'd like. It's yours.'

'Only for a short while and then I'll put it back,' she said and left the room.

He wondered if he would be able to move again.

Chapter Ten

Bellona fought, inside the dream, pulling hands from her throat, her grasping fists closing over emptiness. She struggled for air—ale-scented breath suffocating her. His darkened pupils expanded so that she could see nothing else. She scrambled back as her own vision clouded into black, reaching for her weapon, the world of the ship fading, changing to the bedchamber. The image of the crewman fell away into the recesses of the room.

Her eyes opened. She sat against the headboard of the bed, her heart pounding, fingers gripping the knife she'd had under her pillow. Her throat ached, the press of thumbs indenting her throat still choking her.

She swallowed slowly, trying to get air, but keeping her movements still so she could be aware of the room. Shadows brushed her skin with the lightness of spider's legs. Beyond the walls, something creaked.

Slipping one foot from the bed, she braced for her ankle to be clutched. She had to escape from the room, yet the hallway would be dark and someone could be waiting.

She dashed to the door, her back against the wood, the knife held close to her body. Listening. Watching. Waiting.

Wind blew against the window. She forced herself calm. Over and over the dream found her in the night.

Questions would throb in her head until morning. What if the pirates hadn't been defeated by Captain Ben and his crew? What if they had continued to pursue the ship intent on making another attempt to capture Bellona and Thessa? Or what if the gamekeeper had got angry at her because she had been accepted into the house as a guest and he broke in to attack her?

She touched the door latch with her left hand, gripping the cold metal. Listening. She had no reason to fear. None at all. But blood still raced in her veins.

She leaned back, feeling a vibration as she painlessly thumped her head once against the wood. She could not traverse the room and reach the bell pull. Her feet wouldn't let her.

The room didn't feel safe. She couldn't stay long enough to summon a maid. The pirates would not go away. She could not make them leave her dreams and in her dreams she had nothing to fight with.

Soundlessly, she opened the door and put one foot into the hallway. Nothing. Still darkness. No movement.

She couldn't shut the door behind her. Even though the room could trap her, she couldn't close even one possible way of escape.

Sliding her body out, she moved down the hallway. If she called from the library for a servant, the butler would arrive. He stood tall and she could ask him to check her room for a mouse. She'd heard something. She'd heard a squeak or a creak. A noise had stirred her from the terror.

Or perhaps she'd only dreamed it. The figure of the man squeezing her neck had vanished as she woke, disappearing, as the nightmare always did, taking the stench of death with him. Leaving her room as quiet and still as a crypt covered in dust.

Standing, she waited, making sure she heard nothing again. She forced her imagination away. Those endless fears that plagued her had merely returned, but she didn't want to be alone.

She clutched the knife close to her body, and ignored the chills seeping through her thin shift.

'What—' A gruff voice—behind her—right behind her. Her mind froze, but her body did not. She swirled around, bringing the knife up. His hand rose, clamping on her own, holding her clutched fist with the strength of a vise. In the same instant her hand was caught, he moved forward, pushing her, her right shoulder crashing into the wall. He trapped her with his size.

Neither moved.

'Bellona,' the duke gasped out. 'What the hell are you doing?'

She could not speak. She could not.

'Bellona.' He called her name again.

It was Rhys. Her brain knew it. But her body wouldn't move. Her pounding heart took all the power from her voice. Pushing against him made no more difference than hurling herself at the strongest rock on Melos. Fear overpowered her, and her mind could not free itself from the terror.

'It's me. It's Rhys,' he said. 'Bellona.'

Shudders racked her body.

He still held her knife hand, but his other arm pulled her into an embrace. 'You're safe.' His voice rumbled softly, a caress in words. 'It's me. I won't hurt you. I'd never hurt you.'

The bulwark of his strength didn't frighten her, but terror still controlled her even though her mind translated the scene into the reality of the moment. She rested her head against his shoulder. The only movement she could make.

He pulled her even closer. He murmured to her and he lightened his clasp, cradling her now. Her body shook and he didn't speak again, just held her.

Minutes passed. The knife handle was pulled from her hand. She had no strength to hold it. She didn't have the ability to stand without his help. His other arm went around her.

Her face stayed buried against him, the silken threads of his waistcoat against her cheek. His male scent soothing her. He didn't clench her tightly, but she burrowed into him, regaining her composure as the shaking stopped and her heartbeats slowed.

'I thought…' she whispered.

'You thought to hurt me?'

'No. I did not know. I could not think,' she said. 'I did not know it was you.'

'Who else would it be?'

She whispered again, 'I did not know…'

He kept her folded into his arms, crushing her against the fabric of his clothing, surrounding her with the fortress of his strength.

His chin rested against her forehead. 'I didn't mean to frighten you.'

'I didn't recognise your voice at first.' She shut her eyes, taking solace from his hands clasping her back, holding her.

'Sweet, much as I'd likc to hold you, I have something I must attend to.'

'I don't want to be alone.'

'I understand.' He squeezed her. 'We can talk about it later.'

She gripped him. 'I could have hurt you.'

'I know.' He mumbled the words, his lips against her hair. 'You could have.'

He pushed himself away from her. 'But you must get to bed now.'

She reached out, unable to let him go, and confusion hit her mind. She felt the sleeve of his arm, but he jerked back.

Something was wrong.

'I…' She clenched her right hand, letting her own fingers brush her palm. Wetness.

'I— Did I—?'

'Yes, I believe you did.'

'You're cut?'

'It does feel that way. I appear to have grasped the blade before I was able to get to your hand.'

She gasped. He stepped further away.

'Rhys—we must get a light. You're bleeding.'

'I'll attend to it. You go back to your room.'

'I'll summon help.' She turned to run, but he captured her arm with his right hand, grip warm and tight.

'Shh… I. Will. Attend to it.'

'But, Rhys… Are you hurting? We must—' *He must not be hurt. He could not be hurt.* Her breaths gasped from her.

'Bellona. The servants. I do not want talk, but really I should look at it. There is a light in my chamber.'

'Yes,' she agreed. She slipped from his grip and caught the fabric of his sleeve, pulling him in the direction of his room. 'Quick.'

Inside the room, the stain on his white sleeve looked like nothing more than a shadow until he stopped by the lamp.

Blood dripped from the hilt of the knife.

Red. She gasped. Death. She could hear the screams of the women of her homeland. She could have done to Rhys what the man who'd killed her uncle did.

Her knees weakened, but she did not fall. He put the knife on the bedside table and opened his hand. The skin parted where his palm had slid down the blade.

'You cannot die.' She appraised his body, looking for damage. 'You cannot.'

'I am not planning to.' He pushed the skin together and held it. 'Bring me a flannel. I need to stop the bleeding.'

She rushed to get the cloth and took the fingers of his hurt hand in hers, and he moved his free hand aside while she pressed the cloth against the wound.

'You must remove the blood from yourself as well,' he said. 'You look as if you have been in a fight. Are you cut?'

She noted the red splotches on her arm for the first time. Her own fingers showed red. She examined her arms and hands. 'No.'

'I'm thankful.' He shut his eyes briefly and shook his head. 'I'm thankful I am the one that felt the blade and not both of us. That would be hard to explain.'

'It should be stitched,' she said, bending over his hand. 'I will do it. I know I can.'

He took a step away. 'Damned if I let you near me with a needle. I've seen your embroidery.'

'I will be slow.'

'Bellona.' His eyes widened. 'We have a physician. I have been bled before and I survived. It is merely releasing some of the humours. I do not like it, however. Your method is a bit painful.'

'I will take care of you.' She moved to the washstand and splashed water from the ewer into the basin. She swept her hands through to remove the red. The water turned a bloody tinge, but no cuts showed on her own skin. She turned back. His eyes were on her and his gaze didn't move as she watched him.

She took a cloth, her hands dripping water, and rushed to his side. 'I'll care for it. Sit. Sit on the bed.'

Keeping his hand clasped over the cut, he held his elbows wide, still standing. 'Would you undo my cravat and the buttons on my waistcoat? I'd prefer not to get more bloodstains on the fabric…'

She wiped her hands dry, tossed the cloth to the bed and stepped closer. With a quick tug, she slipped the knot free. Then a swift snap.

The force of her pull on his neckcloth jerked him sideways.

'Damnation, woman. Do not break my neck.'

'Pardon. I did not realise it was wrapped around so many times.'

'You almost snapped my head from my body. You do wish to kill me,' he muttered, then leaned forward again. 'So unwrap it or merely slip it free by pulling *gently* at the sides and front.'

She finished her task, surprised at how comfortable she was this close to him. To be alone with him was quite different from anyone else.

She folded the cravat and put it on the bed.

Reaching up, she slipped the delicate buttons of his waistcoat free, moving back so he could raise his hands as she finished.

At the last one, she stopped, looking up into the dark eyes as she undid the final clasp.

'Are you…' she asked, 'in pain?'

The lightest nod.

When she turned, her eyes locked on his hand. She sucked in air through her nostrils.

'You look a bit rattled,' he said. 'Do not have the vapours.'

'Your Grace. Please. Sit.'

He looked at her. 'Bellona, I believe you can call me Rhys now.'

She paused. 'I am sorry I hurt you.'

'I know. I believe you.' He held his hands clasped a bit more and stepped away. 'What I don't understand is the knife. I thought your weapons were taken.'

'Not the one I carry in my boot.'

'Ah, yes.' He nodded. 'How remiss of me. The blasted boots. Your reticule knife was removed, but it was strictly an oversight on my part not to have someone collect the knife from your boots. That's their charm, isn't it? That's why you wear them?'

She answered with her eyes.

He stared at her bare feet and his eyes trailed up her body clad only in her thin nightdress, leaving warm currents in their wake, causing a *frisson* in her stomach. 'I would say that you do not have another knife hidden about you right now. Is that a safe assumption?'

'No—yes, I do not have a knife.' The words. They scared her. She'd just told a man she was unprotected. The walls in the upper rooms were solid… The duchess would not hear a scuffle. No one could answer her if she called out for help. In the servants' quarters, there was a chance someone might respond, but not here.

He watched her, but without the darkness she feared. 'You should go so I can summon assistance.' She lost all thoughts he could ever harm her. He was injured and he cared that she not be discovered in his room.

The red on his hand reminded her.

She had done that.

'I will summon my valet,' he said.

As he moved forward, she threw her body between him and the pull. 'I cannot go to my room.' He stepped to brush her aside, but she flattened her palms on his chest. His eyes widened. He felt rather like a wall. A wall of muscle and skin and male. 'Your Grace.' She thought it best to address him such at the moment. 'I will worry.'

He leaned close. He'd been drinking brandy some time in the evening. His eyes shone with an emotion that jumped into her and caused a heating sensation that somehow managed to touch her entire body.

'Sweet. It's his job. I will tell him that if I die he

must alert the entire household. So, if you do not hear, then you will know I am well.'

'I am not leaving. He may care for you if you wish, but I am to stay and see that it is done right.'

'You cannot be found in my chamber in the middle of the night, particularly with blood on both of us. The man is discreet. He will not speak of it, but I fear he would have an apoplexy keeping silent on that. I would then have to replace him and I simply do not have the time.'

She lowered her eyes to her palms still resting on his chest and then slid her hands away, before looking up again. 'I will care for you.'

'You will?' He smiled. 'Just as you cared for me a few moments ago?'

Surely he would live if he could jest. She nodded and took the cloth from the counterpane, holding it towards his clasped hands. 'Yes, Rhys.' She daubed at the smears on him, taking the red from his knuckles.

When she indicated that she wanted to reach the cut, he did not open his grasp, but extended his fingertips to clutch the cloth.

'Let me,' she said, refusing to release it.

'You've already attacked me once in the night. Don't struggle with me now. I might stumble backwards and knock myself in the head.'

'If you stumble now, you will land on the bed. Sit on the bed so I can see the wound better.'

He sat on the edge. She was no closer than before until she perched beside him, her shoulder aligned with his. She wiped the cut clean.

'What happened to bring you out into the hall with a weapon?' he asked.

She pressed on the wound. 'I awoke from a nightmare and thought you were…someone evil.'

'And you only cut my hand?'

She pressed harder.

He flinched. 'Go more lightly with the cloth. You're making it worse. Leave and I will send for my valet. I just do not wish for him to know how this happened, but I suspect he will notice the cut and the shirt will have to be burned.'

'How dear are the lamps?' she asked.

'I have no idea. They're lamps.'

She sighed. 'Break the glass of one and tell him you stumbled.'

'I can do that. But when you turned to get the cloth, I noticed a bloodstain on your back. How will that be explained away?'

'The maid will not notice after I finish with the garment.' She peered at the cut. 'Move your fingers.'

He did.

She rested her forehead against his shoulder momentarily, then straightened again. 'That is fortunate. Now do not move them again.'

She held the flannel tight against his hand. He reached to pull it away, but she clasped it. Determined, he took the cloth and put it against his palm, closing the fingers of his right hand over it.

'You don't have to tend this. I'll break the lamp, call the valet and now you can go back to your room and get some rest.' Then he pushed her aside so that he could stand, reached with his left hand, picked an unlit lamp from the side of the bed and crashed the globe against the table. The glass shattered and he sat the base back on to the table.

She met his eyes. 'I'm still not leaving, Rhys.' She rose and moved, planning to search out another flannel. But before she left, she gazed over him to reassure herself he was not about to die.

He returned to the bed, stretched out lengthwise, his head at his pillow and his ankles crossed. 'Sweet, you may return to calling me Your Grace at any time.'

She spoke over her shoulder. 'You must recover. You would need a big spot to be buried in and the man who cares for the gardens would grumble if I asked him to dispose of you.'

'Bellona, you do not just dash a duke into a hole in the ground. You must have a bit of a ceremony first.'

'Yes, Rhys. I suppose it would take some time just to dig a hole for your boots.'

She could feel his eyes on her as he digested her words.

'Even if you address me as Your Grace, I suspect you've always seen me as no more privileged than one of the sailors on the ship that brought you to England.'

'That's not true.' She shook her head. 'I've always seen you as a duke.' She continued searching for a useful cloth, only stopping to look at him. 'But the men at sea are quite skilled in things that matter. You are skilled in books and learning, and I suppose that has a place besides writing letters.'

She found another flannel inside the washstand.

'Thank you.' He exchanged the reddened bandage he had for the new one, pressing it once more against the wound. He shut his eyes. 'Would you bring me a brandy glass and the bottle?'

She went for the drink, splashed some in the glass and then returned. He pushed himself upright with an elbow, his injured hand still gripping the cloth. He downed the liquid and held out the empty glass. She re-filled it with the same amount. He looked at it, frowned and drank more slowly before handing the glass to her once again. The fresh blood smears on the flan-nel pressed to his injury caused her stomach to clench.

Putting the glass and bottle on the table, she re-turned to the dressing chamber and found another flan-nel for his cut. When she returned with it, he took it from her and placed it over the other one.

His eyes moved over her, reminding her of the way water in a stream followed the movement of the current.

'If you wish to get the dressing gown from my ward-robe, you may wear it,' he said. 'I would not want you to catch a chill.'

She moved to the dressing chamber. She didn't feel cold at all and she didn't think he'd been overly con-cerned about that. When she opened the wardrobe, she reached out, running her fingers over the silk and linen in front of her. Nothing looked as if it had ever been touched, but everything had rested against Rhys's body. She took the banyan, wrapping it around herself, amazed at how well shaving soap smelled. The gar-ment drooped from her shoulders and dragged on the floor, but felt like a royal robe.

'This is so…' She snuggled into it. Then paused when she met his eyes. They'd narrowed, but she couldn't see behind them.

Padding back, she sat in a chair, looking across at him.

'You can't sit there all night and stare at me.' He pressed against the flannel. 'That will surely enough do me in.'

'If you die because I'm looking at you, I will take note of it, since I have never even been able to pain my sisters by giving them my harshest look.' An army couldn't have taken her from the room. 'I need to stay to make sure if you fall asleep, you don't get blood on the covers.'

'You sound like my mother. You have been spending too much time with her.'

'I think she will agree with you and so do I.'

He adjusted the pillow with his left hand. 'I suppose I should not have been traipsing about in the dark, but I have done it often in the past year. If I walk enough, then I sleep without my own dreams and I prefer that. The nights are so long after I have finished with my ledgers.'

'The dark frightens me. I always had my sisters close by when I was young. I had never been alone in the night until I sailed here. Sometimes I feel smaller than Willa. And now it has caused your injury. I didn't want to hurt you. I would rather my hand be cut.'

'I believe you. I didn't mean to grab the blade. I didn't know you had a knife in your hand until I reached the hilt. Then it was a little late to reconsider.'

'You could have been hurt much worse.'

'So could you.' His voice rose in exasperation. 'Granted, you did me an injury, but do you realise what could have happened?'

'It's better to have a knife than nothing. Even the

smallest man is stronger than I am.' Rubbing her fingertips together, she examined them for red. 'It is important I protect myself.'

'Why? Why do you feel it is so important?'

She looked at his hand and let her gaze linger over the rest of him. Tall. Shoulders the same width of Stephanos's. But he tried to see her and not just the reflection of his power from the fear in her eyes.

She shook her head. 'It is...how I must be,' she said. 'How I have always been. At least for a long time.' She crossed her arms over herself.

'The ship?'

'That was the second time I knew I could die at a man's hands.'

The memories she kept in her thoughts always, of the island, and that day of violence, flashed in her mind. 'One day when I was young, I heard shrieks. But I thought it was happy noise. I wasn't close enough and I wanted to see what was happening. I ran to the people and saw them crying, but I could not go on.' There had been more than tears. There had been wailing—begging the heavens to reverse time and bring her uncle back to life.

'I could not see my uncle breathing his last,' Bellona explained. 'I could not believe that it was real. This time the truth felt like a dream. I could see and hear but I could not...feel. You cannot undo something like that. You wish for the moments to go back just the smallest time, but they will not. You long to know it didn't happen, but it did.'

She remembered stopping, and sitting, wrapping her arms around her knees. She could hear the words, and see the people, but they blocked her view of her uncle. More screams. Louder this time.

'So much noise,' she continued. 'Then Stephanos was walking away. Swaggering, away from everyone. Towards me. On the trail, he stopped and watched me. He was not even a true man yet, but he was tall even then. As big as the men. His eyes were evil. *"Your uncle is dead,"* he said. *"I killed the man who stabbed him."* He laughed. Blood was on his face and where his knife was tucked in his sash. *"I could kill everyone on this island and no one could stop me. Even you, little one. I could cut your throat."'*

She'd watched him and felt no fear. But she had known he was thinking of death as a prize—someone else's life a bounty. A proof of power.

'He laughed. He threw back his head and raised his fists into the air. Like a rooster crowing to greet the morning. He was not sad my uncle died. He was happy for my uncle's death because he could kill the murderer in front of everyone. He didn't care about justice. He cared that other people feared him.'

'Not all men are evil.'

'Stephanos was. And only one evil man can cause so much pain. And he liked it. Years ago, Melina was to marry him. She had no choice. He had decided to wed. He was going to marry one of us and he didn't care which one. Melos was too small to escape him. Melina sailed away to bring us funds to help, but when she didn't return, he noticed Thessa and would not stop watching her. She agreed to marry him to stop him looking in my direction. But then the ship came and we escaped. I still have dreams about it. About all of it.'

'Anyone could have nightmares after seeing such things.'

'I see too much in my dreams.' She wrapped her arms around herself. 'Again. I see a man's face with nothing in his spirit but death. The happiness of having power over others.'

'You cannot be feeling true danger from me. You cannot.' He pushed himself up. 'I could not hurt you. I could not.'

She shook her head. 'I don't believe you could. But there is something in your thoughts you are not saying.' Something she couldn't decipher. 'When you meet my eyes, I see… I am unsettled. If you are in the room, I know where you stand. I cannot think of anyone else when you are near.'

He shook his head from side to side. 'That is just a… Something that happens between a man and a woman. It means little.'

'I cannot think it means nothing.'

'Not everything a person feels or thinks is to be spoken of. That is why thoughts reside in the head. Some things are to be kept silent. No one tells another person all the things inside.'

'My sisters and I, we did.'

'Perhaps women do. Men do not.'

'So they do not think of important things that need to be told?' She moved so she could see the light flickering on his face.

He closed his eyes. 'A man doesn't need to prattle on.'

'It is not prattle,' she said. 'I don't know what it is, though.' She shrugged. 'But perhaps it is not good.

Your mother talks so much of death and hurting. And now you are injured. If you do not get well, your mother will never forgive me.'

'I doubt she will forgive you anyway if she finds out the truth,' he teased.

'My sisters and I had a saying, "There is the truth, and there is the truth we tell our mother."'

He smiled. 'My brother and I said it a little differently. "If you tell Mother, I will kill you."'

'I suppose they both mean almost the same.' She leaned closer, seeing his lashes against his cheek. The way the soft fringe and the strong jaw, lean nose and stubbled chin all formed the man.

'I am aware the duchess is on the mend,' he said. 'But I don't want to risk her learning of this.'

She rose and got another flannel and took it to the side of the bed, looking down at him.

He opened his eyes, peering into hers. 'Stop staring at me so.' He reached for the fabric. 'You might as well lie beside me. You're already ruined if anyone sees you here. It will probably look more innocent if we're on top of the covers, looking irritated, anyway. You might as well relax.'

She didn't want to go back to her room. To the dreams. She might have even talked to a pirate to keep from being alone. To be alone with Rhys, though, she would have fought sea savages.

She walked around the bed and sat on the other side, resting against the headboard, snuggling into the dressing gown. 'I wanted to make sure you are not hiding pain.'

'I'm not hiding it at all. It aches. But less than other

hurts I've had.' He paused. 'Where were you going when you were in the hallway?'

'The servants' quarters.'

'Were you searching for someone?'

'No. I sometimes sleep there. In my big room, sleeping is difficult. A few nights ago, I could not get the door to latch properly and I could not rest. My bedchamber seemed so large and open that someone could have walked in on me in my sleep and I felt that I had nowhere to hide. So I took the book to a smaller room I had found. I felt safer there.'

'You felt safer away...away from the rest of us?'

She nodded. 'The room is more like my home on Melos. A place so small no one could hide and a single lamp could light to the very edges of the room. In Melos, I would have thought it so grand to have the plainest chamber in your house. It is far better than what I once had.'

'Bellona, do you not respect the servants' world?'

'I do.' She smiled. 'Even your servants would think me far beneath them if they had stepped on Melos and met me right before I left my home. On Melos, the animals lived under my home and the stairs led to the two rooms above, where we lived.'

'You'll never have to live like that again.'

'I miss it,' she said. 'I long for it every day.'

'How could you want to return to that?'

'I miss my sisters and my *mana* being together. The waves. The blue. The smell of the sea. The sand under my feet. But now I must be happy in England. I just do not know how to do that and it has been two years.'

'It takes a bit to recover when you lose what you hold dear.'

'I wish I could share with Mana and I wish she could see the riches here. The only thing I know is— if she had to choose and could, she would have chosen to be poor in order for us to have much. She would be so happy looking down from the heavens, although I don't know if it is possible.'

'Perhaps she does see this.'

'She would not be happy I hurt you.'

He chuckled. 'Of course not. A woman is not like that, especially a mother.'

'Gigia. You did not know her. She would think it humorous or perhaps be angry that I let you so close to me in the hallway.'

'I can understand a grandmother not wanting her granddaughter to be close to a man in the dark.'

'Oh,' she said and chuckled. 'Gigia was not at all like you think. Not at all. She was not at all like the English and their proper ways. If she were here now she would be angry with me that I had not—'

Silence again. She knew he thought of the same thing she did. Gigia would have been angry that Bellona was not pushing her body against Rhys. But what he didn't know was that she would have been most angry to know Bellona had not been whispering a price in his ear.

Chapter Eleven

His hand hurt like blazes where he'd cut himself on her blade—which was the only thing allowing him to keep a decent thought in his head.

No, he didn't have a decent thought. But keeping his hand pressed against the makeshift bandage while reminding himself that he might still die of a fever kept him from pulling her against him.

She slept completely wrapped in his dressing gown, only her head poking from the top of it, concealed more chastely than any woman he'd ever seen.

She wiggled around, towards him, and the dip in the bed helped him roll ever so slightly towards her.

Miss Roman Warrior Goddess could have killed him with her very sharp knife, but he'd immediately wanted to reassure her when she'd discovered she'd accidentally sliced him.

Flames nicked at him everywhere, but he wasn't feverish.

His body still had the cravings of a youth, but his mind had advanced somewhat. He had rules. He had managed for quite some time to keep out of a woman's bed. He turned over. But now one was in his bed and she was sleeping peacefully.

He should have married before now.

He just wished… He just wished he had wed the previous year. He should have. Then his wife would have been settled by now. Most likely, a child would have been on the way and Rhys could have threaded his fingers through his wife's mussed hair and rested his cheek against her skin.

His boots were on so he couldn't get under the covers. He'd have to call his valet to be undressed. If he did that, she would have to leave. He wouldn't be able to sleep. He'd be lying there, bleeding and thinking of her.

She turned in her sleep. Her arm went around his midsection, jolting him, and he rested his clasped hands at the side, his arm just against her hand, keeping it snug to his body.

It would be for ever until morning, but the time would pass too soon.

Bellona awoke with a dim light flickering in the room and the sound of rain pounding against the house. Rhys sat in the overstuffed chair, which had been turned towards the bed. His left arm propped his head and she couldn't tell for sure if his eyes were open.

She pushed herself into a sitting position.

'It's morning,' Rhys said. 'Or it will be soon. You should leave before someone discovers you.'

'Your hand?'

He held it closer to the light. A blood-caked slice went from the bottom knuckle of his forefinger to the heel of his hand. He waved his fingers.

She put a foot on the floor, and looked at the night table. 'Will you return my knife?'

'Do you truly believe you need it here?'

'No.'

He reached to the drawer, pulled out the knife and handed it to her, the blade facing himself.

'I'll put it away,' she said. She held the cold handle and looked at the weapon. The crumpled flannel, coloured with darkened red, lay on the nightstand.

The knife no longer made her feel safe or secure. Now it felt poisonous. The men who had frightened her in the past had hurt her from a world away.

Next, he picked up one of the shards of glass from the floor and put it on the table. 'You should take the real weapon from this room. My valet will believe the culprit was the broken glass. But I don't want him to see a knife in my room where there has been none before because he would surmise something. What exactly, I don't know, but I don't want to take the risk.'

He lowered his voice. 'Bellona, if you have fears in the night, I will check to make certain no one is there.'

'When Thessa and I were taken on the island, it was from our beds in the dead of night. I fear what happens when I sleep. But this time waking was the most dangerous course. I am sorry.'

She rose, reached for the tip of his fingers and examined his hand, putting the image of the injury into her mind as strongly as she could. This she would remember when she thought of the blood and felt fear, because this could result. She must control herself. She couldn't live in terror any longer. 'The hallway is long. If I have trouble sleeping, I'll sleep in the room below stairs. I feel safer there. If I shout, someone will hear. I don't want to see anyone's blood again and know I caused it. I can't.'

'You should not be below stairs. You are a guest. We have family rooms all about.' He waved his arm, then he dropped it to his side, grimacing. 'Just no family to fill them any more.'

She turned away. Only one person had the task of filling the rooms and she did not want to think about that.

'I will be leaving to go back to Whitegate soon,' she said. 'There I'll sleep in the nursery near the children if I need to. When I watch them, the world doesn't seem quite the same dark place. It seems like there's sunshine in the night.'

'I know how much better you've made the duchess while you've been here,' he said. 'I suppose there is a reason the mourning time is a year. Perhaps that's just how long it takes for everyone and I shouldn't have been so concerned. But after Geoff passed, she crumpled, seeming to fall into the past, and even I could not rouse her.'

Bellona knew the duchess had been moving about Harling House more. She even talked of other things besides her grief. Bellona could leave without concern, and if she stayed it would be foolish. Being at Harling House when Rhys returned with a wife would not be wise.

'I am enjoying speaking with you.' He spoke softly. 'But if you don't leave soon, someone might see you. I'll walk you to your room. I don't want my dressing gown left about for the maid to see so I'll return with it.'

'We did nothing wrong.' She pulled the clothing tight around her, tying the belt. 'Except I did cut your hand.'

He moved to the door, waiting to open it. She stopped beside him. His hair had been finger combed and his shirt, rumpled, hung loose from his trousers. She reached, smoothing the sleeve, pressing a hand against it, but the wrinkles were fixed firm. 'You look like you have been in a war.' She didn't release his arm.

'It will certainly not be perceived as innocent if it is known you spent the night here. The talk would rumble about for the rest of our lives. You in my room. My hand slashed. Tales could get quite grand about that. Even I would have trouble believing it all innocent and I am here to see that it is. It might be assumed I attacked you. Or that you meant to hurt me and I had to restrain you. I don't know what would be said, but it would not be good. You'd be ruined. Quite ruined.'

She wouldn't admit the thoughts running through her mind, but she didn't care if she were ruined. She didn't. But for his sake she didn't want any tales put out about her hurting him and people speculating on what had really happened. She didn't even want to remember the night because of the pain she'd caused him and the fear that he might become feverish.

'I am so sorry,' she said.

He cupped her cheek in his hand. 'I see it in your eyes. You don't have to tell me.'

Everything shifted and it was as if his spirit stepped behind her, beside her and all around her.

'I'm leaving Harling House soon,' he said. 'And this will be the only chance I have to tell you goodbye.'

'You would vanish without taking your leave of me?'

'Yes. I would and I should.' He leaned forward. He brushed a light kiss on her cheek. 'I won't forget you.'

'You can't. I've put a mark on you.'

He moved, pressing another kiss on her cheek, lingering this time. His lips touched her as he spoke. 'You certainly have. Deeper than you know.'

He did not say he cared for her, though, and the knowledge washed over her in the same way a winter wind entered the cracks in the wall and enveloped everything inside. She had to make the feeling of unease disappear. She had to warm herself and only by stepping closer to him could she find any comfort at all.

She examined his eyes and he did not move, just looked back at her. Brown. Chocolate. Aged wood. Perhaps not as dark as the men on Melos. But a gaze softened by his lashes. He stood patiently, not speaking, and he didn't smile, but the small lines at the corners of his eyes relaxed.

Then he did smile. 'You shouldn't examine a man so closely. It does things to him... It is the same as if your fingers had swept over me.'

She reached out, putting her palm over his heart. The fabric didn't prevent her from feeling the strength of the man beneath, of the skin covering taut muscle.

He reached up, taking the barest grasp of her fingertips. He shut his eyes and pulled her hand up so that her knuckles brushed against the roughness of his cheeks.

No clock ticked. No sound from beyond the walls reached them.

He snaked the other arm around her waist, using the strength of his forearm to hold her against him, sending shivers into her that she could feel every place her body had ever touched anything and all those senses changed into something burning inside her.

His kiss was her first true kiss. His tongue, warm and hungry, took her, tasting her, melting her into his body and swirling her from her feet and giving her the feeling of when she swam just underwater and sunlight heated her back, only stronger.

He turned her, the door at her back, holding her up and himself, not ending the first kiss, but changing it to a treasure trove of smaller ones, moving to her jaw, her ear and burrowing down her neck, his left hand pulling open the top of the dressing gown, heated fingers pushing the barrier away to make a path for his lips over her skin.

He pulled back, released her, and her knees almost gave way, but as her body seemed to dip, his arm kept her upright.

His eyes stayed on hers, but when he opened his mouth, it took a second for him to speak.

'I am not myself.' His voice roughened, the words barely reached Bellona's ears. 'I do not know what is the matter with me.' He gave her a tight bow of his head. 'Forgive me.'

Bellona muttered. 'You have marked me, too.'

She stepped to the door, stopping only long enough to throw the dressing gown back into the room as she left.

Chapter Twelve

The palm of his hand tingled and burned. The cut had opened twice in the morning, but each time he'd cared for it and the bleeding had stopped.

His morning meal had not gone well. The rasher of bacon left a tallow coating in his mouth and he'd had to wash it away with a drink of chocolate—even that had not been quite right. He'd almost sent to have the cook try again, but he just was not hungry. Eating with his left hand made everything taste off.

The day's lashing rain splattered against the window and Rhys only had the ledger books in front of him so he could look busy if someone walked in. The sums were not terrible, but rather the way he'd hoped them to be. Everything soured before his eyes because of his thoughts concerning Bellona. The woman had injured him and he had fallen at her feet. If his mother had known how simple it could be, she would have been arming all the ladies of the *ton* with knives in their reticules.

This morning, he did not expect to see Bellona moving about the house. She wouldn't be going out to practise archery because of the weather and she'd not slept much.

The decision to leave for London had been taken out of his hands. The roads from his home would be difficult for a carriage and the trip wasn't a good idea. He would get stuck. But he was already mired.

How many times must he go wrong in order to recognise the right path?

His proximity to Bellona had merely misled him. Misdirected him. Natural enough.

He'd relived a certain kiss a thousand times and cursed himself a thousand-and-one times. What if he'd only kissed her because he'd been so long without a woman's touch? Or worse, what if he had kissed her because she was like a meandering stream, winding and winding and seeming to be just a trickle until it pooled into something so wondrous the eyes could not believe it?

He could not do this to her.

His father would have counselled him. He would have shaken his head and closeted himself in a room with his son. They would have discussed the events. Or rather his father would have guided Rhys.

His father's main responses would have been, *'I see. That sounds interesting. I hadn't thought of it that way. What of the other people involved? Your future children? What kind of mother will best raise your son to be a duke? Help your daughters to make the best marriages? This is not a decision for you. It is a decision for your future heirs. And what of Bellona? What is right for her?'*

He forced the thoughts away, determined to make the best decision for everyone.

His sister, his father and Geoff's deaths had pounded his heart into dust. He could not resurrect it and expect to have the strength to carry on with his father's legacy. To let the lands and the estate go to a cousin, while the remains of all those he'd loved would reside here for eternity, was something he could not risk.

He had no choice but to marry a suitable woman, and he had no true heart left to give her. Perhaps that was why Louisa was the perfect wife. He'd not seen any real affection for him in her eyes.

If Louisa died in childbed, and left a child behind, he would be able to care for it and continue on.

He had courted her quietly while his brother was alive, knowing that his brother wanted Louisa—and why not, she was the perfect duchess. Geoff was no fool. Louisa's head wasn't easily swayed. Her thoughts were not altered by a duke pulling her one direction or his brother tugging her another, determined, on this one thing, to win.

When Geoff had died, the letters Louisa sent Rhys had been written in almost the same tone he would have expected from his man of affairs and he had responded similarly. Letter after letter exchanged—with little more personal nature than those he might have sent to Simpson. He'd saved every letter. Every one, and read them over and over, and each one convinced him even more of her suitability. The guilt he felt at courting the woman Geoff had planned to wed only flared occasionally. Now he wanted her for another reason. After he observed the mourning period, he had told himself, he would ask her to marry him.

Rhys had once believed his heart was in the right place. Perhaps. He no longer needed to think about that or question himself. He needed to go forward. Perhaps putting his body in the right place would cause his heart to produce the right response. Louisa knew what was expected of her in the role of duchess. Knew the ways of society. She was pleasant. Kind. Thoughtful. Perfect.

He didn't love her. To love someone else—to release his heart to them, was impossible. He could not give what he no longer had.

'Rhys.' His mother stood in the doorway, whispering loudly. Rhys jolted as if caught in an illicit embrace.

He collected his ducal mien and with his left hand scratched a jagged figure on the page before him. His mother had not entered the library in a long time. 'Yes, Mother?'

'The maid said…' The duchess rushed to his side. 'She mentioned a cut on your hand. The footman saw it when you were eating.'

'It's nothing to concern yourself over.'

'Let me see it.'

He held out his hand, keeping the palm almost closed so the slice wouldn't open again.

She gasped, her thin fingers reaching out to hold the sides of his hand. 'How…?'

'It was just an accident.'

She clasped her hands to her heart. 'I cannot. I cannot lose you, too.'

'I am planning to stay alive for quite some time, Mother. Please do not try to get rid of me so quickly.'

'This is not a jesting matter. You—' She turned and reached to summon a servant. 'I am sending for the physician now.' Her voice rose to almost a scream. Her body shook.

'My babies. They cannot all die. I cannot be left by all my babies, Rhys. Can you not see that?'

'I am almost recovered now, Mother. It is not my time to die.'

'We must have the Prince's physician. We must.'

He took his time with each word, hoping to calm her. 'If my hand becomes infected, we'll send for the man, but the roads are too bad for him to travel.'

'It will be too late by then. Look at it,' she said, again clasping her hands to her heart. She collapsed on to the sofa, her voice rising. 'I cannot live through this again. I cannot.'

Bellona ran into the room. 'Is he bleeding?'

'Bellona. He is injured. Badly. His face is feverish. His hand must be infected.' She clasped her head. 'My baby.'

'He is dying?' Concern flashed in her face.

'No more than I was this—last—yesterday.' He did not wish his mother to know the truth. 'I have a cut on my hand, Bellona.' He spoke precisely. 'A simple cut. That is all.'

'I did not mean for this to happen. I cannot live with myself if you die,' Bellona said.

'He is my only…' The duchess stared at Bellona in bewilderment. 'He is all I have left.'

'Ladies.' Rhys's voice calmed them. 'I am only

slightly injured. Not dead. Please do not hurry my demise along by wearying me to death.'

His mother rose, pushing herself up. 'A mother should not outlive all her children and have no grandchildren to carry on. It is not just.' She looked at Rhys, but her question was directed to the winds. 'What have I done to deserve this?' She put her arms out. 'What have my children done?'

'Nothing, Mother.' He moved to her and held out his hand. 'See. A little cut. I'm fine.'

'You promise me you will not die. You must promise.'

'You have my word.'

She snatched his wrist. 'I will keep you to it.' Tears pooled. 'And you will give me grandchildren? Soon, Rhys. Promise you will give me grandchildren soon. I want to hold them before I die. You must go to London as soon as the roads are safe.'

'Yes, I will.'

Chapter Thirteen

Bellona put her hands over her ears even though no one spoke in the room and she was alone. How many times in how many ways had the duchess said how much she missed her family and how Rhys must wed someone from his own world? And how many times had his mother expressed her fear that he might now die if the cut in his hand became putrid?

Rhys had spent the morning calming his mother while Bellona listened, watching his hand to make sure it no longer bled. After he'd left the room, his mother had talked of nothing else but her younger son for hours. Then the discourse had travelled through each deceased family member and five handkerchiefs.

Bellona waited until the duchess tired herself into a nap. *Robinson Crusoe* was in the room at the servants' quarters. Perhaps she had found a man whom she could spend the rest of her days with, this Mr Crusoe, not that she particularly cared for him, but at least he did not have a mother nearby.

Rhys was in the library. She knew it. She could almost follow his movements inside the house without ever seeing him. He varied little from his usual paths and when he did she could tell by the activity that changed in the household. A different servant would be at the stair or she'd hear his horse outside, or a scent of some baked treat brought upstairs would waft her way.

He had told his mother the roads would be better the next day and he would leave for London. Bellona could not let him go without seeing him again.

She walked into the library.

Rhys sat at his desk. He didn't have the usual ledgers in front of him, but a chessboard with several pieces resting to the side and most on the board. His right arm lay on the desk and he moved a white pawn with his left hand.

He turned to her. Sensations of their kiss returned to her body, but this time, his eyes created the warmth swirling inside her.

She could stay at the door, safe, far enough away from him, or she could step inside. She moved forward, unable to do otherwise. 'The duchess was quite fractious today—your injury on the anniversary of Geoff's death.'

He nodded. 'I thought to leave so she might not learn of my hand, but decided it was not for the best, because of the date.' He moved a black knight.

'You have no opponent?' she asked.

'Not for this game.' He grinned at her. 'If you are unarmed, you may join me.'

'I have no knife,' she said, then answered the question in his eyes. 'Or weapon of any kind. Nothing that can jab or hurt you except my hairpins.'

'I suppose one must take progress where it is found.'
He nodded to the board. 'Do you wish to play?'

She shook her head. Another thing she could not
do. 'How is your injury?' she asked Rhys, stopping
near his hand.

She waited, moving closer. He turned his palm towards her. The gash was closed, the skin around it
slightly puffy, but reassuringly healthy.

'The valet has told me he has seen a man recover
after having his leg cut off,' he said, 'and that his own
father died from a toothache. He said when it's my
time to go, something will find me. But he said it's
not my time to go. He knows this because he peered at
the whites of my eyes and pinched the top of my foot.
The best check of all, he said, was to slap a cold cloth
across my face. I almost let him, but when I declined,
he said I passed his test.'

'I have hidden my knife, even from myself. It is with
my bow and arrows.'

'Do you continue with the nightmares?'

'I have had dark ones, but I'm fighting back with the
knife in my dreams now. It's much better, and when I
wake I tell myself I can shout for help. I remind myself I can scream out.'

'Is my mother treating you well?'

'Well enough. She asked me to read to her again.
A letter she'd saved from your sister this time. I could
read most of it, and when I did not know a word she
was able to tell me without looking. She said I have
progressed much with my reading.'

'She is correct.' Gently spoken words.

'As a mother must be,' she said. 'When I have my own children she assures me I will understand.'

'I think you understand perfectly well now.'

She stepped to the mantel and noticed a vase, not as tall as her hand, had been added. Primroses were tucked into it, their perfume so delicate she'd not noticed until she stood near the flowers. She brushed one yellow petal, feather-soft. 'Yes. I do.'

'You didn't want to leave your island. But you did. It was for the best.'

'Best for me?' She let laughter into her words.

'Yes. It has not turned out so bad, surely?'

'No. I cannot mind. I know how things must be.'

'I cherish those thoughts. I would not want you unhappy.'

'I'm not. Though I don't know that I wish to live on Warrington's estate any longer or live in London. I do not think I should stay here now. I want to have true contentment.'

'Do you truly know what you need for that?'

'Yes.' She met his eyes. 'I have known since I was a child.'

She went to the bookshelves and knew just where to find the *Cobwebs* book, seeing that she had placed it back there. She pulled the book out and looked at the title again. 'I thought about how Mana would have rejoiced to see her daughters so well placed. She would have bargained with the heavens that she would suffer so her daughters would not have to. And perhaps she made a bargain in another way to give us more. So when I feel sadness, because she could not share this life with me, I tell myself it is not so bad. She would have been joyous to know how bountiful my life is. And I will not let her struggles be for nothing. I will not.'

She traced a finger over the cover of the book where his hand had rested. 'I even know what would cause me the greatest of unhappiness. The union my mother had.'

Rhys had to gaze at her. He had no choice. He turned. That crown of hair she wore would topple around her shoulders some day and the man who could see it every day would fall to his knees and give thanks.

'What did your father tell you about love?' she asked. 'Your mother has mentioned it to me.'

'He said if the head could lead, the heart would follow. He said many men have lost their families, their lives and their world by trusting the most untrue organs of the body. He said the heart lies. A man's body lies. But he must separate himself from that and look from a distance. I thought them wise words, but he could not have known he did not need to say them to me.'

'The *Robinson Crusoe*. It was your father's book first?' Her lips quirked up and her expression nearly felled him. This moment was the most precious one of his life. He felt the strength of the world inside him as some mystical force flowed from her eyes, igniting a flame within him.

'I'm certain,' he said.

'Mr Crusoe. A man who wanted adventure and then spent most of his life alone. I don't think I will finish it after all.'

He looked at her long enough to see the smile in her lips and the sadness in her eyes. 'I want you to take the copy of *Crusoe* when you go. You may sell it if you wish. I will never read it again. It would always make me think of you alone on the island of Melos.'

'I would not sell this book. Perhaps I should read it at night when I cannot sleep. I could see how truthful the book is.'

At his side, she took his cut hand, examining it closely. 'I think you will live.'

'I think we both will,' he said.

He reached out with his other hand and let his forefinger touch her skin. She accepted the movement as one might let raindrops linger on the face. His caress slid over the contours of her cheekbone, feeling the silk. One fingertip was not enough. He stretched his hand so he could sweep more of her into his senses.

'I never thought dark colours could be so bright,' he murmured. 'Your eyes. They shimmer.'

His fingers moved to the valley at the side of her temple, where her cheekbone rose. 'They linger in my sight. They take my soul and hang on to it.' He ran his touch over her nose. 'You were created for a warrior god.'

She shook her head, but not enough to move from his fingers, but to brush against them. 'I am blemished. More so than my sisters.'

He chuckled. 'Marred? That could not be possible.'

Her nod moved her closer. 'I have a longing mark.'

'That cannot be bad.'

'My sisters' marks are brown, almost the shape of hearts, but mine is red, more like a scrape that never goes away. With my sisters we believed my mother wished for love for them, but for me, we could not think what she wished for.'

He moved, the smallest bit closer to her. 'Did you ever ask her?'

'Yes.' She stumbled over the word. 'She said she had wished for love for my sisters, but by the time I was born she said she had realised her error. She told me the two red blemishes on my skin are where a heart was torn in half. She said she wished that I would never fall in love. She said it hurts too much. She thought like your father. Perhaps you and I are in agreement on the foolishness of possessing a heart.'

He'd touched her lip when she spoke. She could no longer move. This was not the same immobility of fear, but of an embrace of security. He was fire you could walk into and never be burned, just feel the tingle and caress of the flames.

Now the fingertips from both his hands rested on her skin and his breath whispered against her. 'Your mother was wise for you.'

'She was. I know. Because I already saw my father leave my mother and I want no man near who will not stay with me all his life. Who will not place me above everything and everyone else.'

His hands slid from her face and he closed his fingers. 'I hope to remember the touch of your face. You're the magic I will hold within me for the rest of my life. In a secret part of me that keeps me whole and gives me breath. But I cannot give you what you need most.'

She touched above her breast. 'And I must have a man who puts me above…his father. His mother. Even his children. Who loves me with all the intensity of the sun's heat and his love reaches to the stars.'

'You ask—'

'For what I wish for. Why should I ask for less? I am happy to be alone before I will be with a man who does not cherish me as I wish.'

'A man can say the words easily enough. Words, Bellona. But how will you know if he speaks the truth? And what if he's not sure about his own future? What if he does not even know if he can feel for a woman what you wish him to?'

'If he does not know—then he does not feel enough.'

He swallowed. He moved and his elbow touched an inkpot, knocking it askew. He caught it, but not before splashes destroyed the paper.

Turning, she moved to his desk. Ink had pooled on his work. She put the stopper back on to the empty bottle.

He shrugged and touched a blot on his sleeve and frowned, still staring.

She put her fingertip in the obsidian pool. She paused, studying the letters scratched on the piece of paper. Taking her time and reading. The list of things he planned to do in London. The places he would go and the people he would meet. She dotted her finger over the letters, obscuring them. Then she put another spot at the side of the first one, letting her finger drag over, smearing the lines into darkness.

She looked at his eyes.

Her index finger touched the back of his hand and she left a faint mark.

'Have a pleasant journey.' She walked out through the door.

Chapter Fourteen

A storm brewed, but not in the clouds. The sun warmed the morning, turning the day into a spring confection of promise. Bellona didn't want to go back inside the mansion. Rhys's carriage had just left the estate.

The air moved aside for her arrows, creating the perfect pathway for each tip, taking them so close they clustered together, fighting for room. One *thunk* after another. She stepped back to give herself more of a challenge. It didn't work.

'Miss Bellona.' The shout screeched into Bellona's ears.

She turned. The maid ran from the house, skirt clamped in both hands raising it enough to allow swift movement. 'She's fallen. She's fallen.' The maid stopped. 'The duchess. Down the staircase. She won't open her eyes.'

Fear leapt into Bellona's chest. 'Send a rider after Rhys's carriage.' She dropped the bow. 'Let Rhys know the rider will need to continue on for the physician.' She rushed into the house and found the duchess lying at the base of the entry staircase.

The cook's bulk bent over the older woman, with only the duchess's feet visible. The servant talked softly to the still form. The butler stood at the ready.

The duchess's eyes fluttered. Then she blinked, looked around and studied her surroundings. A puff of air escaped her lips. A sigh.

'Are you hurt?' Bellona knelt beside her, relieved she was breathing. The lifeless form had plunged the memory of Bellona's own mother into her heart like a knife.

The duchess pushed herself up, looking at them all, but not speaking.

'Are you hurt?' Bellona repeated.

The duchess held out a hand to Bellona. 'I had thought to see what heaven might look like. You are not it.'

Bellona smiled and put her arm around the older woman, her ribs feeling as though they were hardly covered by skin. The woman winced, but managed to stand. She reached up and touched her cheekbone. A bruise would be evident soon, but for now there was only a scrape. Then she clasped her wrist and wiggled her fingers. 'I'm fine. Fine.' She pulled out of Bellona's grasp and grabbed the banister. 'I'm going to lie down.'

She took each step up the stairs with great care.

Bellona followed behind her and the cook did as well.

'Just leave me,' the duchess said crossly. 'I fell. Simple enough. I didn't watch my feet. I stumbled. Others cannot stay alive and I cannot die. I cannot *die*.'

The sharp turn of Cook's head alerted Bellona that the servant was checking her reaction to the duchess's words.

Bellona schooled her face to show no emotion, but she didn't think it worked.

'I'll fix a purgative for Her Grace,' the cook offered.

'No. I'll keep my bile and whatever else I have inside me right there. I just had a fainting spell. I'm fine just as I am.'

The cook looked again at Bellona, and this time she grimaced.

They'd hardly settled the duchess into a chair, with a maid sitting beside her, when Rhys burst into the sitting-room door.

'How is she?' he asked anxiously.

'We don't think she's more injured than a few bruises.'

'What caused her to fall?'

'I am not sure. She said the world turned black around her.'

'She has never fainted before…'

'I fell, Rhys,' the duchess snapped, eyes closed. 'I fell. Do not worry about me. The house could burn around my ears and I would still be standing. Festering boils could appear all over my body and I would still see the sunrise every day.'

'Mother.' One strong reprimand.

She opened her eyes. 'I didn't mean for you to have to return. I am just sitting around every day, waiting for the end.'

He turned. 'You may slap her, Bellona. We will see if she can chase you.'

'Don't be ridiculous.' She shook her head. 'I just fell down the stairs.'

'An accident? Or on purpose?' Rhys said grimly.

'Neither. I was crying over Geoff. The tears were in my eyes and I had to go to the garden. I had to pick some honeysuckle. I'd almost forgotten to pick the honeysuckle for him.' She waved her arms about, her white sleeve billowing. 'I might not have done it on purpose, but I certainly wouldn't have minded waking up somewhere else. When I opened my eyes, I realised the truth. I am in a different kind of purgatory. My back hurts and my face aches. My wrist burns.' She sniffed. 'I would like some port.'

'How will I know you won't stumble again once you take a sip?' Rhys asked.

'Because I cannot die. A thousand times I have asked to be with my husband and children and I cannot. One year ago yesterday Geoff was taken from me. They are all waiting in heaven and cannot be happy without me and yet I cannot join them.'

'I would have thought you might wish to stay here on earth with me,' Rhys said quietly. He strode from the room. Bellona followed.

Outside the door, Bellona caught his sleeve.

'She is just distressed. She means none of it.'

He stopped, face stone. 'I understand that.' He pulled his arm from her grasp and strode to the stairs.

'Rhys,' she called at his heels.

He turned to her on the stairway. 'You don't understand.' His face rested near hers. 'It is not my title. It is not my estate. It was never meant to be. Never.' His words flowed faster. 'I do not know why Geoff did not marry and have children. I was not supposed to have it all. I don't know whether to feel guilty for taking it or angry that it's now mine and I cannot escape it.'

'That has nothing to do with this moment.'

'It is everything to do with it.' His eyes darkened. 'If he were here none of this would be happening. Things would be as they should be. They would be—controlled. The world was taken and torn like little scraps of paper and tossed into the air. All scattered and in bits that cannot be mended.'

'Do you wish to tumble down the stairs as well? Would that make it all better? Leaving a cousin to inherit. Would it be his destiny either?'

He raised his hand, the mark showing. 'I do not care at this moment. I must get to London, find a wife, bed her and produce a child. Hopefully before nightfall.'

'Oh…' She dragged out the word. 'More's the pity.'

He lowered his chin.

'From where I was born,' she said, 'even the people who cannot read have no trouble with that.'

'You witch. It is not quite the same for me.'

'I imagine you will find some way to have pleasure doing it. I have heard it can be done.'

'An unmarried woman is not supposed to know about these things.'

'And what turnip were you born under?'

'Not the same one as you, apparently.'

'Now go to London and do as you must.' She put a foot beside his and moved down the stairway, turning back to him. 'Safe journey.'

'Bellona.' He rushed after her and caught her arm. His voice softened. 'I cannot leave you like this.'

'Yes, you can.'

'I don't want to be alone now, and there is no one in the world I would rather be with than you. And perhaps you are right. Perhaps you are the one able to see this clearly without the heart being involved.'

She didn't answer, but her hand grazed her skirt, above the red blemish hidden from view.

Chapter Fifteen

She continued down the stairway and heard his footsteps behind her. She rushed ahead, moving to the
servants' quarters where she could shut out the world
above the stairs. No one was about and she moved to
the small room she'd taken over.

Only the door didn't shut when she pressed it. Rhys's
hand caught it and pushed it open again.

'So this is the room where you feel safe,' he said,
stepping inside and shutting the door behind him.

'Yes. It is more my world than any other room in
the house. You can see it for what it is.' Even as he
looked around, she knew he could only see the room.
He couldn't see the truth of her past. This room was a
palace compared to where she'd grown up on Melos.

Nothing marred by salt from sea air. Nothing
marred by life. This room had belonged to a scullery
maid and it was the closest she'd found in the house
to what she'd had.

His eyes furrowed. 'I did not know such a place
even existed in my home.'

The small bed had a washstand beside it. Resting

on the washstand was a small mirror propped against the wall, a tallow candle and Robinson Crusoe's tale.

'This is how most of the servants' rooms are.'

The bed covering wasn't torn. The walls were solid. She raised her eyes to the ceiling and saw no stains. At the washstand, she pushed against it. No wobble. 'I am sure Mr Crusoe would have been pleased to have such a place on his island. I would have.'

Rhys sat on the bed, elbows on his knees, fingers steepled and his chin resting on them. He raised his eyebrows. 'I have been angry these last few years. Enraged that my sister died, my father and then my brother. Now I anger at even my mother, who suffers deeply.'

Brown eyes, more rich than any silk or sable, peered at Bellona. He smiled. 'But it doesn't matter. Nothing changes. I tried shaking my fist in the air. Pounding the wall. It changed not a thing. Didn't make me feel any better, only more angry because it was senseless.'

'I did not mourn my mother after she died. But I did not need to. While she was ill, I cried and thought my life could not go on. But she talked so much with us towards the end. We talked of everything and she prepared us. I missed her, but the hardest part was her suffering. The last week of her life. That was cruel. She hurt so.'

In front of him, she rested her hand on his shoulder and then let the back of her hand move upwards, along his cravat, to the skin above it, letting sensations engulf her as she talked. 'Your mother will get over this. It is just the valley before she climbs back up the hill of life again.'

'I thought if I went to London I might be able to put the loss behind me. But when I return, there will be even more. You will be gone.' His eyes flicked to her and one side of his lips turned up.

She brushed his hair from his temple. 'There is the duchess you must find.'

'Do not remind me.'

'Why not? You will do it. You have put your mind to it. Don't tell me you do not think of the woman. How you will approach her. What you will say. How you hope to feel something for her in the way you used to feel before Geoff passed away.'

'When I close my eyes at night, it's not her I think of. When I open them in the morning, she is nowhere in my head.'

'Truly?'

He turned to her. 'Look at my face. What do you think?' He touched the earring at her ear. 'I notice you always wear these.'

She nodded. 'Yes. I think it makes your mother feel better.'

His hands clasped her waist. Warm bands. Strength that made her feel delicate.

'I want to make certain you are provided for,' he said.

'It is not needed.' She held her chin up.

She shook her head and turned her gaze from his. 'When you wed, I will never again see or speak with you. It is for the best. I will not forget the past. The good or the bad. Yet I will not fall into the same trap of the heart that my mother fell into. When it is done, finished, it is over and done with.'

She didn't raise her eyes, but kept the expanse of his chest in her view. The cravat rested close to his heart, but she didn't know what emotions lay inside the man. No words of love reached her ears and only the warnings of her mother sounded in her mind. She would heed them.

Rhys's hand slid up, sparking eruptions she had only heard about in myths. He cupped her cheeks in his hands. One kiss. Then another. So light. Lighter than the one before. Soft. The barest moment of contact and then he pulled back.

She kept her eyes closed, her chin upturned, and savoured the softness of the lace on his sleeve against her face.

Opening her eyes, she said, 'You dressed so fine to go to London.' She grasped his wrist, trapping the thin cloth so that she kept it between them. His jutting wrist bone rested under her fingertips. Then she stepped back and let her hand fall slowly, and land on the buttons of his waistcoat.

'Bellona…' He said her name, but it wasn't really a word. More of a caress. He paused. 'I cannot. Not now. Not ever.'

'Cannot?'

The words sounded pulled from him. 'I cannot touch you because I cannot…*touch* you. You deserve the promise along with the touch.'

Her gaze stopped at his face. She could see him more clearly than she had ever seen another person. Her eyes even caught the tenseness at the corner of his lips and the slight sheen of moisture at his brow.

His eyes darkened, but with an emotion that didn't

frighten her in the least. But he still did not move one bit—even one hair closer.

Then she waved fingertips over the silken waistcoat. The fabric working as a barrier between the life of him and her hand. He took in a breath yet still didn't move towards her. Nor away.

He made her think of the statue of an armless woman she and her sisters had found on Melos. If the artist had carved a male, Rhys could have been the perfect model. His face. The stance. Unmoving.

She trailed her hand up, turning the palm so that the back of her knuckles moved past his cravat and caught the slightest bit of roughness on his cheek. He was strong enough to have moved away at any time, but she knew he couldn't. His eyes closed. The back of her fingers stroked his chin. His lashes rested just above her touch.

With the lightness of a feather, his fingers clasped over her wrist. Eyes still shut, he pulled her hand away. 'You must go to Warrington's estate.'

Slowly, his eyes opened. Her heart crashed alive in her body, flooding her with such pounding she could hardly take in air.

She had an arrow, of sorts, and she carefully aimed it. 'When I do, your mother has said there is a kind vicar…that you provide a living for…who might be looking for a wife. I should meet him.'

His lips barely moved as he spoke. 'I will see that he calls on you.'

'You do not have to. I will.'

She pulled back from his grasp but she couldn't walk to the door.

His body remained still, but his gaze didn't. The thoughts she couldn't touch were there, showing in his eyes.

It wasn't fear of dying without him that overtook her when she looked into the brown, but the truth of living without his touch. And she took the strength he used to stand still and captured it in her body to stand there immobile.

His hand reached to her face, but she flicked her head back out of reach.

'You must not forget, I'm not an English society miss,' she said, 'which your mother tells me is important to you. I have tried for two years to want to be one and I see I am not, and will never be. I will be always free. I may not be a lady by birth, but I *am* worthy to walk the same earth as you.'

'You are.'

'I saw my mother cry when my father left us and I swore I would never beg for a man's attentions. I would have them freely or not at all. Whether he is a vicar or a soldier or a carriage maker, I will find a man who falls to his knees and thanks the heavens for me. And when he speaks words to me, they will be true. How I feel for him is not so important—as how he thinks of me. I am not a goddess. I do not wish him to think I am such. But he will have me in his heart as if I am.'

'I would like to see you with your hair down…' His voice was a whisper with a rumble that could only come from a man's throat and hardly touched the air, but swirled around her at all sides, as if an artist with a thousand brushes had taken her as his canvas and danced his brushes lightly over her body.

She pulled one pin from her hair.

He took it and held it between them, letting it linger in their vision, and she couldn't take her eyes from the fingers that held it so lightly.

'Your hair always looks as if your next movement will tumble the locks around your shoulders. I catch myself holding my breath, waiting. The wisps dance with your body, but the rest of it stays, looking soft and...like you. But even with the pin removed—' instead of returning the clasp to its place he palmed it '—it doesn't fall.'

His hand fell away, as if he'd forgotten what it held. His gaze moved over her tresses before returning to her face. 'A meadow. Did you know, it is always as if meadows or forests surround you? When I was a child, I would lie in the grass and look up at the puffs of clouds, and then close my eyes. Sunshine warmed my face. The grass softened the ground beneath me.

'The world had the same scent of an oak leaf held to my nose. At that moment, if a bird flew over me, it was as if its wings brushed my face and I was alive and everything was quiet in a way it had never been before. I could feel the poetry of the world and now that same verse surrounds you. I can feel the warmth of your hair against this pin.'

She reached out, putting her palm on his chest, cloth caressing her fingers. 'You have been reading—too much of that man who writes about women walking softly at night. Byron.'

'I would never say you walk softly in the night. *"She walks in beauty like the night..."'* His eyes flicked back to her face. 'Those words I do recall and they do apply.

I'm sure there's more after that, but when I look at you, I cannot even remember who I am.'

She stood so close she could even see the way his pupils seemed to fade into a softer colour at the edge. But she could not see herself reflected. She shook her head. 'I do not think Byron knows the true meaning of love either. Words. Perhaps that is why I have had so much trouble thinking of reading. It is bad enough when false words are spoken. To put them down on paper is even worse.'

'I admit, words do not do you justice.'

She stood immobile, and one edge of his mouth moved up. He took a step and reached up, and both his hands went to loosen her hair and she felt strands against her skin. Finally, her hair fell around her shoulders as he stepped away, but he wasn't truly moving from her. He was using his eyes to remain close, looking at her lustrous hair.

Taking her hand, holding it open, he dropped the pins into it. Then he closed his fingers over hers and pulled them up, dropping a kiss over her knuckles.

She put the pins on the table and stood with her back to him. The mirror reflected from his shoulders to his waist.

She took a breath, watching him worry the edge of his sleeve in his opposite hand. Then he straightened his fingers, flexed one hand, relaxed it and ran his forefinger along his opposing thumb, softly brushing back and forth.

She couldn't take her eyes from the mirror.

'If I were to choose one minute in my life,' he said, 'to live over and over again, it would be this one.'

'You say all the right words—almost…'

'I know. I say the easy ones. How hard can it be to tell a woman she is beautiful?' His fingers slowed, curling into a soft, unmoving clutch.

'But you are honest to us both.'

'A man must be more than his wishes, his dreams. He must set his path and follow it. He cannot let himself be swayed by what…he desires.'

'Words of your father.'

His reflection tensed, but his words held no emotion. 'True words. Words I believe.'

'I know. And I do not know if I hate you or love you.'

'Perhaps it would be best if you hated me.'

'I have seen how love withers when a man marries a woman who cannot follow him in his life,' she said. 'I know I am not your idea of a duchess and living that life is not what I see for myself. This simple room is how I wish to live. I am like my mother, except I know not to walk her path.'

'What are you trying to say?'

'Do not think if you lie with me, there will be a wedding to follow. I would not be compromised. I do not have to bow my spirit to anyone. The dowry I have has made that true for me. I do not have to listen to your society's rules and I am not staying in London either. I will find a small place and have a simple life. I will plant my own flowers and cook my own meals. I will work side by side with my husband to make a home that is ours alone.'

She stopped watching his reflection in the washstand mirror and turned, examining his eyes. Her lips turned up, but it didn't feel like a smile. 'I suppose I will feel differently when you leave tomorrow to find your duchess. But today I love you.'

Her lips were soft under his. She tasted of nature. Perhaps it was the spiced scent which always seemed to cling to her, or perhaps it was because she was so different from the women of his past and future. But he didn't care about the reason. Just for a few moments he wanted to experience her.

She clutched at him, pulling him to her. He ended the kiss too soon, leaving their faces pressed cheek to cheek, feeling their breaths mingle. Then he sat on the bed and took her by the bottom, skirts and all, pushing them up just enough so he could sit her astride him. He kissed her again and ran his fingers up her back, through the thin material of her gown, until he touched one of her shoulders. The feel of her under his hand captivated him.

He buried his face in the cleft of her bodice, awash in the heavenly sinful friction of cloth covering soft, delicate skin.

Keeping his lips against her skin for all but the briefest moment, he slipped the shoulders down on her gown, revealing a corset contrasting against the flesh that blossomed over the top of the stiff fabric. Her breasts, like her hair, barely stayed in their constraints, as if waiting for the smallest movement to free them.

Hooks unclasped under his fingertips. The corset ties hardly needed a tug, and when she stirred against him, the corset fell open and the chemise had already slid down her shoulders.

As he removed her clothes she slipped from one form to the next, becoming a woman from another land, a world he'd never seen, and a magical being, female, feminine and with the ability to hold him captive with her spirit.

His hands grazed over her back, taking strength from her body, filling him with a sense of power. She arched against him.

He had not known it could be like this. To be inside this realm of another person, gaining strength from them.

She increased the distance between them just enough to capture this moment in her vision. To see him. His eyes were shut. Defenceless. Innocent. Never had she seen such a captivated look on a man's face. His nose, aquiline, and lips, soft. She moved, brushing her forefinger over them, and he kissed her and kept one arm at her waist while he pulled back the counterpane and watched as she slid into the bed.

He swept the coat from his shoulders, removed his waistcoat and pulled the cravat away in a silken whoosh. He whipped his shirt up and over his head— stopping her breathing for a minute. He tossed the garment aside. For half a second he stood motionless.

He sat beside her and the narrow bed, not made for two people, sagged with his presence. She placed her hand in the very small of his back, savouring the feel of his muscles beneath her fingertips while he tugged at his boots and then his stockings. The buff doeskin slid from his legs and he lay almost over her, propping himself on his elbows to keep his full weight from her, skin heating skin.

He kissed her and she could taste him, and her heart beat stronger, igniting the volcanic smoulder inside her. Her blood transformed into a lava heat, seeming to flow from her body through his body and returning to her.

His legs melded with hers, and his whole body surrounded her. The shaving spice on his skin mixed with the barest hint of wood smoke and she didn't know what kept her from actually igniting.

He twisted to his side, pulling her almost from the bed and into his complete grasp. The pillow slid to one side of the floor and the coverings to the other. The bed had no room for anything but them. His every movement against her increased the deepness of her breathing, and sent her higher into a cloud of pleasure. Molten.

Fingers explored her, claiming each curve of her body, and the feeling of his hand rolled over her so that even the places he did not reach responded as if he had caressed them.

He touched her softness, her wetness, and she erupted into spasms, lost to everything.

Rhys sat with his shoulders against the bed frame, looking at Bellona. Her hair wreathed around her— more appealing than any he'd ever seen graced with a tiara. He tapped her chin when she closed her eyes and let his knuckles rest at her arm when she looked up at him—sated, he hoped.

Twining his fingers through her hair, he lifted it and

let the locks slide free. The second time, he brought them to his face, the delicate ends caressing his cheek. Savouring every strand.

And then something clattered outside the door, hitting the wood.

He knifed his body around, jerking the counterpane from the floor to toss the covering over her, and when he did his elbow hit the washstand, jarring it, skittering the mirror over, and the glass clattered to the floor. The fabric slid in place, partly, just as the door opened.

But it wasn't the aged housekeeper's head, the one with discreet quiet acceptance in her demeanour, who peeked around the door, but one of the underservants holding a wooden pail. Peering in with a question in her eyes.

Her expression changing, her eyes opened wide and her mouth fell into what appeared to be a near scream, but came out as a strangled gasp.

No, of course it could not be the housekeeper, a woman known for her silence.

He closed his lips and watched as the thoughts behind the girl's eyes embedded the scene before her into her mind for ever.

'Leave,' Rhys commanded.

The girl nodded, gave a gasped 'yes' with the uptake of her head and then she snapped shut the door.

He swore, words he'd never said in front of any female before, and the moment they fell from his lips, he knew as Bellona's head turned to him. He saw a different look in her eyes and he much preferred the servant's shocked gaze to the black one befitting a coiled snake about to strike.

He blinked to gather his thoughts because his next words were so very important, but before he could speak them, she pulled ever so slightly from his side. Her eyes. He'd never seen a darker stare.

Chapter Sixteen

Her hands clenched. Trapped. But she would not be snared. She had lain with him, knowing he would go to London and she had not once asked him to stay. She had wished him well. She had been in his bed and then he swore when they were discovered.

He was not the one who would be destroyed by their actions becoming common knowledge and he well knew it. She was. But he swore. Because now he must do the right thing and offer for her hand. She'd seen how a man could be a treacherous husband and father when he did not wish to be wed. Her father had followed the dictates of his body and had then been angered because he blamed her mother for his lust.

'So, Your Grace, this is a first for you as well.' Soft words.

'In a sense.' Controlled, he said, 'I will instruct her that she is not to speak of this.'

'You may instruct her,' Bellona said calmly, 'but you know how the talk will travel. By the time we have dressed it will already be flying around the estate.'

'We will marry.'

'I would not wed you if you were the last duke on earth.' She reached for the pins at the bedside and in one quick twist she'd secured her hair and pinned it almost in place. She pulled the covers around her and moved from the bed. 'I can do better.'

'The Prince is taken.'

'I am not talking of rank, as you very well know. You trapped me like a hare.'

'No. I do not have to do something like that to get a wife and you know it. I can wed any one of a score of women. A fortnight of courtship and a proposal and I would be married.'

The words buzzed in her head so loud she could hardly think to form her own thoughts. They were true, but for him to speak them, unforgivable.

'Yes. But I am here. You desire me. Your head tells you I am the wrong woman, but your body does not care. And now you think I have no choice. That I must marry you because my reputation will be soiled for ever. You also have no choice—you can say that later, too.'

'No.'

'You heard the maid and you knocked the mirror askew.'

'That was an accident.'

'Accident.' She followed with an expressive gesture. 'That is what I think of your accident.'

He jumped to his feet. 'You cannot for one moment believe I did this to trap you.'

'Oh—' she shrugged '—why should I not? You had a brief moment to think and you didn't. You acted.' She cocked her head to the side.

'You are wrong.'

'I refuse. Refuse. Refuse. To let my children think their father was forced into marriage with me.' She could not control her voice. Let the world hear. 'That he purchased me in his own way. Oh, I have seen that. How many *drachmas* am I worth? Five hundred. Oh, but you have much more money. A thousand, then. And will you shout at me in front of my children to tell me how you paid too much for me? No, you will not.'

His voice softened. 'I would not.'

'No, you will not.'

She stood, securing the coverings, a Grecian goddess draped in white, as in times of old, proud as any statue. She brushed a tangle of hair from her lips.

'I will walk naked down St James's Street before I turn my back on my heritage and before I am trapped into a marriage I don't want.' She swirled the cloth and controlled her words. 'But thank you for asking.'

He inclined his head to her and reached for his own clothing, thankful she did not have a spear and that her bow and arrows had not been returned to her. That was the only thing from this situation which he could be happy with.

'I—'

Her words cut across his before he could finish. 'I will say, *Stubble it, Your Grace.* Or perhaps, *Rolleston, hold your tongue*, seeing that I can only call you Rhys when we are alone because we have no ties at all.'

'Except the ties of marriage,' he added.

'And this is written where?'

If he did not tread very carefully, he knew that not only the servants, but the tongues of the *ton* would get more than a splash or two of *on dits*. This would make the notorious tales of Lady Lamb fall by the wayside. He slipped on the trousers that had been dropped beside the bed. He picked up the shirt he'd tossed to the floor and donned it. She stood draped in rough-woven bedclothes, and the small amount of light found her, sparkling on the earrings, cloaking her regally.

'In society's eyes,' he said, 'you'll be able to wed no vicar now. You will be a woman known to have been… been in my bed…in the servants' quarters…'

'What about you, Your Grace? If you ask another to wed you too soon, what will you think of her if she says yes? She will be marrying only your title. Your funds. Your estate.'

He continued with his shirt and trousers. 'Warrington will insist on our marriage. Your sister, the countess, will expect it. I will acquire a special licence before first light tomorrow morning.' He held his boot and sat on the bed. He stared at the leather. 'With Warrington and I both in accord, we can have this completed by nightfall. It is not unheard of for a man and woman to share a bed on their wedding day.'

'This is not my wedding day.'

He raised his eyes…waiting.

She smiled. At least her lips did. Her eyes, not at all.

'Yes. It is.' He paused, seeing steel in her face. 'You cannot…' He paused. 'You cannot *refuse*. Warrington has control of your dowry.'

'Yes. Warrington has control of my dowry. I cannot get it at the moment, but I am sure he will give it to me eventually. That was a mistake my father's wife regrets. She has promised she will correct it very soon.'

He knew where this was going. 'And your father's wife…'

Her shoulders flicked up and then down. 'We have talked. Her relative has the wealth so that my father cannot touch it. It was done that way before her father died because he did not want his money in the hands of her husband, my father. My father's wife can do exactly as she pleases because her cousin moves the funds as she instructs. And when I told her in the past of my wish to be free…' Her chin tilted. She might not have a spear in her hands but she could use her words as one. She tossed the words out and they landed as a challenge. 'My father's wife understands. She understands my need to make sure I am safe at night and that no man can get near me if I choose not to let him. She has a spinster aunt in Scotland. My father's wife owns the house and she would like me to live there with her aunt. That is who I spoke of before.'

'Bellona. You must be my wife.' He looked at his boots again. The floor. The crumpled neckcloth. The waistcoat lying beside it, but even they did not make sense to him now. Could she not understand? Did she not know how many ambitious mothers would put their daughters before him—a virginal sacrifice the daughters would willingly become? His wife would be getting the same life of wealth he shared. The same deference from the whole of society. It was the way of the world. He had no more choice in it than they did.

'I will cherish that request—those words—just as I cherished the words in the books I sold to the sailor.'

'It isn't a request as you well know.'

'And I am not refusing you.' She swept the cover

around her as she turned, her cape of bedclothes swirling, and he realised she was about to walk out of the room into the servants' area clad as a heathen goddess. He did not think she would walk quickly up the stairs. Oh, no. She would possibly meander. Every servant in the area was going to get to see her dressed like this.

'I am merely taking a lifetime to decide. You may wait patiently for my answer.' She opened the door wide and he was suddenly thankful he was mostly dressed.

She pointed to the floor. 'I will be sending someone for the dress.' She indicated the clothing he had removed from her body. 'Please do not let it be misplaced as I will be directing a servant to this room.' Her eyes. No woman had ever looked at him in such a way.

'You cannot go about like that,' he commanded.

The door closed on his words.

The mirror lay at his feet. Unbroken. He picked it up. Hair mussed. No cravat. He looked more heathen than she did.

He slung the mirror on to the bed behind him, put on his boots, kicked the pillow into the wall and looked around the room. Let the servants talk.

For the first time in his life, he was thankful his father was no longer alive.

Chapter Seventeen

Bellona bypassed the servants' stairs, fearing her covering might get caught in her feet on the narrow climb. In the main stairway, she bundled the covers closer and moved towards the family rooms. She reached the top in time to see the duchess open a door and stand with her hand at her neck, and a bruise on her forehead.

'I heard such shouting…' the duchess said.

The woman was not picking good times to leave her room.

Her eyes closed, opened, and then closed again briefly as she spoke the first words. 'My dear, you appear dishevelled.'

Bellona nodded. 'Yes.'

'As if you have been…' The duchess swallowed, examining her.

Bellona met the older woman's eyes. 'I was thinking of taking a bath.'

'It is always sensible to disrobe on such an occasion.'

'I should also like a carriage readied…' Bellona paused. 'I will be returning to Whitegate.'

'I agree.' The duchess nodded. 'But might I speak with you first?'

The duchess stepped back inside the door, keeping her hand on the wood. Bellona followed and sat, pulling the covering with her, kicking it with her feet to clear it from the pathway.

After shutting the door, the duchess stood across from Bellona. 'And should I...should I assume you have been walking about my house like this? And perhaps even been seen?'

'Yes. I heard the butler sputter just now so perhaps he saw me.'

'Were you bathing alone?'

'No.'

'Is there to be a marriage?'

'No.'

'My dear. Even being able to read, dance and embroider adequately will not rescue you from such actions if there is not to be a wedding.' The older woman's head tilted low, but her eyes remained straight ahead. 'You have no choice. You rather agreed to that when you decided to bathe.'

'No.'

'We must consider all options.'

'I am only considering the ones which do not include your son.'

She swayed and grasped the wall. 'It is worse than I feared. Rhys. Rhys saw you dressed such?'

'I assume he saw me quite well.'

'In the servants' quarters? The duke was with you in the servants' quarters?' She panted. 'Well, you certainly made a fine kettle of fish. To trap him into marriage is one thing. *But in the servants' quarters?*' She made a fist. Her eyes narrowed in a way that said she could have easily tipped a boiling cauldron on to Bellona's head. 'I should never have let you step foot in this house. You planned this all along.'

'Not all along. I waited until after I had met him.'

'So you *bathed* with a duke and then walked around in view of the whole household?'

'Yes.'

'Well, that explains nothing.'

'A maid did not knock…when I was unclothed. The bath was not a private matter any longer.'

'Did you pay her to open the door? In all my years a maid has never interrupted my bath. Possibly because a decent woman knows to bathe at night.'

'So do all decent men.'

The duchess raised her hand and reached for the bell. 'Do not move. I will send for your clothes to be packed. You will not believe how fast the servants can have the carriage readied when I am on a tear. You can dress or not for the carriage ride. It hardly matters.' The duchess's hand stopped. She struggled for words. 'And there could be a little…' She blinked. 'Have you and Rhys been *bathing* together…regularly?'

'I would not speak of such things with his *mana*.'

'Nonsense. I *am* his *mother*. It is not as if I did not instruct his father how to handle that little indiscretion Rhys had with one of the servants.' Her eyes narrowed and, this time, she used one finger to jab her own chest. 'And I was *wed* to *his* father and that shackle had to be kept clamped on *his* leg.'

'The duke and I have agreed not to marry.'

Rhys walked swiftly through the doorway, the door knocking back against the wood. His cravat was looped in the most unsettling knot Bellona had ever seen. His hair had somewhat returned to its place and his waistcoat was buttoned. He had her clothing draped over his arm.

'Mother, Bellona and I are betrothed. We must go immediately for the special licence.' He looked at Bellona's covering, took in a full breath and held out the dress. 'And she forgot what she was to wear—in her excitement over the marriage.'

'Rhys,' his mother said, voice high. 'We have more rooms on the upper floors than can be counted. You could have been in one of those where you wouldn't be seen. I cannot believe this of you. I cannot believe it of *her.*'

'However, it is done. Bellona and I are to be married. I have sent the maid to instruct the carriage to be prepared. Mother, please start writing notes to all your friends telling them how I could not wait a moment longer to make her my wife.'

'*Never.* I don't need grandchildren after all. In fact, I've decided I don't like babies at all. They're never well mannered. Cast up their accounts. Spit on silk. Then they grow up and—it—gets worse.'

Bellona took the chance to turn to the door, but Rhys was between her and the exit.

He spoke softly. 'We must wed.'

'I have never heard of so many proposals in one day.' She spoke more words, in Greek, and from the tightening of his eyes, he had certainly learned those from his tutor.

'Bellona. Consider…what we have done.' His words were soft and his eyes gentle, but she had heard the harsh tone from him when the maid had opened the door. The one that came from his heart. That one she agreed with.

'I am not thinking of the past,' he said. 'I am thinking of the future.'

'Mine is in Scotland,' Bellona announced.

'Sometimes travelling is very good for you,' his mother grumbled. 'It is a pity it just did not start soon enough.' She held her hands up. 'And none of this would have happened if not for my fall.'

'I must go.' Bellona struggled to reach out her hand while keeping her breasts covered. 'I need...the dress...'

He moved forward and she extended her hand, taking care not to hold it out too far. He placed the garment near her and she fumbled to hold everything together. He frowned, waiting while she managed.

'I would have liked to have wed you, Your Grace,' she said. 'But—you will spend your days looking at me as if I am less than you. As if I trapped you.' She shook her head. 'I knew every moment we were together you did not plan to marry me. Only because of the maid outside the door did you finally consider it.'

'Rhys. Did you not learn anything from that past indiscretion with the servant?' his mother asked. 'Did your father not explain the word *mistress* means to pay and go away? One does not soil one's own home.'

He frowned at her. 'It is not like that, Mother.'

'You took advantage of Bellona.' The duchess swept forward as if she'd suddenly gained strength from all the disappointed mothers of the world, the silver knot of her hair shaking as she walked to him. 'You took advantage of...a woman practically alone in the world and her supposedly under my guidance and care. I can forgive her more easily than I can you.' She stared. 'You were not raised to behave like this.' With each word her voice strengthened. 'You know better. I cannot believe you did this.'

She stopped in front of him. Her hand swung out, palm open, and she slapped his cheek. 'Get out of my house.'

He didn't flinch and his expression did not change. 'As you wish, Mother.' He turned and left.

The loudest thing in the room was Bellona's thoughts. The duchess had her head averted and stood away from her.

'It wasn't like you think,' Bellona said to the duchess finally. 'He didn't take advantage of me. I needed... I wanted...'

'Do not say it. The two of you created this wrangle and I cannot slap you because you are not my child.' The duchess sighed. 'The only thing I want to hear from you is that you will leave immediately.'

'If the servant hadn't heard Rhys drop something in the room and walked in to discover what made the noise, no one would know. Nothing would have changed.'

The duchess turned to Bellona and the lines at her eyes and mouth had deepened. 'And if the black plague hadn't happened—well, then we would have missed all that death and dying.' She put a hand to her chest. 'I would not usually compare this to the destruction of so many lives, but right now, it feels about the same to me. Get dressed. I have had enough of being a mother for one day. For one lifetime. I am going to have some wine and lie down. And *if* I wish to speak with you when I wake up, I will take a carriage to visit you at Whitegate.' She made a flitting movement with her hand, as if sweeping Bellona out through the door. 'I would not stand by the door and wait if I were you.'

Rhys sat at his desk, examining the black-ink mark Bellona had made on the page he'd kept. One smear, with another beside it. A heart, or rather two halves of one. Not joined. He tried to find the right oath for how he felt. There simply wasn't one strong enough and even stringing all the ones he knew together hadn't worked. Whoever invented swearing did not make words strong enough.

His father had once said that being a duke was no different from anyone else except one had to always appear perfect. Wise words. Not quite accurate, however.

His father did not mention days when one did not know exactly how one could be so imperfect and not decipher any of it. He could not jump over a broom and then try to leap back to undo the action because then two errors had been made.

'Your Grace.' A footman stood at the doorway. 'The carriage is readied as you requested and Miss Cherroll—' His gaze dropped. 'She is also asking to be taken to Whitegate.'

Rhys felt no surprise. If he did not miss his guess from the flustered servants who had been darting to and fro, his mother was trying to manage the tales to reflect her family in the best light. Bellona would not fare well.

But he would change that. 'We will travel together,' he said. 'Let her know the vehicle is ready.'

The footman darted away.

Rhys stood and walked to the front of the house. He stepped outside and into the carriage. In a few moments, the door was opened. Bellona was half-inside the carriage when she saw him. She halted, but then continued and sat beside him, or rather as close to the other side of the carriage as she could get. She pulled her reticule into her lap and crossed her arms over it.

'Lovely dress,' he commented.

'Thank you for returning it.'

'I see your reticule does not have a blade poking from it.' The carriage jolted forward.

She ignored him.

'Are you going to London?' she asked.

'Eventually.'

'I'm going north.' She looked out of the window.

'Not in this carriage.'

'I do not need your carriage. I must tell my sister goodbye and arrange the trip.'

He grunted. Warrington might have other ideas. And he wagered her sister would as well.

'Are you…wearing a weapon anywhere about your person?' He watched her face carefully.

'Will I need one?' she asked. She didn't turn from the window.

'I might wish to borrow it from you. I don't think Warrington is going to be pleased when he hears of the recent…events.'

'I expect him to be more upset when he discovers his carriage missing and on the way to Scotland.'

'Bellona. Do not be surprised if he is aware something has happened before you even arrive. My mother had many servants scurrying to make sure she got in her side of the story first.'

'No.' Her head snapped around. 'Surely the news… would not travel that fast.'

'I think it moved as fast as it could be written on paper and carried through the woods by the fastest runner at Harling House. Accept that we are to be married.'

'I accept that *you* are to be married. That is no surprise to anyone. You have no choice, Your Grace.' She smiled and touched her earring. 'I do.'

He studied her. 'Well, it is best I find out your disagreeability before we wed. I would hate to be surprised.' He studied his palm before glancing at her. 'Again.'

He was not sure he wanted any wife at the moment. A woman could appear as sweet as the finest confectionery, but then one error at the wrong moment and she stubbornly refused to do the sensible thing and correct it.

'You know that no one can force me to marry you.'

'Fine. That might be safest,' he said. 'Don't marry me. But Warrington will not be pleased. Your sister will not be pleased. Your niece and nephews will miss you.'

'I can write enough words now to send them letters. It is how I will practise.' She tapped her hand to her head. 'Thank you for helping me read. It will be very useful now.'

The face which had been so soft in his hands earlier had changed. Her eyes no longer had the sparkle he'd seen in them before.

He tried to think how he would advise someone else to sort out this problem, after he'd told them they were an arse for getting in such a bramble.

Fine. He knew he'd been foolish, but he couldn't condemn himself for that.

He glanced at his puckered palm, wondering if his senses had bled out with his humours. The memory of her would go with him to his grave. And *if* he ever needed to be reminded he could simply hold out his hand.

'I don't regret what we did, Bellona. I only regret the knowledge of it being something for people to whisper about. If you wed me, and continue in the ways of a duchess, then society will accept you well enough. Your sister, the countess, is quite adept at moving in society. You can be as well.'

'No. If you think because we are sisters, that we are similar, you are wrong. To be a sister means only the faces are near the same. Our thoughts are our own.'

'What is wrong with you that you do not relish the chance to put yourself in the highest tiers of society for ever? To wed me?'

'As I said, I can do better.' She spoke. Quiet words. His second slap of the day.

The carriage rolled up to Whitegate and she jumped out before the door was properly opened for her.

She ran towards the steps. He would not chase after her. At a sedate pace, he followed. The groom watched from the corner of his eye. The servants would discuss this tonight. At least she had looked lovely draped in bed clothing. He hoped that had been noted.

The butler opened the door for her and waited for Rhys.

Bellona was not in sight by the time Rhys crossed the threshold. 'Summon the earl,' he said to the servant.

'I do not think it is necessary, Your Grace.' The butler spoke in the distant way of a well-trained servant, showing no awareness in his face of any upheaval in the household. 'He dispatched a message summoning you at half-past and he did not speak quietly.'

Rhys brushed by the man, not waiting to be announced, and moved up the stairs as easily as if the home were his own. He slowed at the sitting-room door.

Bellona sat on the sofa, not speaking. Spine firm—lips the same.

Warrington stood, arms clasped behind his back, staring at a painting of the three children playing. One chair was overturned.

'Rhys.' Just the one softly spoken word. Warrington didn't move.

'War.' He paused. 'Would you like to travel with us to procure the special licence?'

The pop of Warrington's jaw preceded his answer. 'I don't think you need do so, Rhys.'

'Why?'

'No one will expect you to.'

Bellona's chin tilted a bit, defiant, but her knuckles were white as she gripped the reticule.

Rhys stepped inside and shut the door.

Warrington exhaled sharply. 'She tells me she led you to the room. When you suggested marriage, she refused.'

'I will leave England,' she said.

'You cannot run away from this, Bellona,' Rhys challenged.

'My sisters and I ran from Melos.' She shrugged. 'It has not turned out too badly for them.'

'It doesn't have to turn out badly for you either.' Rhys gestured with his right hand for emphasis.

Warrington's eyes locked on his palm. The earl gave a sharp intake of breath. 'Arrow?'

Rhys immediately dropped his hand, turning the wound away from the earl's gaze. He shook his head in answer and kept his eyes on Bellona. 'Do not make this worse for yourself.'

'I won't,' she said. 'I'm leaving.' She paused for a second. 'It will be best for you, too. You will not have to concern yourself that you could do better.'

'I have never said such a thing. You are the one who keeps saying that. Not me.'

'You don't have to.'

Warrington huffed. 'It is as if I have my children standing in front of me. You both need to listen.' He righted the chair, thumping the legs on the rug. 'I have known for a few days, but I hoped it would disappear. It hasn't. Lord Hawkins has been drinking. The man appears to be losing his mind—perhaps he is succumbing to some sort of illness. Unfortunately, it is also loosening his tongue. He claims Bellona has been trying to get money from him. Claiming she will say she is his daughter to discredit him unless he pays her.'

She jumped to her feet. 'He *is* my father. The funds have been organised by his wife and she gives them freely.'

'I know that,' Warrington said. 'But he is splattering every handful of mud he can in your direction.'

Chapter Eighteen

Warrington snorted. 'Don't look so…gutted, Rolleston.' Warrington's eyes narrowed. 'Neither my wife nor Bellona can help their birth. None of us can, *Your Grace*.'

Your Grace. He heard the sneer in Warrington's voice, but it reminded him of who he was. And he realised who Bellona was. He'd never cared about the *on dits* that Hawkins had a mistress he visited when he left England. When he found out Hawkins was Bellona's father he'd not really cared. But the truth had been secret for so long and now Hawkins was spouting it everywhere.

Warrington closed his mouth and paused before speaking to Bellona. 'Perhaps you should consider the special licence. Even Rhys can't change a marriage after the deed is done. His property joins mine. You would be close to Melina. And when Thessa returns from sea with Ben, you will be near to her as well. If you go away now to Scotland, it will be assumed there is a child. If you stay here and wed the duke—perhaps you can geld him.' He shrugged and gave a pointed look to Rhys's hand. 'Just a thought. I'm sure she'd eventually think of it on her own.'

'His Grace and I would not get on well.' She reached up, pushing an errant lock behind her ear. 'He doesn't even like the way I dress my hair.' She shrugged. 'He does not know how to live for himself, only for others. I do not know how to live that life. I have seen what happens to a woman who falls in love and marries a man when he does not love her back—or think her above his tracks in the dirt.'

'I would not treat you ill.' The duke's words bit into the air.

'But in your heart you would. Now you can promise—anything. Everything. That is easily done.' She looked across at him and slipped a pin from her hair, and tossed it to the table beside her. 'My father promised to return to my mother. He would hurry, he said.' She stared at Rhys. 'He promised most sincere *agape*, love, when he meant it the least. And do you know what my mother's last words were?'

Rhys blinked, forceful. Jaw firm. Solid, unmoving.

'She asked if my father was on the ship in the harbour. But he was not. He was never returning. I knew it.'

'You cannot judge other men by your father.'

'You judge other men by yours.'

He shook his head, causing a strand of hair to fall across his eyes. He put his hand to his temple and thrust the lock back into place. 'I know he was a stickler for convention. But that does not mean—' He used his flat palm to indicate himself. 'He *was* a good man and I can follow his example. All men make mistakes. Even him.'

'You made a mistake and now you must correct it?' She tilted her head.

'We must be married. You cannot hide away in Scotland.'

'I find it nobler to be a spinster than to throw myself under your feet. I do not care who you wed, Your Grace. As long as it isn't me.'

'You should tell him everything, Bellona. Rhys isn't worth much, but he can keep his counsel,' Warrington advised.

Bellona stared forward. Rhys thought she'd looked much gentler when she'd held the arrow to his stomach.

Warrington left the room, his grumbles mixed with curses at her father.

Rhys stood, his face with so little expression she could not read it. Behind his eyes he was secured alone with his thoughts and she suspected they were not charitable ones.

She refused to discuss any more of her life with him. Warrington said Rhys could keep silent, but the earl didn't realise Rhys was the one person she most did not wish to tell.

'We are finished here,' she said. 'You've done as much as you can to help me. You've tried to correct what you see as an error. You should go about your duties and remove this from your thoughts.'

'Remove it from my *thoughts*? And how might I do that?' He moved to stand in front of the painting and pointed to the smallest girl. 'If I wave my hand over the canvas, will it make the scene disappear? Will it make the memories I have go away?'

'Memories are the past. Thoughts are what are in a person's head at the moment. I do not care what you do with your memories. You may polish them until they outshine the sun. But do not keep me in your thoughts.'

He whirled from the painting to look at her. 'You think I am so uncaring a person that I can bed you in my home and just toss that aside.'

'Did you not do that to a woman once before—a servant?'

'Even that was not as simple as the way you speak of it. It was not.'

'My mother loved my father so much. And she thought she could not live without him. But he was not to stay and she died. Perhaps she spoke the truth of her love. Which showed me so much. The warmth faded from her body while my father painted. I was not with him, but I know—at the very moment my mother died, my father had a brush in his hand, a canvas in front of him and more concern about the light than my mother. She never meant more than being a subject for a painting to him.'

'He will pay for that.'

'He cannot. It cannot be done.'

'You do not have to worry about your father, Bellona. I can ensure he has a set-down. It will be his word against mine. You and I can face this together and it will never be more than a rumour. A tale we laugh away.'

'No.'

'He cannot spread such tales if we are wed. It will be ridiculous for him to do so. I will take care of him for you, Bellona. He cannot cross a duke and get away with it,' Rhys said.

'No. Do not add more coal to the fire.' Bellona shut her eyes. She should have left England earlier. Now her father would feel he had successfully chased her away if she left, but she did not know how she could stay and watch Rhys wed someone else.

'It is not about increasing the gossip. I will see that he ceases it altogether. We all have our weaknesses, Bellona. All of us. And I can find his.'

'Searching them out will not be hard. They flutter about him like birds over grain. I do not want you to be pulled into his mire. He relishes such things.'

'I will relish this.'

'Do not meddle. I am his daughter.' If she confronted her father, he could tell more truths. More truths she did not want known. She could not lie away the truth. 'His actions do not truly surprise me. I do not wish to be near him and he feels the same about me.' She ignored the way the air seemed to have the scent of her home again and she could hear the waves. 'I am so much his daughter that we cannot bear each other.' Rhys could not get involved in her past.

'You are not like Hawkins.'

'Oh, I am.' She put her hand over her heart and patted. 'I do not use mine to guide my actions. It is to beat and keep me alive, nothing else.' She shut her eyes. 'The letters my father sent my *mana*… My sister read them aloud to her so many times we could recite them. Such words of love. Tears in Mana's eyes. Hope in Melina's voice. Thessa and I would later go to the sea, fall on to the sand in front of the waters, and repeat the words, each of us speaking with all the sincerity we could bring to the speech. None of the fish ever changed the direction of their swimming. The waters continued on as before. Gold did not fall from the heavens. The words were worth nothing. They were not love to Mana. They were words for himself. A painting he created on paper instead of canvas.'

'Words may disappear into the air, but a special licence is binding.'

'My father married twice. Two too many times, but he married for a reason each time. His first wife's funds and my mother's beauty. I will not marry you for your title. Or for your protection of my name.'

'You cannot tell me you do not care for me.'

'No. I cannot. I would say I care for you more than anyone in London does. But no matter what feelings I have, one person's love in a marriage is not enough.'

Chapter Nineteen

She held out a hand to brace herself against the thoughts buffeting her, but nothing fell into her grasp. Rhys stood there, not speaking.

But his past gripped him as strongly as hers held her tight. She'd been marked on the outside and the inside.

Her mother might have called the spot on her body a longing mark, but it wasn't. The mark was her strength. A reminder not to repeat her mother's broken heart. All her father's children had the blemishes—her father's London wife had told her how each of her children had been born with similar marks. They were a legacy, just as a title was. But where her sisters had brown marks, hers had red in it—like a scrape, as if the blood had risen to the surface on her hip and never healed. A heart that was broken.

Now she truly believed that her mother had wished for a torn heart for her daughter.

Better to have a broken heart than a broken soul from loving someone who could not love her in return.

If she didn't turn her back on him in that instant, she would not have the strength to do it at all. She turned. She could not look at his face.

She left him behind.

Rushing up the stairs, she went to her sister's chamber, not knocking but running inside. Melina sat in there, her son's toy soldiers arranged on the table, and Willa stood at the side, moving the toy men into rows. A governess sat in a corner chair.

When Melina looked up, Willa ran to her aunt and wedged herself against Bellona. For a second, the hug erased the pain deep inside her, but then when she looked at the little girl's tousled curls and cherub cheeks, she realised she had given up her chance to have a child by the one man she loved. Sharp spasms of pain hit her body and she forced herself immobile to let the hurt pass.

Melina looked at her sister's face. 'Take Willa to play in the nursery,' she said to the governess.

'Warrington told me about Rhys.' Melina stood as the governess and Willa left. 'When you moved to Harling House to be a companion to the duchess, I knew you were taking a risk, but how could I warn you?'

'You could not have. I already knew. When I met Rhys in the forest, I knew. No one had ever unsettled me the same way he did.' She'd pointed the arrow tip at him to keep herself safe, but not in the way he'd thought at the time.

She couldn't stay at her sister's house. Rhys had even taken that from her. To see the children grow and watch her sister's family flourish while she stood on the outside looking in would wither her spirit. She had to leave.

'You will survive,' Melina said, walking to put an arm around her sister's shoulder.

'How would you know?'

'You have no other choice.' Melina reached out as if to pat Bellona, but instead pinched her sister's arm.

'Stop it.' Bellona pulled away.

Melina reached out, fingers poised to nip Bellona again.

Bellona took a step away. 'You had better not.'

'It is only because I care for you.'

'Do not let us get in a competition to see who loves the other the most. Your children do not need to see such behaviour.'

'If you do not want me to hurt you, then you must remember that you would not want a husband who does the same.'

'I know. My mind knows that.' She put her hands to her head, pushing back the hair that had fallen at her brow. 'But my head cannot find a way to tell my heart. I do not understand why it will not listen.'

The man of affairs still sat in front of him, patiently awaiting the return to his duties. Rhys didn't know how a man could smell of roses and be content in life, but Simpson seemed to have mastered that. Rhys felt he could kick the chair legs from under the man and he would receive only an apology from Simpson for having placed his chair in the wrong path.

Rhys's jaw hurt from keeping his words careful and precise and all emotion banked.

He began looking over the ledgers again. He spotted an error. One he'd made. He crossed it out, irritated. He couldn't have been paying attention to have made such an obvious mistake.

Voice ever so solicitous, the man of affairs said, 'I wish to speak with you about a private matter, concerning a bit of rubbish currently being batted about.'

Rhys nodded. Apparently the man of affairs had heard the *on dits*. Rhys could sense a change in the man—an awareness of unsaid things.

'So—' Rhys relaxed his body in the chair, interlaced his fingers behind his head, and fixed his eyes on Simpson '—what is the talk?' Might as well get the words on the table, so to speak, and then get on with things.

'Talk?' The voice was just a tiny amount too shrill. 'I would not call it that. Only small minds repeating things heard. Embellished, I'm sure.'

Rhys didn't speak, but let his eyes pull out the words. He waited. And in the same manner of a gust of air blowing over his body, he viewed his physical self. He'd never sat in a chair in such an informal way. Rhys put his feet flat on the floor, hands on the desk, straightened his back and leaned forward.

'It's said the dark-eyed foreign woman had wild ways, and you, well—' his head swiveled sideways '—did as a normal man would and partook of her favours.'

'That's all?'

'It's said she's even claimed to be that Lord Hawkins's daughter—the one who paints. Trying to disgrace him—though you know how he's viewed by the *ton* as full of himself and rather like a belch that's gone on too long.'

Rhys let his palms feel the smooth wood.

'And we all know,' he continued, 'that the sisters come from Grecian high-born people on an island where the French have been claiming treasures abound from the past. But people are supposing the youngest one is unsettled.'

Rhys's lips firmed and he glared at the man.

'You asked.'

'Yes, I did.' Five heartbeats of silence followed and Rhys reminded himself he had offered to wed Bellona. She had refused.

'One other thing.'

Rhys waited again, wanting to throw an inkpot at the man to hurry him and strangely upset at the thought that the man would not pick up the tossed inkpot and hurl it back.

'Lord Hawkins, he doesn't seem to be taking things well and is blaming the girl. He's said she's hurt his children with her tales.' The man put his fist loosely to his upper lip, as if to blunt what was said next, concentrating on his words. 'Of late, it's said he can't even get along with himself.'

Rhys only response was his usual flick of the brows.

Lord Hawkins wasn't cracked. He knew him. The man didn't have an *un*selfish bone in his body. He could lecture for hours on a bird's beak, as if no one but he could see it. As if everything he saw, he saw in brighter colours and with more meaning than mere humans could digest.

'He's not doing...' The man's words trailed away.

Rhys met his eyes and forced him to continue.

'He's not doing her any good at all, Your Grace. He's talking about her in a way no lord should talk about a girl who has been a guest at a duke's home.'

Rhys placed his right hand on the desk, above the

drawer, and knew that underneath lay a newspaper, with the words neatly printed, not only the reference to *a certain duke*, and most of the things his man of affairs had just said, but repeated several times, as if once wasn't enough.

Bellona was referred to as the Untamed Grecian Temptress from a land of Saturnalian delights, ready to leave a trail of women in tears as she danced about for their husbands.

The simple-lined caricature did not look like her, but a Gillray sketch, hair flowing as a brief covering swirling around her, while she held a tambourine, dancing. The goddess of beguilement. He hoped to be able to return a copy of the newspaper to the artist, personally.

'We're through for today,' Rhys said.

Simpson shuffled the papers together. 'You'll do fine, Your Grace.' He coughed. 'Not a life about doesn't have some struggle from time to time. You've just had more loss than most of recent. Time for a spell of good luck.'

Rhys waited until Simpson left and returned to his examination of the man's meticulous records. Truly, he wondered if Simpson hadn't managed better alone.

Rhys wanted to return his life to normal. To erase the impact of tales that might be told, before the whispers grew louder. To gauge the look in the faces of others and listen, and steer the conversation if they mentioned anything of the improprieties he had caused. But most of all he wanted to forget.

Folding his arms flat over his desk, he rested his head on them, closing his eyes and trying to trick himself into sleeping. In the night, whenever he'd lain in bed, his mind had darted alert, thinking of all the mistakes of the past few days, and the woman whose image he could not erase.

The sound of a rap on the door caused Rhys to raise his head. He brushed his hand over his eyes, uncertain of how long he'd slept. A servant stood there, holding a salver with a calling card.

Rhys straightened, and reached out. The tray was moved to him and he pulled the pasteboard card into view. Lord Hawkins. Bellona's father. He'd sent for him the day before. He tossed the card back on its resting place.

Rhys brushed a hand across his cheek, feeling the bristles.

The grimness of Jefferson's face alerted Rhys. Jefferson had been trained well. With just the briefest narrowing of his eyes, and the extra-precise steps he took as he moved backwards to the door, he told Rhys this was not a congenial guest.

'Show him to the sitting room,' Rhys said, 'and serve him cold tea. Collect me when he has reached a proper temperature to boil the water.' Rhys put his head back on the desk.

He felt he'd just shut his eyes when the sound of Jefferson clearing his throat woke Rhys.

He pushed himself up from the desk, stood, pulled his waistcoat smooth and reached for the coat he'd tossed on a chair, donning it.

'Would you care for a comb, Your Grace?' Jefferson asked.

Rhys shook his head and walked out through the

door, running a hand to smooth his hair, but not really caring.

When Rhys walked into his sitting room, the scent of a painting just completed lingered around the man, perhaps linseed oil or painting pigments.

Bellona's father sat, holding a cane, gnarled fingers grasping it, a birdlike flutter to his movements. It felt as if someone had left a raptor in the room and it had flown from place to place, leaving feathers and droppings about. A chair had been moved a bit. A tea cup sat half-empty with crumbs scattered. Rhys examined Hawkins's face, looking for a resemblance to Bellona. He saw none, except perhaps a bit of the chin. And they both tilted their head to the side when showing displeasure.

Hawkins stood. 'Rolleston.' His bow was more the semblance of movement than anything else. 'I have wasted near a day waiting on you.'

'Greetings to you as well, Lord Hawkins. I am going to make you pay for what you did to Bellona. It is nothing personal, you understand. It is justice. You left your daughters to fend alone. You left a family without funds to live in little more than a shack on an island while you lolled about here.'

'I did no such thing.' His lips twisted. 'My only family has always been in England.'

He thumped his walking stick on the floor. 'I hate Warrington for giving refuge to those women when he should have packed them back on the ships they arrived on.'

'They're your daughters, no matter how much you deny it. You know it and I know it.'

'I know no such thing.' He chuckled. 'It's possible I spent some time with their mother while I was away from home. So I can understand how they might be under the impression I am their father. Ridiculous as it is.'

'You make this easier for me.'

'You let her gull you. You couldn't keep your hands off her.' He frowned and looked to the ceiling. His voice softened. 'Not that I don't understand. I had the same problem with her mother. Couldn't leave the woman alone. I'd sail from Melos thinking I'd never see her again and then I'd go back. I couldn't stay away.'

'You were a married man.'

He chuckled, shrugging. 'Only slightly.'

'You are going to *only slightly* pay for deserting your daughters.'

Hawkins raised a pointed finger and softly shook it in the air. 'Oh, no, no, no. You cannot do a thing to me or I will remind everyone how you soiled her. I am no different from other men. I even kept my number of visits to the island to a reasonable amount.'

A flush of intensity blasted Rhys's body.

'You would do well to follow my example.' The voice hit Rhys's ears with a clatter that rang on and on.

Rhys's stomach churned cold.

Hawkins strode past Rhys. The walking stick brushed Rhys's leg. Hawkins looked back over his shoulder. 'She's been nothing but trouble since she arrived. Calling on my wife. Not settling into suitable English society as her sister did. She's nothing to me. My children—she let my *real* children see her. My daughter cried. Un…for…giv…able.' He dragged out the syllables as if he spoke four words.

Hawkins stopped in the doorway. 'And you…' He pointed the cane at the painting over the mantel. A work by Lawrence. 'Wouldn't know a good painting if you fell over it.'

Rhys didn't speak. He didn't want to give the man even the smallest response, afraid of what his voice might reveal.

Hawkins's walking stick crashed against the door frame. 'You lie to yourself, Rolleston. You think you're better than me, but you're not. Your brother was born to be duke—not you. If he'd been wise enough to wed and sire a son before he died, you'd be living off your nephew's whims. Now you toss crumbs about instead of scrabbling for them. Your dead brother's crumbs. I bet every morning you say a prayer of thanks that he died.'

Hawkins left, pulling the walking stick up and putting it under his arm.

Rhys didn't move.

The foundation of his life cracked, turning into rubble.

Chapter Twenty

Rhys went to a soirée. Louisa was there. She turned her shoulder to him when he walked near and relief surged along with guilt. The relief won when she danced twice with someone else and her eyes shone on her partner. Watching her, it was as if he'd never *seen* her before. This woman he'd hoped to marry, but had never really seen for who she was—because, he now realised, he'd never truly loved her.

He forced his attention to the man who was speaking to him, Lord Andrews.

Lord Andrews leaned closer, winking and smiling. 'So what of the bit of muslin you—?'

'Stop.' Thoughts pummelled Rhys from the inside, causing him to need a moment to sort through even half of them. 'I asked her to marry me. She refused.'

Lord Andrews stared. Rhys didn't think he'd ever looked at Lord Andrews properly either. The man was commanding, of fair face and quick-witted. Yet, Rhys would have compared him to a toad, waiting, watching for insects. They'd shared brandies more times than Rhys could count.

'I am pleased we spoke,' Rhys said. 'But I must be away.'

On his way to the door, he dropped the brandy glass he held on to a footman's tray.

He had to wait for his carriage outside, the unseasonably cool air brushing his face and waking him up to feel even more.

How many times had he truly looked at himself through his own eyes? Possibly never. He'd always used the eyes of others to gauge himself. His father. His older brother. His mother. The things he did privately were deemed to deserve no judgement. No censure. No introspection. After all, he was the second son. It did not matter. Nothing mattered until after Geoff died and then everything tilted in a different direction.

The town-coach door was opened. Rhys stepped inside and made himself comfortable. Even in darkness, he knew exactly what the crest on the door looked like. He'd had the colours corrected as they faded. But he didn't know the face of the man who'd held the door. Didn't know his name.

Rhys touched his cheek with his marred hand.

He had thought, when he'd first discovered that Bellona was not the offspring of someone in the Greek upper classes, that she was scarred by her birth. Perhaps in a way like the statue without arms the sisters had found on Melos. The one that Warrington had told him about and said the sisters thought an ancestor of theirs had posed for. Supposedly, the statue favoured their mother.

But blemishes and perfection did not always appear in the expected forms. The white line at the top of Bellona's nose made him want to kiss it. Her hair tumbling about called to him in a way perfection never would.

He was marred. Bellona had risen from a world of struggle and became someone of strength. He had been handed the world and only had to continue on the path already cleared for him, yet he'd been unable to choose the right steps. She'd made her own path and tossed her head back and fought with all her strength to survive, becoming stronger.

He'd become weaker. Softened by the world giving him his wishes as he indicated them. He supposed—but he would not wish to repeat it—if he had true strength, it had been gained when he'd watched Bellona follow the rules she created for herself.

The feeling of a funeral surrounded him, and now he felt he knew what it would be like to attend his own last service, and see the crypt surround him on all sides, with the grim knowledge that he had done this to himself.

Bellona sat in her room, the needle slowly going into the fabric and moving out on the other side. Her eyes not rising once. Holding the embroidery high into the light, she examined the stitches. She would be better letting the maid sew while she attended the washing. Cleaning she could do well, which no one wanted her to do. Embroidery, which everyone expected of her, was a tangle of threads.

If not for the war with the Turks, she would be wishing for a return to Greece. She couldn't safely sail to Melos now. Or ever. If she did, she'd not be able to see her nieces and nephews grow. She'd not see her sisters again.

Warrington's voice didn't carry through the walls any more. She wondered if her sister had finally quieted him or if his throat had simply given out from the exertion. This was the one time he seemed to have forgotten his rule about servants not hearing family matters.

She looked into the grate. Only ashes left. No more of the vile newsprint.

She wished for more words to burn. Burning the papers somehow seemed to ease the ache in her heart. She could not even look at the mark on her body any more. Once, it had made her feel stronger, the memory of her mother—a trace of the past. Now, even the blemish ached.

Just like her heart and all the rest of her that mattered.

Ruined. That word had carried through the walls a few times.

'She could not be more ruined.' That had spewed into the air and cloaked her with a feeling of being unwashed.

The needle jabbed her finger and she didn't spare her grumbles. She could be more ruined. Warrington was wrong to think otherwise. If not for her sister and niece and nephews, she would be finding out where the scandal sheets originated and marching there with the largest hammer she could beg from the stable master. The printer would be having a holiday from his work long enough for repairs. Then he could write about the angry woman who'd smashed his press and stopped him from being able to put his cruel words on paper.

Rhys could not be sailing easily through this either. He could not.

'A visitor for you.' Her sister spoke from the hall.

Bellona's heart pounded. Rhys. She thrust her sewing to the side.

The quick sideways shudder of her sister's head paused Bellona's movements.

'The duchess.' Melina frowned. 'She's…'

'She's in quite high dudgeon,' the duchess said, walking in behind Melina. Melina rolled her eyes and left.

The older woman's skin hardly covered the bones of her face.

'Embroidery again?' She walked closer, the black crepe of her skirt reminding Bellona of a raven's wings fluttering about. Her reticule matched the clothing and her bonnet completed the effect.

She peered at the sewing while opening her reticule. 'You should conquer reading first. Then dancing. Perhaps leave the sewing to someone else.'

She held up the folded paper and tossed it on to Bellona's sewing. 'I received this unsigned note, but I believe it is from Rhys's man of affairs.' She knotted the ties of her reticule. 'I believe the words are simple enough for you to make out. I brought it for your own good.'

'Your *kali thelisi*, good will to me, is kind.' Bellona forced her lips into a smile and refused to touch the paper, uncertain if she could read it. Refusing to let the duchess see her stumble. 'But I was going to send my sister to tell you I am not at home.'

'Oh, my,' the woman said. 'Neither am I. The stairs weakened my knees. I'll be in bed the rest of the week.'

'You shouldn't overtire yourself.'

'You'd like that, wouldn't you—if I left?'

'Yes. I don't wish to be near you.'

'The house is quiet without you. The servants seem to miss having you about. One of their own has left them.'

'Your maid was very kind to me.' Bellona glanced at the messy fabric beside her. If she'd known what was to happen, she would have stolen a piece of Melina's perfect embroidery and worked on it, pretending to complete it.

'I'm sure the staff here is also kind to you.' The duchess looked around the room. 'The maid does know where her loyalty lies, though.'

'As you know yours.'

'True. I do.' She held her head up, again reminding Bellona of a bird. 'I'm a duchess. I'm well suited to it. But I am a mother first and I only have one offspring left.' She sighed. 'Are you with child?'

'It is a little soon to know.' She shrugged. 'And when I do know, I will not inform you.'

'I will raise the child for you.' The duchess picked a bit of fluff from her gown.

'I will bear that in mind.'

'I'm excellent at selecting nursemaids. I have a gift for it.' She lowered her lids. 'I made sure my children had the best of governesses. Ones that suited them.'

'Perhaps you should have cared for the babies.'

The duchess frowned. 'Child. Think about it. If you were a babe, would you want me or a governess comforting your tears? I am not suited for that duty.' She raised a brow.

Definitely, Bellona would have chosen a servant. 'I see.'

'Even now, I know to put the needs of my son first and let someone else handle the task of giving him direction.' The duchess's chin bobbed. The lines at her eyes deepened. 'You must go to London and speak with Rhys. He's causing a disgrace to our name by lowering himself to squabble in public. He is not maintaining his dignity at all. You caused this by your presence and you can correct it.'

'But it would not be—'

'Proper?' the duchess inserted. 'Child. You two lost that chance already. I would hope that you could be a bit discreet. Perhaps leave your bow and arrows behind and travel in darkness.' She examined Bellona. 'I'll send a quiet servant with you and you can wear my veil and dark clothing. If anyone sees you, they'll assume I'm visiting him.'

Bellona didn't speak. She shook her head.

'It's not that I particularly like you,' the duchess continued. 'But I think I could—even though I cannot imagine you would ever be a true duchess. But I must have grandchildren and I want them now. There is only one way I know to get them and I will have to accept someone, so it may as well be you.' She shrugged. 'No one's good enough for him, but then no one was good enough for my daughter or Geoff either. You see where that has left me.'

She shook her head. 'I could accept someone as unschooled as you because of the grandchildren.' She leaned towards Bellona. 'I have decided I want the babies strong most of all. I want them to survive. You would have a spirited child.' She sniffed. 'You're tolerable for short lengths of time. And you sing well.'

'I doubt I would let my child meet you. Rhys is not going to be in my life again so you must pick out someone else to breed the next heir.'

The duchess chuckled. She examined Bellona toe to head.

Fingers splayed, the duchess put her palms together and then she interlaced her fingers. 'The butler did the unthinkable. He started a betting book with the staff concerning Rhys and you. Even taking in the possibility of an heir. I am not supposed to know of it, but my maid understands the importance of her duties.' She extended her forefingers towards Bellona. 'All sorts of wagers are being bandied about. I plan for my maid to do quite well. The maid has been informed that she is to wager on you marrying Rhys inside the month and that the first child will be a daughter, because I know you will do that just to spite me.'

'I liked you better when you were crying,' Bellona said.

'Well, child, you should have thought of that earlier. You should have thought about the consequences when you…bathed with my son. The butler has not yet recovered his senses or he would not have started the betting book.'

'You have no say in this.'

'Fine. But you need to alert Rhys that you mean nothing to him.' Unclasping her hands, she stood.

'I have.'

'You have not convinced him.'

'He's a grown man. He can do as he pleases.'

'Oh, he is,' the duchess said. She smiled. 'I have it on good authority—since the staff in London knows I must be informed of events—that an interesting tale could be bandied about at any day.'

'What about?' Bellona couldn't help herself.

The older woman's lips turned up. Bellona thought of Gigia.

'I shall win that wager,' the duchess said.

She didn't walk to the door like a woman with a sore knee. She looked back. 'My son has to have some tenderness for you or he would not be so bound on destroying your father.'

Bellona paused two steps from the room's entrance, listening as she brushed the black veil from her face. A murmuring voice, a male, answered Rhys's bursts of command.

She took a deep breath, moved to the doorway and saw Rhys and a smaller fellow. The diminutive man, face wan, needed a razor, although he had been near one much more recently than Rhys.

'Your Grace,' Bellona spoke, pulling Rhys's eyes to her.

His eyes showed no reaction to her presence. He stood. 'I beg forgiveness that I cannot entertain you. But as you can see we have much to finish.' Papers mounded his desk and a small stack rested on the rug.

She tossed her reticule into the empty chair. 'So no shop owner may dare exhibit any of my father's paintings or they will have the Duke of Rolleston's wrath visited upon them. Even the tradesmen are afraid to sell any artist's supplies to him, for fear of reprisal. His every step outside his house is noted, and should anyone extend any favourable notice to his art they are warned away.'

This time, his face turned directly towards her and his eyes sparked an inferno. Then he switched his attention to Simpson and the man jumped back in his chair. Even Bellona could see the guilt in the face of the man of affairs.

'Rolleston.' She snapped the word out, pulling his gaze. Even though she did not fear him, she didn't like the look he gave her—the calmness a bit too scorching.

'My dear. I am impressed.' Then he pointed a pen to his man of affairs. 'Simpson. For your tale-bearing you are let go without a reference.'

The man's jaw dropped and he gathered his papers as he stood.

She stepped back into the doorway, feet firm. 'Stop,' she commanded Simpson.

'Oh, I could not, miss.' He caught a paper that had slid from his fingers, grasping it before it hit the floor.

She put a hand out, palm against the wood. No one could move through the doorway without pushing her aside.

Simpson stood, looking at her, eyes wavering but feet immobile. 'Pardon, miss?' His eyes begged.

'Tell him,' she commanded the duke. 'Tell him there will be no repercussions for his actions.'

Words knifed the air. 'There will be.'

'Then he may wed me for my *proika, my* dowry.'

Rhys coughed. 'His wife will object.'

She shook her head in frustration. 'You cannot blame this man for his concern—if he did write to Harling House to mention your behaviour towards my father. You have a houseful of servants here and I have noticed that your staff at Harling House cares for you. Or perhaps they just fear the duchess and only pretend affection for you.'

'I am quite well, thank you.'

Her eyes raked over him, and she pressed her palm tightly against the door frame.

Well groomed, he looked like a duke and commanded a woman's attention in a discreet way. Unkempt, his appearance made a woman's hands beg to straighten his clothing. Or loosen it some more. His eyes looked into the depths of her being.

Rhys need never question whether a woman would only want him for his title and his wealth. But he should always question whether she wanted him only to pleasure her senses. The days Bellona had not seen him had taken her strength and weakened her for his touch.

Simpson needed to stay in the room. She needed to keep him there, for her own well-being. The granite in the duke's eyes told her he would not back down and she could not lose her strength.

'It's said you have been about town, seeing that no man near you has a parched throat, and you've been more affable than people are used to seeing.'

'I see no reason to hide from anyone. My life is my own. To live as I—' Then his breath swooshed on the last word, echoing it in her ears. 'As I wish.'

'Your cravat is a sight,' she said.

'Well, dash my wig,' he said, words light. 'And I have been wearing it in public all day.'

Silence dragged.

'Miss…' Simpson said tentatively. 'Might I pass by you?'

'Not until the matter of your employment is settled.'

'Simpson.' The duke's voice was a commanding boom. 'You will return in the morning to take up where we left off.'

The man took a tentative step towards Bellona.

She left her hand at the door.

'Bellona—' Rhys spoke low, voice curling about her '—must I toss him out of the window?'

Predatory eyes snared her, but she wasn't afraid. Well, not in the mortal sense, anyway.

Rhys made sure he truly looked at her. He needed to see past the hair, the memory of her body and the opinions of other people.

Her fingers slid from the wall and Simpson snaked out through the door before she had fully stepped aside.

'So you are here to tell me all that I have done wrong. You do not have to. I am well aware. More so than you, I suspect.' Rhys put the chair against the desk, but did not release the wood.

'You have enraged my father.'

On that he had not been blinded by any foolishness of his heart. On that one thing he knew he was absolutely right. 'Surely you cannot have concern for that man who did not even give you his true last name, but one he simply pulled from the air.'

'I have no care for him,' she said. 'But his wife has

been as kind to me as any *mana* would. I care for her. She suffers with him. It is the way of the world.'

'She's strong. She will survive.' He gave the chair an extra shove.

'If he shoots you, as it is said he has threatened, you might not.'

One side of his lips went up, a smirk. 'It is not in his best interest to be near me. If I die merely from choking on a bone, he will hang. If he does try to do me in and I live, he will be hanged. I have seen to that already.'

'You have convinced people to speak ill of his paintings.'

'I have viewed a considerable amount of them in the past few days as I visited most homes in London where I knew the owners had his drivel displayed. I could not help but notice the subtle flaws in his work, which of course, I asked about before I viewed them. I only spoke the truth. Had he not had the funds of his wife as his patron, he would not have been able to survive on what his paintings earn and he is certainly not worth notice as an artist. Not only my opinion, but the men I talked with.'

'It is in the scandal sheets that the Duke of R. mused about whether this artist painted with his toe or his elbow and suggested he be shown what a brush looks like.'

His lashes flicked down and then up. 'That is actually a compliment compared to what I truly think. They would not even improve the look of a dust bin.' He looked at her.

'Not all of them are that bad.'

'Enough are. Most are. Someone should have taken pity on him and broken his paintbrushes long ago.'

'You are trying to do so now.'

'Yes. The man had left you alone for years. He should have continued to do so.'

'You brought even more attention to the situation.'

'If I did not stand against him, I could not have lived with myself.'

His gaze locked on her so hard she might have become afraid, except something deeper behind his eyes showed a private agony. 'I would not have injured you for the world and yet I live with, every day, how I caused your name to be sullied.' He looked at the ring on his finger. The one passed from duke to duke.

He changed the direction of his gaze. 'What does the crest on my carriage look like?'

She shrugged.

'Tell me about the servants?'

Her eyes tightened. 'Why do you change what we are talking of?'

'Just tell me about the servants.'

'Fenton, I do not like at all. He broke the scullery maid's heart. Thompson makes sure to keep him in hand, though. He thinks of all the women on the staff as his daughters.'

'And the maids. What are their names?'

'Julia. Honour. Susan. Eliza, although she prefers to be called—'

'Enough.' He raised his hand.

'Yes. I know their names. I saw them daily at your house. How could I not?'

'That is just it. How could you not? I dare say you

have no thought of the art in the house which could fund a small country.'

'I do have some notion of the paintings on your walls,' she admitted. 'I have never imagined paintings could be so beautiful. Before I left the duchess, I walked through the house to view the art and that took her grief from my mind.' She lowered her chin for a moment before looking back at him. 'Days after I refused you, I realised I had turned away a chance to live with those works.' She shook her head as if she could not believe it.

His response was half-chuckle, half-snort. 'The art tempted you to say yes more than I did.'

She didn't answer.

To speak took more strength than he could immediately garner. Words choked inside him in a way they'd never constricted before. Then everything vanished from his mind except for what mattered most. 'I love you.'

Chapter Twenty-One

He'd not expected the deep intake of breath and the way her lids dropped causing her narrowed eyes to spear him.

He wondered if perhaps he'd been right to let his thoughts be directed by the opinions of others. He could not see what Bellona thought or meant or wanted.

'You say that. But you have not shown it. You have made things so much worse.' Quiet words from soft lips, but with fervour attached.

The words. He had to roll them around in his head to make certain he heard what she was saying.

He struggled to sort things in his mind and then he spoke again. 'I believe that my art collection is one of the best in a private residence anywhere in the world.' He watched her face. 'In case you are wondering.'

'Stubble it, Your Grace.'

'Yes, sweetness.'

She moved within arm's grasp and he could not help it. He moved enough to brush back the hair that had fallen to her temple.

The puff from her lips censured him, but she didn't retreat.

'You are trying to destroy my father and his family,' she said. 'You have no right.'

'I have every right.' She'd taken all his resistance to her and reduced him to the rank of a schoolboy. But then, she'd truly done that days ago. 'The man—he may not have meant to, but he could have caused your death. He left you on that island to fend for yourself.'

'You had no cause to interfere. I told you not to hurt him.'

'His arms and legs are all attached, as well as his head. I would say he is unhurt.'

'How my father treats me is my concern. I will deal with him, but how can I do that now when you have struck out at him and reduced him?'

'And just what were you going to do—thank him for nearly causing your death by deserting you on Melos with no food? Forcing you to use whatever means you might find to survive.'

Rhys was taken aback that she was not more grateful to him, but he didn't care. He cared that she was standing in his house and thought enough of her father's wife to be concerned.

'You are not my protector. You have no right to my life because we kissed.'

'We did more than just kiss, Bellona.'

'And the women before me—did you jump to their aid in this way, too?'

'They did not have such problems as you, but I did not abandon them without a thought. Perhaps the first I did not stand by when I was very young and that

cured me of the inability to do so again. I cannot hold
a woman near my heart and then forget she exists the
next day.'

'That is a poor excuse.'

'Really, sweet? I feel you owe me a bit of understanding. We shared something together I have never
shared with anyone else.'

She raised her brows.

He lifted his palm, the cut towards her. 'A very painful bloodletting. I should think you'd have some toler-
ance for me for that reason alone.'

'You know that was not intended.'

'Just as my actions towards your father are not intended to bear you any ill will.'

She shook her head. 'You have meddled.'

'Meddle? I did not meddle. The man, he needed to
be punished. Any man who can cause such harm to a
woman should suffer.' He stared at her. 'And you are here
now—why? To what purpose? I cannot undo anything
that has already happened.' He held his palm where he
could see it. He gave a dry chuckle. 'This memento. It
will never go away.' He raised his eyes. 'I suspect the
true mark you have left on me is not on my palm.'

'That does not give you the right to denigrate my
father.'

'I let him off lightly.'

'You destroyed him.'

'He still can sit at a fine table and drink fine wine.
I feel no pity for him.'

'You do not even tell yourself the truth.'

He turned from her, shaking his head, and then
faced her again. 'If someone strikes at me, Bellona,

they can expect me to strike back. It is the nature of the world. It is how one survives.'

'Revenge. That is what you did.'

Her words rasped against the inside of his skin. 'I make the heritage I will pass on to my children. With that in mind you can understand why it is so important I uphold the beliefs I hold close to me.'

He had upheld them. Most of them. Until his world had become fodder for the tongues of the *ton*. But he could trace his madness back one step further than that. When a woman had put an arrow tip to his stomach. 'I had thought to make amends to you by holding your father responsible for his actions,' he said.

She merely shook her head. 'You took away his belief in what he loves most.'

He whispered, 'What he loves most should be—*you*.' He walked forward. He grasped her arms. 'We have both abandoned you, Bellona. He and I.'

'No. I only thought I needed him. I did not. My life is better without him. I did not need his love. I did not. I did not need his presence in my childhood. I only needed food. The funds he did give us came from coin his wife had given him, though I did not know it at the time. When I had nothing, she agreed to give me a dowry, which I now have. She has been my friend even though she could view me with distaste. I do not want her hurt. And you have added to her disgrace. The woman who gave me all she could and asked for nothing. She has treated me with the same kindness as my own *mana*.'

Just like the chimes of the clock sounded too loud in his ears, Rhys heard the pounding of regret in his body.

He loved the woman who had taken away every

part of him he believed in and put a mirror in front of his soul.

'I did not tell you all the truth either. My father could hurt me even more and I did not want him to decide to tell you everything.' She stood in front of him and when she moved, the shoulder of her dress drooped. She pulled it back into place. 'My father came to Melos to paint my mother,' she said. 'He had heard tales of her beauty and of the island's. My mother had no funds and had been forced to sell her body so when my father decided to keep her she insisted he marry her. He did not mind the fact that he was already married. As far as he was concerned it was just words.'

Unthinkable.

The old duke would not even have welcomed Bellona as a guest in the house once he discovered her origins were so tainted. Her mother, selling her body, and her father a bigamist.

The tousled goddess stood in front of him and, like the shattered statue recovered from her homeland by the French, she was indeed more marred than only a dent on the bridge of her nose. But also perfect in a way he'd never seen.

'I don't care about your mother, your father or your grandmother.' Rhys reached out, his forefinger looped under a lock of her hair which barely remained constrained. He slipped the brown strands free. They fell to her shoulders. 'I wish I could be perfect for you. I'm not. Who your father married, or what your mother did to survive, does not matter to me.'

'Rhys, your mother told me how angry you were when a servant did not wear the proper livery once.'

'I was very young when that happened. I was trying to… I don't know what I was trying to do, but I was not acting as I should. That was not the correct way to handle it. I was in error. As I have been many times.'

He held out his left hand. 'Forgive me?'

She didn't step forward right away, but when her body swayed in his direction he moved to her.

'It is not idle words,' he said. 'I do not do that. It is not who I am. It is not what I believe in.'

He rested his forehead against hers. 'I am sorting out who am I to be. What I am to think. All I believed about myself has been a lie. I thought I could forgive myself anything. I was the second son. A second son did not have the responsibility of the first. I am still the second son by birth. I will always be, and yet I am the duke. The thing I wanted most of all, but knew I could not have. Knew I was not worthy of. If I married the perfect duchess, she would hide my flaws. Instead I found the woman who would show me my weakness. You hold it to my face, Bellona.'

'I do not. I would not do such a thing.'

He moved back. His eyebrows rose.

'I could be wrong on that,' she muttered. 'Before you met me, you imagined yourself too grand.'

'Yes. I did want to be grand. Every day I thought of my father and how he would act, or Geoff, and what he would do, and then I did as if they directed me. Mostly. Until you. I could not keep you from my thoughts.'

'What of the woman you courted?'

'She has not even missed me this past year nor I her. But, if I married a woman such as her, without my heart involved, it would be the same as your father did when he wed Lady Hawkins. He married the woman who could give him funds and increase his status, but he could not forget the island woman. I am like the man on the other island. The one in Defoe's book.'

'Crusoe.'

He shook his head. 'No. The one who lived to serve him. I can't be rescued without you, Bellona. I need you every moment of my day.'

'You do not think me good enough for society.'

'Bellona, it is not you that is not good enough. It is me. It was fine for me to be in a woman's bed if the doors remained closed. I felt no guilt at all. But the minute the door opened and others could see me for who I was—then it was different. I didn't ask for marriage to protect you. You were closer than I to that truth. *"Ah, the duke is caught with a woman, but of course His Grace married her. Noble man."'* His words were a sneer. *'"Sacrificed himself to protect a woman."'*

'It is no surprise to me. I told you near the same.'

'You may have told me, but I didn't listen.'

She curled into his chest. 'Put that as another flaw of yours. Along with not listening. But you are very appealing to the eyes...'

'You could not say, *Oh, Rhys, you are perfect just as you are.*' He couldn't help pushing her.

'I do not lie.'

He circled his arms around her, putting a soft kiss on her cool lips before moving back. 'You are here. Why not stay? As my wife?'

Eyes, darker than the darkest stone flickering in the bottom of a pool, looked up at him.

'How do I know you are different now than you were only a fortnight ago?'

He shook his head, letting her slip from his arms, but taking her hands in his. 'Perhaps I am not. Perhaps I cannot truly change. But now instead of using the eyes of my father and brother and mother to look at the world, I wish to use your eyes. I wish to see people the way you see them. Even how you see me.'

'I will think about it.'

'Take the time you need,' he said. 'I am not going anywhere.'

Quite without asking, she moved into his house with the same amount of fuss a mouse made when taking up residence. She found her own room and changed it as she wished. A chamber with the best light which now smelled of linseed oil and paints. She said she wanted a painting of her homeland and wanted to create it herself. He'd instantly sent for a tutor and she'd not said one word against the man.

No one could see evidence of her anywhere else about the house and he did not think she went out often, but contented herself in the room.

She did not come to him in the night. Not once. So finally he went to her. He could not help himself.

Rhys looked in her chamber. All her paints were scattered about and the canvas was there, but he could not find her and the hour was late.

He puffed a breath out through his nose, knowing it could not be a good thing for her to be gone. His jaw tightened.

Rhys returned to his bedchamber and summoned his valet.

'Your Grace?' the servant asked when he walked in through the doorway.

Rhys realised he'd been standing with his hand still on the pull. 'Miss Cherroll, is she about?' He released the rope.

The valet's long face became even longer. His words were spoken as he breathed out. 'I believe you are the only resident of the house, Your Grace. Miss Cherroll received a message and had to rush away.'

'Where did she go?'

'I believe Lord Hawkins has taken ill and she was called to his bedside. It is not certain if he will recover. If you are to request a carriage, I am to instruct you that her father's wife does not want attention called to the matter and it has been suggested that you not follow.'

Bellona stared at the face of her father, noting the bluish tone around his lips. Her oldest sister had already visited him—a quick discreet visit in the night. Their middle sister, Thessa, might never see him alive again because she was at sea. But the ship could dock any moment, or a year hence.

His condition was uncertain. She had asked his wife if she might stay a bit longer and her father's wife had agreed. They had sat, side by side, watching him breathe.

Lady Hawkins wore a dressing gown and no rings or jewellery of any kind. Her face had little more colour than her husband's. Her shoulders stooped. 'This is the end of our years together, I suppose. He is falling more and more away each day.' She took the cover and tucked it closer at his side. 'I don't think he is here any more.'

Bellona tried to think of questions she would ask her father if he roused, but none mattered. The answers would not change anything.

If he hadn't acted so badly, she wouldn't have been given life.

But it had seemed uncaring of her to leave him. Much like he had left them on the island. She stayed at his bedside, if only to prove to herself that she would not do as he had done.

She'd met her half-sisters and brother, and knew they'd only spoken to her begrudgingly after their mother had insisted. She'd felt no kinship for them at all, and yet, for his wife, she did.

'There are no secrets between him and me any more,' his wife said to Bellona, looking at the wan face of her husband. 'They were his secrets, yet he was the one who could not accept them being displayed.' She shook her head. 'The truth of his skill, though, that is what concerned him the most. When he discovered he had no true gift for painting.'

'I am sorry for my part in that.'

'Nonsense.' She waved the words away. 'It's not as if he'd not had it pointed out to him a thousand times before. He just finally accepted it now.' She leaned forward and let her hand rest on the bed. 'His paintings have rarely sold for more than the price of the canvas and frame. The best ones, oddly enough, were the ones of his children and your mother. If he has any talent, it is for capturing people, and of course, he thoroughly detests creating anything but landscapes. Endless landscapes. He doesn't like people. To paint them would mean he might have to look at them. Spend time with them.'

She put her hand on the counterpane covering his arm. 'He lied as much to himself as he did to everyone else. He sneered at the knowledge of others—only believing himself capable of thinking correctly. If he had gleaned from others and used his dedication in the right way, then perhaps he could have had what he wanted most. No one worked as hard to destroy his talent as he did.' She shut her eyes. 'I am only sorry for the pain of my children. For all his children.'

'I cannot begrudge him the past,' Bellona said. 'If I did, then I would be saying he changed me and he does not have that honour. I am who I am because of my *mana* and my sisters and myself. I thank you for what you have done for me.'

'I hated the thought of you children living with nothing. I am sorry he told such lies of you and destroyed your chance of marriage to Rolleston.'

'He did not. Rolleston asked me to wed him. I told him I could not. I was not sure.'

'Bellona.' Her eyes opened wide and she leaned forward to look in Bellona's face. 'After… When you were discovered together, the duke proposed?'

Bellona nodded. 'Yes, but I did not wish…'

'Oh, you may be a bit more your father's daughter than I realised,' she said. 'He turned down his chance to create art because he did not wish to follow his talent of painting portraits. And you turned down a chance to become a duchess—because?'

'I thought he felt he was doing me a boon just asking for my hand.'

The woman took her hand from her chest and clucked her tongue. 'Well, you have the attitude of a duchess already.'

'I will not be married because of pity, or duty or any reason I do not like.'

'Something—perhaps my knowledge of this world—tells me that Rolleston could have tumbled his choice of women into bed and yet he chose you, and then he had the brazenness to ask you to wed him. The cad.'

'He told me we should be married.'

'Perhaps he's a bit fonder of you than you think?'

'He could be. He thinks he is.'

'I've known his family my whole life. Rolleston is, or was, rather a stick. Much more the saint than most. Pleasant to look at, I thought, but as interesting to talk to as a land steward—'

'He is actually very interesting to talk to,' Bellona snapped.

Her father's wife paused before continuing. '… And quite the duke, until the last fortnight when your father began to denounce you as an extortionist. Then tales about Rolleston's fury began to blossom like weeds in a garden left untended. He became terribly unsettled for a man who'd never caused any kind of stir before.' She raised her brows and looked at Bellona. 'Terribly unsettled.'

'But he was included in the tales. It was said I was using him for gain as well.' Bellona could not keep the pique from her voice.

'He could have easily shrugged it off. Perhaps you should go to him and ask him what madness has grown in him that he had to be restrained in White's because a man dared speak slightingly of you.'

'I had not heard of that.'

'My sister has tried to schedule as many soirées, nights at the theatre and morning calls into her world as she can the past few days to keep me abreast of all the *on dits* because she considers it her duty to know what is being said about her family. Particularly when it concerns my husband. The duke, whether he means to or not, is not letting the talk wither away. His anger over you causes people to note you even more.'

'Rolleston can do as he wishes. I don't know that he cares enough for me even though he says he loves me. I don't know that I can love him enough for both of us if he does not.'

Lord Hawkins's wife looked again at the bed. 'Whomever you marry is a risk. If you don't marry, it is a risk, too. You might look back later and have missed so much.' She took her eyes from her husband and looked at Bellona. 'At least the duke doesn't like to paint.' She smiled.

Bellona didn't nod, or acknowledge the words with anything more than her eyes, but the next morning, as she walked to the carriage, she longed for Rhys more than she'd ever longed for anything in her life.

After directing the servants away, Bellona stepped into the duke's library and saw him at the desk with his man of affairs. He looked up and twisted a pen between his fingers, his eyes fixing on the movement. 'Leave us, Simpson.'

The man stood and hurried by Bellona, but his eyes flashed concern as he passed her.

'I don't think you need worry yourself about my father saying anything bad again,' she said.

'Are you well?' he asked.

She nodded. 'I left before the end came. His children did not want me there. I knew his wife understood. I do not need to be present. As I sat with him, I realised that when he sailed from Melos the last time, he died in my heart. It is as if he is someone I hardly know.'

The duke placed his pen atop his papers. He shifted in his chair and his knee hit the desk leg, but he caught the ink bottle before it tumbled over. 'Blast it,' he muttered. 'I can't keep these things upright any more.'

Still he held the liquid in his hand. He looked at her. 'That never used to happen before.'

She walked to him and took the bottle, their fingers brushing, shaking her in a way she would not let him see.

He put his elbow on the desk, his jaw on his fist, and his eyes flicked her direction. 'What day of the week is it?'

'I'm not certain,' she answered.

'Simpson would know,' he said.

'You can always ring for one of the servants.'

'And let them know I am unaware of even the date? If they have not surmised it already, I will not enlighten them that I am completely distracted.'

'Rhys, why did you ask me to marry you?'

'If you had said yes, we could have discussed it in

detail. For years perhaps. But as you said no, I decline to even think about the moment, much less speak of it.' He stared at her, then he took the ink bottle back off her and set it aside.

She put fingertips under his chin and guided it in her direction. 'I have tried to sketch you, but I don't have the skill. I'll learn, then I will always have a likeness of you.'

Eyes, weary with sleeplessness, watched her until his face turned into her hand and he pressed a kiss to her skin. 'You will always have me in person, Bellona, if you wish it, wedding or no. I have committed my heart to you and you will always hold it. You are truly my first love. My only love. If you do not plan to marry me, I understand. That does not change my heart.'

'You think you can continue in your life without a wife?'

'I have not been married in the first decades of my life and have managed very well, and when I look at you and know that it leaves me free for you, I'm very thankful.'

He pushed the chair back as he stood, his body brushing against hers. His hands rested on her hips. 'I will only ask you once more, today, but the question will remain open every day for the rest of your life, if you do not say yes now. Will you marry me?'

She nodded.

Epilogue

Bellona could hardly believe the change in her sister. Thessa had returned from her sea voyage with a young son and enough tales to keep them all laughing for hours, but somehow the talk had changed from the voyage to the husbands, and had become something of a verbal competition to see who had married the most delightful man.

'He talks in his sleep,' Thessa said of her husband, Captain Ben. 'And I find it most entertaining.'

'Rolleston… Well, I do not know if he talks in his sleep or not,' Bellona admitted, covering a yawn, and then aimed a smug smile at Thessa. 'He does not sleep.'

Melina grimaced. 'You are not learning how to be a proper duchess and he is acting more like you every day. You both disrupt all around you.'

A young female shriek of laughter sounded from outside the room.

'See what I mean.' Melina shook her head. 'Willa,' she called out, standing to move to the door. 'Do not—'

Warrington walked in, carrying his daughter under his arm, snug against his side and grasped around her middle, her hands and feet flailing as she laughed. 'I don't know what we will do with her. She thinks she is as big as her brother Jacob,' he said, bending enough so she could put her feet to the floor and right herself. 'Willa, you must not shout when I toss you about. Jacob does not.'

'He does,' she said. 'And he has a pail of worms hidden under his bed.'

'No,' Melina said, rushing to the door.

Warrington put out an arm, catching his wife at the waist. 'Don't worry. I have told him we will go fishing. I'll see to the worms.' He gave his wife a kiss on the forehead.

Ben walked in behind him. 'Rhys and I have decided to teach Jacob how to fish. We cannot trust his father to such a simple task. And we all know—' he looked at his wife '—that I am very good at catching things from the sea.'

Warrington snorted. 'But we will be fishing in a pool and you always claim the fish are not biting.' He looked over his shoulder at Rhys. 'And you claim the sun is in their eyes.'

Rhys shrugged. 'That was when we were children. I say now that the fisherman who fares worst will be tossed into the pool by the other two.'

'Challenge accepted,' Ben said.

'Wait.' Warrington held out a hand. 'I will be the judge of the winner. You two can compete.'

Ben looked at Rhys and winked. 'Certainly, War. We will see that you do not fall into the pool and get your cravat wet. But I suggest you wear old boots.'

'You could use a dunking as well. You hardly look

like a sea captain,' Warrington said. 'You are all Brum-melled.'

Benjamin shrugged. 'I had a portrait sitting in the library. Thank you, Bellona, for recommending your tutor.'

'I think Ben looks quite dashing,' Thessa said. 'And the blue waistcoat matches his eyes so.'

Warrington made a choking noise. 'A good reason not to choose it.'

'I'm only too happy to wear it for my wife, even if it is a bit tight under the black coat.' Benjamin's smile broadened. 'It was worth the trade —worth standing for my own portrait just to have a painting of my wife as I saw her the first time.' He straightened the sleeves of his coat. 'She'll always be my mermaid.'

Melina frowned. 'I've seen that painting on your ship of Thessa in the water. Not something that didn't happen every day on Melos.'

Warrington turned to the artwork above his fire-place of the three sisters on the island. The old painting created in their childhood. 'That is the one I cherish.'

'This is the artist I cherish,' Rhys said, putting a hand at Bellona's back. She looked into his eyes. He often sat near her, reading aloud while she sketched or practised with oils.

She'd never expected to love painting and she didn't care if she ever became any good at it, but strangely, it made her feel closer to her mother's memory and her homeland. During her childhood, their house had always smelled of pigments and she'd learned to mix them quite young.

Her sisters did not see painting the same way, but

they had all agreed to travel to the museum in France when their children were older. They wanted another look at the statue they'd found—now that the armless woman had a home—and they wanted to show their children the woman from Melos.

Melina turned to Bellona. 'I will have a picnic prepared and brought to us at the pool. The nursery maid can watch the children, but we will watch the boys.'

Melina and Warrington left the room, followed by Thessa and Ben. But Rhys lingered a bit, looking into Bellona's eyes.

'Do you wish to go with the others?' he asked. 'I'd prefer to visit the pool in the moonlight with you.'

'Oh, that would not be a good idea,' she said, shaking her head. 'Ben and Thessa are planning a stroll there tonight.'

'Well, then,' he said. 'When we return home, we can visit the small room in the servants' quarters. I've had a good latch put on the door.'

'You did not,' she said, slapping at his sleeve. 'The servants will…'

He laughed. 'I did. I will take a book with us—to give us something to do, of course. I gave strict instructions to the servants it is not to be disturbed. A good book should not be interrupted—ever.'

She shut her eyes and put her hand to her temple. 'What must they think of us?'

He reached and snatched a pin from her hair and palmed it as she tried to take it back, then he trapped her close for a soft kiss. 'I hope they think we are rather fond of each other.'

Her face was not that of a goddess—well, perhaps

it was the face of his goddess. But to him, she was his angel. And when he bent to kiss her he did not care if all the doors of the world opened and everyone saw them together. For ever.

* * * * *

If you enjoyed this story, you won't want to miss these stories by Liz Tyner linked to
Forbidden to the Duke

Safe in the Earl's Arms
A Captain and a Rogue

And don't miss these great new reads

To Win a Wallflower
Saying I Do to the Scoundrel

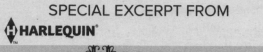
Read on for a sneak peek at
The Highlander's Dangerous Temptation
by Terri Brisbin.

"Athdar?" Isobel said, caressing his face. When had she touched him? When had she risen from her chair and approached him? "Are you ill?" She crouched down closer before him and stroked his forehead and cheek with the back of her hand. "No fever."

"I am well," he said, though he was trying to convince himself of it more than her. "What happened?" He swallowed, but his mouth and throat were parched. She noticed and held out a cup to him.

"You were telling me of your confrontation with my father and then something happened. You looked as if in pain and then ill. Now?" she asked, taking the cup from him and kneeling next to him.

Strange. He had been thinking about the true humiliation of learning the unintended consequences that Jocelyn suffered, when some other memories or feelings surged forward. Now they were gone and he felt fine.

"'Tis a painful thing—exposing a man's youthful stupidity to a beautiful woman who is the daughter of the man who exposed it in the first place. You now know my sordid past with your father, Isobel."

Her hand still caressed his face and, with her kneeling at his side, it would be easy, oh so easy, to lean down and kiss the lips that tempted him so much. When she lifted her head and her mouth opened slightly, he did what he wanted to do.

Her lips were soft and warm against his and he could feel her heated breath against him before he touched her mouth with his. Athdar did not touch her, but she did not let go of his face, stroking it as he deepened the kiss by sliding his tongue along her lips until she opened to him… For him.

God, but she was sweet.

He knew not when it happened, but his hand slid up and he tangled his fingers in her hair. Then he cupped her head and held her against his mouth. His tongue felt the heat deep in her mouth, and he tilted his head, tasting her and kissing her. For a moment, he drew back, but she looked at him with such wonderment in her eyes that he kissed her again and again and again.

Don't miss
The Highlander's Dangerous Temptation
by Terri Brisbin, available now.

www.Harlequin.com

Love Harlequin romance?

DISCOVER.

Be the first to find out about promotions,
news and exclusive content!

Facebook.com/HarlequinBooks

Twitter.com/HarlequinBooks

Instagram.com/HarlequinBooks

Pinterest.com/HarlequinBooks

ReaderService.com

EXPLORE.

Sign up for the Harlequin e-newsletter and
download a free book from any series at
TryHarlequin.com.

CONNECT.

Join our Harlequin community to share
your thoughts and connect with other
romance readers!
Facebook.com/groups/HarlequinConnection

HARLEQUIN®

**ROMANCE WHEN
YOU NEED IT**

HSOCIAL2018